Exploring Gender and LGBTQ Issues in K–12 and Teacher Education

A volume in
Research in Queer Studies
Paul Chamness Iida and Hidehiro Endo, *Series Editors*

Exploring Gender and LGBTQ Issues in K–12 and Teacher Education

A Rainbow Assemblage

edited by

Adrian D. Martin
New Jersey City University

Kathryn J. Strom
California State University, East Bay

INFORMATION AGE PUBLISHING, INC.
Charlotte, NC • www.infoagepub.com

Library of Congress Cataloging-in-Publication Data

A CIP record for this book is available from the Library of Congress
http://www.loc.gov

ISBN: 978-1-64113-617-4 (Paperback)
       978-1-64113-618-1 (Hardcover)
       978-1-64113-619-8 (ebook)

This volume is dedicated to the teachers, teacher educators, scholars, and activists working towards LGBTQ inclusive and affirmative classrooms, schools, and societies.

CONTENTS

Foreword ix
Mara Sapon-Shevin

1 The Rainbow Assemblage: An Introduction 1
Adrian D. Martin and Kathryn J. Strom

SECTION I

EXPLORING GENDER IN K–12 AND TEACHER EDUCATION

2 Troubling Gender Ideology in Japan: Today's University
Students' Views of Breadwinner and Homemaker Status 13
Paul Chamness Iida and Hidehiro Endo

3 The Hegemony of Transition and Transgender Counternarratives
in Children's Picture Books.. 29
Ashley Lauren Sullivan and Laurie Lynne Urraro

4 Pleasure Games (of Truth) in Boys' Schooling: Interrogating
Gender and Sexuality Through a Pleasure Lens 53
Göran Gerdin and Amanda Mooney

SECTION II

EXPLORING LGBTQ ISSUES IN K–12 SCHOOLS

5 Using Literacy to Explore Heteronormativity with Second-Graders.... 73
   Paul Hartman

6 "I Want Them [Teachers] to Treat Us Like Human Beings":
   Educational Experiences of Black Gay Youth 95
   Michael D. Bartone

7 Beyond the Binary in Elementary School 111
   Lynn Bravewomon

SECTION III

EXPLORING LGBTQ ISSUES IN TEACHER EDUCATION

8 Forging Alliances, Becoming-Ally: In Pursuit of Pedagogical
   Virtualities.. 129
   Kathryn J. Strom

9 Battling Heteronormativity in Teacher Education: Reflections
   on a Human Development Course from a Teacher and Student..... 147
   Peggy Shannon-Baker and Ingrid Wagner

10 An Intergenerational Self-Study of Narrative Reflections on
   Literature, Gender, and LGBTQ Identities 163
   Adrian D. Martin and Monica Taylor

   About the Editors 183
   About the Contributors.. 185

FOREWORD

When my daughter was four-years old, a friend of hers gave her a Barbie doll for her birthday. I was appalled, since I had conscientiously kept this toy out of her environment. But, unlike some parents I now know, I hadn't put "No Barbies" on the party invitation.

I was relieved when she didn't seem that interested in the gift. A week after her birthday, I entered her bedroom and found her sitting on the floor with the doll. Because I have never been very good at keeping my opinions to myself, I asked, somewhat pointedly, "What are you doing?" She responded, "I'm dressing and undressing my Barbie." "Oh," I said, "That looks pretty boring."

She looked up at me very seriously and said," Mama, "not being sexist" doesn't mean I can't play with girls' toys. 'Not being sexist' means I can play with anything I want to."

This volume encourages us to ask questions that are challenging and complex—we are asked to interrogate sexism and heterosexism and to ask ourselves what a world that was really supportive of gender and sexual diversity would look like.

We are invited to think about school safety and schools as safe spaces in ways that go beyond simply avoiding violence. We are asked to think about what schools would look like that are not limited and distorted by "heteronormative and patriarchal discourses and actions."

Here are five key ideas that this book raised for me; I share them here and invite you to think about them as you read the excellent and diverse chapters.

DISRUPTING BINARIES VERSUS NON-BINARY THINKING

We know that toys and colors and activities and clothes are heavily gender-bound in our current society. In the story above about the Barbies, my 4-year old took a first step to disrupt the binaries of "girls' toys" and "boys' toys." But what would it be like and what would it take to engage in truly non-binary thinking? What would the world look like if we had evolved enough so that concepts like "girls' clothes" and "boys' games" didn't even exist? When Target department stores decided to eliminate separate sections for GIRLS' TOYS and BOYS' TOYS, they were appreciated by some but reproached by others. We read occasionally about parents who are attempting to raise children without these binaries and the challenges they encounter. The difficulties are rarely with the children themselves, who are often happy and free and choose a wide variety of ways of being in the world; rather, these parents often report that they are criticized and critiqued by other parents: "You are going to raise a child that's very confused;" "How will he/she know what she/ he is if you don't tell him to act like a boy or to dress like a girl?" Some of the violent responses to children who identify as "transgendered" allows us to see how vested many people are in there being separate and easily discernible categories of "girls" and "boys" and the steps they will take to re-inscribe those distinctions.

Challenging regimes of power and privilege will not be easy. Gerdin and Mooney allow us to see the power of hegemonic masculinities and the power of gender policing among young men. Iida and Endo provide evidence that gender stereotyping and injustice are international problems. How will we move forward to create a different world? There is much to do.

LANGUAGE MATTERS

Many of the writers in this volume address the importance of how we talk about sex, gender, gender expression, sexuality, etc. Language is never neutral, and how we use language is both shaped by our understanding and shapes our understanding at the same time. One of the challenges to "normalizing" diversity is that our language gets in the way. How can we both talk about differences and yet not call attention to them as though they were more salient than we want them to be. It's kind of a Catch-22; if we say, "My daughter's kindergarten teacher is a lesbian," one could ask why we are mentioning that. But if we fail to mention that fact, then everyone will assume that her teacher is cis-gendered and heterosexual. When I did research on children's music about sexuality (particularly homosexuality), I encountered this difficulty. Failing to note that "Tony's family" is a family with two dads leaves intact the assumption that his family is heteronormative with a Mom and a Dad. But if we draw attention to the difference by naming that "Tony has two dads," (particularly when we never mention the gender/sexual make-up of other families), it makes it sound like Tony is the exception and thus the only one whose family warrants explanation. The chapter by Sullivan and Uraro on the ways in which transgendered people are represented reinforces the need for expanding our language and avoiding labels. They make clear that even their attempts to categorize books sometimes lead to some of the same rigidities they seek to avoid. What gets called "gender-expansive" and what is labeled as "transgendered"? Who does the labeling? Who has the right to name others' realities? This is complex work. And, as we make progress in thinking about the language we use and the examples we give in our teaching and interactions, there is also the inevitable resistance and push-back. The professor in Canada who refuses to use the pronoun "they" because he claims it interferes with his civil rights is an example of what that resistance looks like.

THIS RESEARCH IS IMPORTANT AND PERSONAL AND POTENTIALLY PAINFUL

Many of the authors of this volume explicitly name their own non-straight identities. In Paul Hartman's chapter, for example, he talks about his exploration of heteronormativity with second graders through literature. Because he names himself as a gay man, however, this research is quite personal, and thus, some of what he hears from his young students can be painful. One of the students explains that teasing is mean, but it's bad to be a sissy. What is it like for a gay man to hear one of his students say that? How can he respond from a position that is educative and not triggered? Those of us who claim marginalized, oppressed identities risk hearing even more homophobic and oppressive remarks when we engage in this research. The authors in this volume care deeply about this topic, not just professionally, but often personally as well. They are to be applauded for the bravery of their research and their writing, and we owe them a huge debt of gratitude for their willingness to share their own identities in order to make a difference.

PUNITIVE APPROACHES TO CHANGE DON'T WORK

The desire to eliminate bullying, teasing, exclusion and oppression leads many people to punitive, disciplinary approaches. In New York State, the Dignity for All Students Act, DASA, which was designed to improve school climate relative to diversity, is primarily a regulatory act; it outlines rules and consequences for dealing with violations in student codes of content.

But it is far less prescriptive about how the school should establish a positive climate and what pro-active steps can be taken to prevent bullying, harassment and exclusion. The research shows clearly that punitive approaches to negative behavior lead to sneakiness, revenge and often to escalation. Students who hear "Don't let me ever catch you calling Matthew that name again" hear "don't let me catch you." They don't necessarily change their understanding of why the word "faggot" is painful or inappropriate. They learn not to get caught; this doesn't lead to a better climate or more understanding. Schools will not become the welcoming, warm, accepting environments we desire without pro-active, far-reaching pedagogical practices and institutional policies that address diversity head-on.

YOUNG PEOPLE ARE MORE THAN EAGER TO DO THIS WORK BUT TEACHERS NEED TRAINING AND SUPPORT

Several of the chapters detail the ways in which young people are willing and often eager to discuss issues related to sexuality and gender. Hartman's students are eager to understand the human variation they are exposed to in the children's books he reads them. Bravewomom describes the enthusiasm with which young students learn to become allies and want to go beyond that to become activists in addressing discrimination and prejudice. And Bartone allows us to hear the voices of Black, gay youth who are desperate for their teachers to do better in acknowledging their intersecting identities and create a safe and welcoming space for them. Students are more than willing to describe the ill-treatment they have received and to articulate what would be better.

In order for students to engage, however, teachers must be prepared, comfortable and committed to facilitating such challenging discussions. Bravewomon describes the teachers to whom she provided professional development who were uncomfortable even using the words "lesbian," "gay," "bi-sexual," and "transgendered," when they began their engagement with her. She explains that teachers need to learn to disrupt heteronormativity; as stated above, however, that "interruption" cannot simply be silencing or sanction or it will be read as "sanction."

In her chapter, "Forging Alliances, Becoming-Ally: In Pursuit of Pedagogical Virtualities," Strom discusses her own growth as a teacher when she is forced to expand her syllabus to include issues of gender and sexuality. Her students lead her and she follows enthusiastically; she details her own recognition of the gaps in her experience and awareness and her growth as a teacher.

And such teacher education must be a permanent campaign, not an inoculation. As Shannon-Baker and Wagner detail, preparing teachers to challenge heteronormativity involves active learning to become allies and create productive alliances. Teachers need to practice, practice, practice. Articulating a commitment is a great start, but the specific skills and strategies required to disrupt patriarchal language and privilege must be modeled and practiced. Simply placing more inclusive children's literature in teachers' hands is not sufficient; they must be trained in how to use these books and how to talk to their students. And mandates to create "gender expansive" practices will do little good unless there is administrative support, peer modeling and non-punitive problem solving when there are difficulties.

Two new children's books, *The Bride Wore Celery* (Gordon, 2016) and *The Purim Superhero* (Kishner, 2013) both provide models of stories that include diverse families without making that fact the point of the story. In the first book, a little girl attends the wedding of two women, and the story centers on her misunderstanding of her role as a flower girl—believing that she will be wearing celery—and her confusion about the "ring bearer" whom she thinks will be a bear. In *The Purim Superhero*, a little boy tries to figure out his costume for the Jewish holiday of Purim with the help and support of his two dads. But neither story makes the families exceptional; they simply describe diverse families who are living their lives. And two new books for children by Cory Silverberg, *What Makes a Baby?* (2013) and *SEX is a Funny Word: A Book about Bodies, Feelings, and YOU* (2015) both talk about bodies and reproduction in ways that include many variations in how babies are made and in what bodies look like. These books bear little resemblance to the children's books I read or had read to me when I was a child. What a huge difference these books would have made for me and for everyone else trying to figure out the world's complexity and their own place in that world.

The last chapter, by Martin and Taylor, describes a process by which teachers reflect on who they are, how they became that way, and how their own experiences and upbringings have affected them as teachers. We see encouraging evidence that teachers can use and transcend their own experiences to become anti-bias educators and promoters of social justice pedagogy.

There are hopeful signs, and it is important to acknowledge how the landscape is changing. The publication of his volume is a positive step in our journey to creating more equity and more justice in the world and to hastening a future in which children can truly be themselves in all their complexity and fullness.

—**Mara Sapon-Shevin**

CHAPTER 1

THE RAINBOW ASSEMBLAGE

An Introduction

Adrian D. Martin and Kathryn J. Strom

ABSTRACT

This chapter serves as an introduction to the edited volume. The authors articulate the need to attend to gender and LGBTQ issues in K–12 and teacher education. An argument is made that despite increasing scholarly attention to equity issues relevant to cultural and linguistic diversity, attention to the experiences of LGBTQ members of the school community is under-researched. Further, systems of schooling are undergirded by patriarchy and heteronormativity. As such, it is necessary to promote scholarship, pedagogical practices, and education policy that enables inclusive and affirmative educational contexts. The chapter provides commentary on the scholarship included in the volume and the productiveness of this work for teachers, teacher educators, and education researchers.

In K–12 and teacher education, it is critical that students, and indeed, all educational stakeholders, be able to participate in academic contexts as valued, welcomed, and included members of the community (Ainscow, Dyson, Goldrick, & West, 2012; Hornby, 2012). Unfortunately, for gender diverse

Exploring Gender and LGBTQ Issues in K–12 and Teacher Education, pages 1–10
Copyright © 2019 by Information Age Publishing
All rights of reproduction in any form reserved.

and LGBTQ individuals, systems of schooling have historically been and continue to be less than inviting, frequently marginalizing, and/or erasing, and at times actively oppressing, their presence and representation (McCarty-Caplan, 2013; Payne & Smith, 2013). Such conditions serve to perpetuate patriarchal and heteronormative discourses that further narrow and limit understandings of self outside normative gender roles and ideologies (DePalma & Atkinson, 2010; Martin, 2014a).

Such phenomena is not exclusive to a particular educative context, but rather, is global in nature and manifests in myriad forms both tacit and overt to discipline bodies into forms acceptable to the straight, cis-gendered, male gaze. These manifestations include (but are not limited to) a lack of LGBTQ and gender diverse representations in school curriculum (Elia & Eliason, 2010), policies that explicitly forbid the hiring of LGBTQ school personnel (Bellis, 2016), the exclusion of students from school functions on the basis of their gender/sexual identities (Kosciw, Greytak, Giga, Villenas, & Danischewski, 2016), the pathologization of non-heterosexual and non-cis gendered identities (Gowen & Winges-Yanez, 2013), and the failure of teachers, administrators, and other school personnel to respond appropriately, or in some cases at all, to bullying, harassment, and violence on the basis of diverse gender and sexual identities (Blackburn & Pascoe, 2015; Espelage, 2015).

Ultimately, these corollaries of hate-based perspectives and bias-laden values are detrimental to parents, teachers, students, and other members of the school community in innumerable ways. They expose children and their families to hate and violence, as experienced by Jane Currie and her partner Anji Dimitriou. As they were waiting to pick up their son at the playground of his school in Oshawa, Canada, a man—the father of another student at the school—approached the couple, spit in Anji's face, shouted a series of homophobic statements, and physically assaulted the couple (Welsh, 2008). Jane and Anji later expressed this was not the first time this individual had aggressively confronted them. These acts of hate often have tragic consequences, as in the case of thirteen-year-old Tyrone Unsworth of Brisbane, Australia, who committed suicide in 2016. A friend of Tyrone reported that he was bullied and taunted for being gay, and was repeatedly called a "faggot" and "fairy" by other students at his school. The friend subsequently disclosed that his peers repeatedly told Tyrone to kill himself (Atkin, 2016). Students are not the only ones affected; in 2014, Jill Grienke, a special education teacher for the Miwaki board of education in Wisconsin, United States, committed suicide. Her mother reports that Jill, a transgender woman, experienced more than ten years of bullying by her colleagues (Kellaway, 2015).

These accounts reflect the horrific and iniquitous hate-based and oppressive contexts endured by many LGBTQ and gender diverse individuals who are part of academic communities. Recent efforts by gender equity and LGBTQ inclusive non-profits, think tanks, and advocacy groups have leveled public scrutiny against such reprehensible instantiations within schooling systems, contending the need for schools to serve as "safe spaces" for all individuals, but especially for LGBTQ and gender diverse individuals (Fetner, Elafros, Bortolin, & Drechsler, 2012; Vaccaro, August, & Kennedy, 2012). This argument has primarily centered on the promotion of classrooms and school environments wherein all students, irrespective of gender or sexual identification, can fully engage in academic instruction and reap the benefits of schooling. While some endeavors to advances schools as safe spaces consider means to dismantle, undue, or minimize hate-based, homophobic or transphobic beliefs, attitudes, and dispositions by directly addressing heteronormativity and patriarchy (Clark, 2010; Vega, Crawford, & Pelt, 2012), the onus for many safe space ventures has predominantly focused on student safety at the expense of attending to the hate-based ideologies that undergird such violence and vituperation.

Clearly, for students to learn, schools must ensure that classrooms are safe and free of violence in any form (physical or otherwise). Safe schools and safe classrooms serve as the foundation upon which productive pedagogical activity can unfold (Reeves, Kanan, & Plog 2010). While we are supportive of and endorse efforts that work toward this aim, we also believe that a strict focus on school safety and schools as safe spaces ultimately does little to advance and establish classrooms, schools, and school systems unencumbered by heteronormative and patriarchal discourses and actions. More is needed beyond LGBTQ day celebrations, gay straight alliances (GSAs), and feel good posters, slogans, or t-shirts that proclaim allyship (Sadowski, 2016–2017; Taylor & Coia, 2014). While certainly bringing gender and LGBTQ issues to the mainstream of educational discourse, these fail to address larger, systemic issues relevant to the marginalization of gender diverse and LGBTQ individuals. We, among others, contend that members of the school community (e.g., teacher educators, teachers, school administrators, and staff professional development providers) must work to not only dismantle the homophobic, transphobic, and misogynistic elements of schooling contexts, but also to proactively engage in professional practices that promote gender equity and LGBTQ inclusive (and affirmative) values, dispositions, and attitudes as the dominant lens that informs curriculum, pedagogy, and policy (Luke & Gore, 2013; Martin, 2014b; Matthyse, 2017; Pinar, 2009; Shlasko, 2005).

This volume, *Exploring Gender and LGBTQ Issues in K–12 and Teacher Education: A Rainbow Assemblage*, seeks to advance scholarly conversations regarding how to transform schools and institutions of learning not just into those with inclusive and welcoming contexts for LGBTQ and gender diverse individuals, but also as institutions that actively seek to dismantle heteronormativity and patriarchy. To do so, the volume provides exemplars of theoretically guided empirical studies that illustrate possibilities for schools as not just safe spaces, but also educational contexts that disrupt tacit and overt normative conceptualizations of gender and LGBTQ identities and practices that reinforce those. Collectively, the chapters can be likened to the Deleuzo-Guattarian (1987) concept of an assemblage. The late 20th century philosopher Gilles Delueze and his collaborator, the psychoanalyst Felix Guattari, theorized assemblages as the joint activity produced through multiple processes among a diverse and wide-ranging confluence of actors (human and non-human) that transverse multiple plateaus (e.g., discursive, psychological, political, interpersonal; Martin & Strom, 2017, 2018).

The authors of this collection reflect a range of education stakeholders in diverse school contexts and global settings. Their scholarly contributions to this volume report on instances wherein multiple elements of a classroom or school settings coalesce to shed light on how these system components serve to reify, disrupt, and/or transform normative gender and LGBTQ perspectives in K-12 and teacher education. As such, the volume itself functions as an assemblage, each chapter supporting the reader's insight on how policy, practice, or future research can be informed by the study under discussion. The diversity of the included material, as well as the constellation of different backgrounds and scholarly interests of the contributing authors are a multicolored collage of voices. In concert with each other, these voices surface as a rainbow assemblage, working towards equity and social justice not only for the students and other members of the school community discussed in the individual chapters, but also gender diverse and LGBTQ communities globally.

COLORS OF THE RAINBOW: COMPONENTS
OF THE ASSEMBLAGE

This volume is the result of our (Adrian & Katie's) ongoing discussions and inquiry on our teaching practices, research endeavors, and commitment towards dedicating our work to further educational equity and social justice. Having initially met as doctoral students, we sought to deepen our understanding of our roles as teachers/teacher educators/scholars and explore how, through our work, we might contribute to more equitable schooling experiences for diverse members of the academic community. Our joint and individual scholarship has encompassed diverse areas relevant to equity, education, and teacher education, including the influence of neoliberalism on classroom practice (Martin & Strom, 2015; Strom & Martin, 2013), teachers' conceptualizations of professional self as educators of English Learners (Martin & Strom, 2016), and equity-oriented practices among novice educators teaching culturally and linguistically diverse students (Strom & Martin, 2016, 2017). As professionally meaningful as such work has been, they have not placed issues of gender and LGBTQ identities at the center of our inquiries. Given our commitment to inclusive and affirmative schooling contexts, this volume directly addresses this area, heralding the call among education researchers and teacher educators to engage in meaningful, substantive, and transformative inquiry to disrupt patriarchy, heteronormativity, homophobia, transphobia, and other forms of bias that marginalize and oppress students, teachers, parents, and others in schooling contexts.

Our volume is divided into three sections. Section I, "Exploring Gender in K–12 and Teacher Education," offers contributions that attend to the realities and possibilities for gender expression, identities, and discourses in diverse academic contexts. The section opens with the work of Paul Chamness Iida and Hidehero Endo, who report on a study that sought to spotlight normative gender role expectations and gender disparity among undergraduate preservice teachers in Japan. Focusing on Japanese gender ideologies, the researchers investigated generational differences in constructions of gender roles and expectations in Japanese society and the implications for disrupting these traditional views among Japanese youth enrolled in an education course. Miller and Endo's work highlight the salience of not only considering individual, micro-level constructions of gender, but also how these align with and/or diverge from macropolitical, dominant, and socially-prescribed gender roles and expectations.

Explorations of gender, and emergent conceptions of gender, are advanced in the subsequent chapter by Ashley Lauren Sullivan and Laurie Lynne Urraro. Drawing from an earlier analysis of children's picture books that analyzed depictions and representations of transgender and gender-expansive youth, the researchers built upon this work in a subsequent study that explored the meaning-making of such texts among transgender and gender expansive participants in focus group sessions conducted in the United States. Employing queer theory as a theoretical framework, the researchers critique master-narratives about the experiences of trans individuals as hegemonic and, ultimately, detrimental to the multiple and diverse experiences such individuals possess. Sullivan and Urraro argue for the need to better represent and understand the schooling experiences of trans students while disrupting hegemonic interpretations of gender by teachers and school personnel and fighting for the inclusion of diverse representations of trans youth in school texts and curricula.

In a related inquiry, Göran Gerdin and Amanda Mooney draw upon Foucauldian notions of power, pleasure, discourse, and regimes of truth to explore the ways adolescent youth at two all boys' schools interpreted and identified with norms of masculinity in relation to sports and physical education. Conducted in New Zealand and Australia, their ethnographic study delves into the pleasure games (of truth) enacted by the boys and perpetuated/reflected in the educational context of which they were part. Gerdin and Mooney's nuanced employment of Foucault's framework renders a theoretically rich and conceptually grounded analysis that demonstrates how pleasure can emerge as an element that serves to perpetuate a heteronormative schooling culture. The work also highlights the discursive qualities of power differentials/relationships, not only in physical education settings, but academic settings at large.

Section II, "Exploring LGBTQ Issues in K–12 Schools," directly addresses constructions of sexual identity and insights generated by diverse education stakeholders to create inclusive and affirmative educative experiences for students and teachers. To begin this section, Paul Hartman examines LGBTQ issues in the discourses of second grade students who engaged with LGBTQ themed literary texts in an after-school program. A teacher action research project, the study employs queer theory as an analytic lens to interpret students' responses to the texts and the representations of LGBTQ characters. Hartman's work reinforces the imperative for teachers and teacher educators to engage in sustained reflection and inquiry in their interactions and practices with students, particularly in relation to the privileging and othering of particular sexual and gender identities.

Michael Bartone's chapter shifts the emphasis from the elementary classroom setting to middle and high school. Through a narrative inquiry approach, the study draws from quare theory and critical race theory to gain insight on the academic experiences of two gay Black men in the metro Atlanta area. Bartone's work emphasizes the intersectionality of identities and the numerous challenges the two participants experienced as they sought to navigate through their schooling contexts. At times embraced for being Black or gay, the two men in the study chronicle both incidents of marginalization and the processes through which they gained a sense of self-possession as a form of self-love, particularly the self-love of one's intersecting identities. This empirical inquiry sheds much needed light on the experiences of Black gay men, whose identities are all too frequently marginalized not only in institutions of schooling, but in education research as well.

To work with gender-expansive and LGBTQ youth and families while disrupting heteronormative schooling structures, teachers need to engage in professional development that supports LGBTQ affirmative and inclusive instruction. Speaking to this need, Lynn Bravewomon discusses a professional development sequence in which she documents her efforts to implement queered professional development designed to support elementary classrooms teachers and their capacity to provide LGBTQ-inclusive instruction to their students. Bravewomon offers an analysis of her experiences conducting the professional development sessions and the teacher-participants' responses and pedagogical adoptions as a result of the sessions through combined frames of queer theory and culturally sustaining pedagogy. A concrete example of the possibilities of pushing beyond school safety in LGBTQ focused school initiatives, this work provides evidence of potential avenues and approaches to teacher learning experiences that professional development providers can adopt in their work with elementary educators to develop LGBTQ-inclusive pedagogical practices.

The third section of the volume, "Exploring LGBTQ Issues in Teacher Education," focuses on the work of teacher educators addressing LGBTQ issues in their practice. The authors draw from diverse sources and theoretical frameworks to inform their research. Kathryn J. Strom's chapter, "Becoming-Ally: In Pursuit of Pedagogical Virtualities," draws on a critical posthuman framework to analyze an experience teaching about issues of identity, social justice, and schooling in a summer youth empowerment program for adolescent girls. Strom narrates her discovery, through a "coming-into-composition" with her students, that her syllabus had neglected to include issues of sexuality and gender expression—issues which were at the forefront of her students' consciousness. Confronting her own heteronormative gaze and lack of knowledge, Strom redesigned her syllabus and offered a set of open-ended activities through which she and her students forged an alliance, investigated their current realities, and constructed new possibilities for ways of knowing and being in the world. Drawing on her experience of this becoming-ally process, Strom describes the importance of educators developing a different way of thinking and teaching—one in which the teacher politically locates herself and her teaching activity, forges a binary-disrupting pedagogy of affirmative difference, and purposefully brings these into composition with students to disrupt harmful discourses and structures in schools that perpetuate heteropatriarchy.

Peggy Shannon-Baker and Ingrid Wagner offer the unique perspective of an inquiry between a teacher educator and preservice teacher that explores the pedagogical unfolding in an undergraduate teacher education course. The authors draw from interactionist theory, queer theory, and the notion of nonunitary subjectivity to explore the disruption of heteronormativity and the implications of this disruption for future pedagogical activity not only in the teacher education classroom, but in K–12 classrooms as well. Shannon-Baker and Wagner exemplify the affordances of and necessity for teacher educators to examine their own practices, to bring the voices of their preservice teacher students into the research process, and to employ diverse theoretical lens in the processes of data analysis. The chapter serves as an example of how the experiences provided to teacher candidates in preservice education can serve as catalysts for combating heteronormativity.

We close this volume with a self-study by Adrian D. Martin and Monica Taylor. Drawing on a bricolage approach that employs autoethnography, narrative research, and co/autoethnography, the researchers analyze their individual and collective lived experiences in relation to gender, identity, and engagement with literary works. In doing so, the inquiry considers shifting perspectives on LGBTQ identities across multiple generations and offers implications for teacher educators to take up LGBTQ advocacy and allyship in their professional practice. Further, Martin and Taylor's methodological approach serves to illustrate the fluidity of identity, temporality, and context as a shaping influence on one's understanding and interpretation of self as educator and teacher educator. The work highlights how a collaborative inquiry endeavor among teacher educators can serve as a valuable epistemological font from which to understand one's professional identity as an advocate for LGBTQ inclusion in teacher education and the dismantlement of heteronormative and patriarchal systems, structures, and discourses.

Our hope is that this collection of research studies inspires and encourages other members of the academic community to better promote LGBTQ and gender-inclusive classrooms and schools through research, policy and practices conducive to this aim. The work described in this volume represents a starting point—one that values the presence and contributions of gender diverse and LGBTQ school members—from which we can further such an agenda. Moreover, from a practical standpoint, we suggest that, if teachers, teacher educators, researchers, and other education stakeholders take up the recommendations in this work, the educative experiences provided and enacted in classrooms may better support the development of LGBTQ allies and advocates as global citizens who are able to engage with others in increasingly diverse, pluralistic societies.

REFERENCES

Ainscow, M., Dyson, A., Goldrick, S., & West, M. (2012). Making schools effective for all: Rethinking the task. *School Leadership & Management, 32*(3), 197–213. doi: 10.1080/13632434.2012.669648

Atkin, M. (2016, December 5). *Gay school boy shared bullying torment day before suicide.* Retrieved from http://www.abc.net.au/news/2016-12-05/kids-at-school -keep-telling-me-to-kill-myself-tyrone-unsworth/8093910

Bellis, R. (2016, March 3). *Here's everywhere in America you can still get fired for being gay or trans.* Retrieved from https://www.fastcompany.com/3057357/heres -everywhere-in-america-you-can-still-get-fired-for-being-lgbt

Blackburn, M., & Pascoe, C. J. (2015). K–12 students in schools. In G. L. Wimberly (Ed.), *LGBTQ issues in education: Advancing a research agenda* (pp. 89–104). Washington, DC: American Educational Research Association.

Clark, C. T. (2010). Preparing LGBTQ allies and combating homophobia in a U.S. teacher education program. *Teaching and Teacher Education,26*(3), 704–713. doi:10.1016/j.tate.2009.10.006

Deleuze, G., & Guattari, F. (1987). *A thousand plateaus: Capitalism and schizophrenia.* Minneapolis: University of Minnesota Press.

DePalma, R., & Atkinson, E. (2010). The nature of institutional heteronormativity in primary schools and practice-based responses. *Teaching and Teacher Education, 26*(8), 1669–1676. doi:10.1016/j.tate.2010.06.018

Elia, J. P., & Eliason, M. J. (2010). Dangerous omissions: Abstinence only until marriage: School-based sexuality education and the betrayal of LGBTQ youth. *American Journal of Sexuality Education, 5*(1), 17–35. doi:10.1080/15546121003748848

Espelage, D. L. (2015). Bullying and K–12 students. In G. L. Wimberly (Ed.), *LGBTQ issues in education: Advancing a research agenda* (pp. 105–120). Washington, DC: American Educational Research Association.

Fetner, T., Elafros, A., Bortolin, S., & Drechsler, C. (2012). Safe spaces: Gay-straight alliances in high schools. *Canadian Review of Sociology/Revue Canadienne De Sociologie, 49*(2), 188–207. doi:10.1111/j.1755-618x.2011.01290.x

Gowen, L. K., & Winges-Yanez, N. (2013). Lesbian, gay, bisexual, transgender, queer, and questioning youths' perspectives of inclusive school-based sexuality education. *The Journal of Sex Research, 51*(7), 788–800. doi:10.1080/00224499.2013.806648

Hornby, G. (2012). Parental involvement in middle and secondary schools. *Parental Involvement in Childhood Education, 7(1),* 61–77. doi:10.1007/978-1-4419-8379-4_5

Kellaway, M. (2015, June 15). *Wisc. trans teacher dies by suicide after being bullied for 10 years.* Retrieved from https://www.advocate.com/politics/transgender/2015/06/15/wisc-trans-teacher-dies-suicide-after-being-bullied-10-years

Kosciw, J. G., Greytak, E. A., Giga, N. M., Villenas, C., & Danischewski, D. J. (2016). *The 2015 national school climate survey: The experiences of lesbian, gay, bisexual, transgender, and queer youth in our nation's schools.* New York, NY: Gay, Lesbian, and Straight Education Network.

Luke, C., & Gore, J. (Eds.). (2013). *Feminisms and critical pedagogy* (2nd ed.). New York, NY: Routledge.

Martin, A. D. (2014a). From Adam and Eve to Dick and Jane: A literary nomadic inquiry on gender and sexuality in teaching and teacher education. In M. Taylor & L. Coia (Eds.), *Gender, feminism and queer theory in the self-study of teacher education practices* (pp.143–156). Boston, MA: Sense.

Martin, A. D. (2014b). Kaleidoscopic musings on a queer praxis. In H. Endo & P. C. Miller (Eds.), *Queer voices from the classroom* (pp. 169–175). Charlotte, NC: Information Age.

Martin, A. D., & Strom, K. J. (2015). Neoliberalism and the teaching of English learners: Decentering the teacher and student subject. *The SoJo Journal: Educational Foundations and Social Justice Education, 1*(1), 23–44.

Martin, A. D., & Strom, K. J. (2016). Toward a linguistically responsive teacher identity: An empirical review of the literature. *International Multilingual Research Journal, 10*(4), 239–253. doi:10.1080/19313152.2016.1189799

Martin, A. D., & Strom, K. J. (2017). Using multiple technologies to put rhizomatics to work in self-study. In A. Ovens & D. Garbett (Eds.), *Being self-study researchers in a digital world: Future oriented pedagogy and teaching in teacher education* (Vol. 16, pp. 151–163). Basel, Switzerland: Springer. doi:10.1007/978-3-319-39478-7_11

Martin, A. D., & Strom, K. J. (2018). Coping as a line of flight in a multilingual kindergarten classroom. In T. Rishel & P. C. Miller (Eds.), *Stress and coping of English learners in the 21st century* (pp. 61–81). Charlotte, NC: Information Age.

Matthyse, G. (2017). Heteronormative higher education: Challenging this status quo through LGBTIQ awareness-raising. *South African Journal of Higher Education, 31*(4), 112–126. doi:10.20853/31-4-890

McCarty-Caplan, D. M. (2013). Schools, sex education, and support for sexual minorities: Exploring historic marginalization and future potential. *American Journal of Sexuality Education, 8*(4), 246–273. doi:10.1080/15546128.2013.849563

Payne, E., & Smith, M. (2013). LGBTQ kids, school safety, and missing the big picture: How the dominant bullying discourse prevents school professionals from thinking about systemic marginalization or...why we need to re-think LGBTQ bullying. *QED: A Journal in GLBTQ Worldmaking, 1*(1), 1–36. doi:10.14321/qed.0001

Pinar, W. (Ed.). (2009). *Queer theory in education.* New York, NY: Routledge.

Reeves, M. A., Kanan, L. M., & Plog, A. E. (2010). *Comprehensive planning for safe learning environments: A school professional's guide to integrating physical and psychological safety: Prevention through recovery.* New York, NY: Routledge.

Sadowski, M. (2016-2017, Winter). More than a safe space: How schools can enable LGBTQ students to thrive. *American Educator.* Retrieved from https://files.eric.ed.gov/fulltext/EJ1123878.pdf

Shlasko, G. D. (2005). Queer (.) pedagogy. *Equity & Excellence in Education, 38*(2), 123–134. doi:10.1080/10665680590935098

Strom, K. J., & Martin, A. D. (2013). Putting philosophy to work in the classroom: Using rhizomatics to deterritorialize neoliberal thought and practice. *Studying Teacher Education: A Journal of Self-study of Teacher Education Practices, 9*(3), 219–235. doi:10.1080/17425964.2013.83097

Strom, K. J., & Martin, A. D. (2016). Pursuing lines of flight: Equity-based preservice teacher learning in first-year teaching. *Policy Futures in Education, 14*(2), 252–273. doi:10.1177/1478210315615475

Strom, K. J., & Martin, A. D. (2017). *Becoming-teacher: A rhizomatic look at first-year teaching.* Rotterdam, Netherlands: Sense.

Taylor, M., & Coia, L. (Eds.). (2014). *Gender, feminism and queer theory in the self-study of teacher education practices.* Boston, MA: Sense.

Vaccaro, A., August, G., & Kennedy, M. S. (2012). *Safe spaces: Making schools and communities welcoming to LGBT youth.* Santa Barbara, CA: Praeger.

Vega, S., Crawford, H. G., & Pelt, J. V. (2012). Safe schools for LGBTQI students: How do teachers view their role in promoting safe schools? *Equity & Excellence in Education, 45*(2), 250–260. doi:10.1080/10665684.2012.671095

Welsh, M. (2008, November 11). Lesbians attacked outside school. Retrieved from https://www.thestar.com/news/gta/2008/11/11/lesbians_attacked_outside_school.html

SECTION I

EXPLORING GENDER IN K–12
AND TEACHER EDUCATION

CHAPTER 2

TROUBLING GENDER IDEOLOGY IN JAPAN

Today's University Students' Views of Breadwinner and Homemaker Status

Paul Chamness Iida and Hidehiro Endo

ABSTRACT

This chapter examines if the gender disparity in work-family planning, that seems to be prevalent among younger Japanese generations, is also found in university youth at an institution that promotes critical thinking and who are beginning to think about their future with work and family. In order to address this topic, the authors answer the following research question: How do issues of gender ideology, entrenched in Japanese society for generations, affect contemporary pre-service teachers' assumptions toward their tacit beliefs about their gender role in the work force? In addition to addressing the guiding research question, this chapter explores how one might disrupt the traditional views that are so deeply rooted in the minds of Japanese youth in a teacher education course.

Exploring Gender and LGBTQ Issues in K–12 and Teacher Education, pages 13–28
Copyright © 2019 by Information Age Publishing
13

There is a common belief that gender equity is increasing around the world. While this may be true in Western societies where women have more opportunities to work in higher status professions and exercise greater power and influence in society than they have in the past (Davis & Greenstein, 2009), in Japan women have yet to achieve such parity with Western women (Ashikari, 2003). For example, in the United States the percentage of women in the workforce has more than doubled since the end of World War II (from 35% to more than 75%), while in Japan the percentages of women working outside the home has not changed, remaining at just under 50% (Lee, Tufis, Alwin, & Teachman, 2010). As Lee et al. note, this is in large part due to the structure of society, where women are expected to quit working once they have their first child. What is more, governmental policy and societal structure dictates that a spouse only benefits from a tax break if she earns less than 1.35 million yen (less than $12,000) per year (p. 188). Additionally, normative working conditions are often unfavorable for a woman who works outside the home, who may need to negotiate challenges such as a lack of childcare for young children, long commutes, expectations to work late through the evening, and frequent transfers to other offices (Lee et al., 2010). Although some empirical studies report a shift in the attitudes toward gender equality in Japan, society's expectations of the roles of men and women have not evolved with these changes in attitude.

Another area where there is significant disparity between men and women is in reference to educational opportunities. Although more than 96% of all adolescents enter high school in Japan, 7.4% less women continue to a four-year undergraduate program than men (48.2% and 55.6% respectively; Gender Equality Bureau Cabinet Office, 2017b). Even though the number of women who choose a four-year college has consistantly increased over the past several decades, roughly 8.9% of women enroll in a junior college rather than pursue a Bachelor's degree. Furthermore, there is a significant difference between men and women who continue their studies after completing a Bachelor's degree, with only 6% of women and more than 15% of men enrolling in graduate programs (Gender Equality Bureau Cabinet Office, 2017b).

Even after obtaining a Bachelor's degree, women who do enter the workforce continue to earn significantly less in the same job as their male counterparts. In 2016, although women's salaries reached an all-time high, they earned 73% of what men earned ("Japan's Gender," 2017). Women are also frequently overlooked for promotion in managerial roles, although that has also begun to improve slightly over the last few years ("Japan's Gender," 2017). The most recent data suggests that as of 2016, women occupied only 3.4% of executive positions in the companies observed in the study (Gender Equality Bureau Cabinet Office, 2017a).

Despite these inequities in education and employment, more recent studies indicate that indeed attitudes toward gender roles are shifting in Japan (Adachi, 2017). Nonetheless, life goals continue to reflect traditional normative gender roles of men serving as the breadwinner of the family and woman as the caregiver and homemaker (Adachi, 2017). Adachi (2017) found that present-day male youth continue to envision their future filled with working long hours, whereas female youth envision spending more time with household work. Instead of aligning with the Japanese government's agenda on gender equity, "young people observe the current situation and, understanding how difficult it is to pursue non-traditional work-family plans, are then persuaded to conform to traditional intentions" (Adachi, 2017, p. 6). Furthermore, the Japanese educational system follows a traditional approach to learning where students spend their lives studying, memorizing facts, and attempting to achieve high scores on entrance exams to attend better high schools, more prestigious universities, and ultimately further exams to gain employment a in a typical Japanese company. This system does little to promote critical thinking among students. Thus, Japanese youth often lack a sense of efficacy to challenge their society's gender norms and gender expectations (Miller, 2017). Therefore, youth typically accept traditional roles that have been expected of men and women throughout Japan's history (Miller, 2017).

The purpose of this study was to examine if the gender disparity in work-family planning that seems to be prevalent among younger Japanese generations is also found in university youth enrolled in a teacher licensure program at an institution that promotes critical thinking and who are beginning to think about their future with work and family. In order to address this topic, the following research question serves as the guide for this study: How do issues of gender ideology entrenched in Japanese society for generations affect contemporary pre-service teachers' assumptions toward their tacit beliefs about their gender role in the work force? In addition to answering our guiding research question, this chapter aims to explore how one might disrupt the traditional views that are so deeply rooted in the minds of Japanese youth in a teacher education course.

THEORETICAL APPROACH

According to Zuo and Tang (2000), breadwinner status used to be exclusively reserved for men, while women were resigned to being the homemaker. However, in testing the "threat hypothesis" where men feel threatened by women taking on the role of the breadwinner, and the "benefit hypothesis" where men benefit from women becoming the breadwinner, they found that in the United States, society is shifting to a more egalitarian view, where men see the benefits they reap from women being in the workforce.

Although some progress has been observed in the Japanese context in terms of society's attitudes towards women working outside of the home, according to Lee et al. (2010), the role of women has remained, by and large, as homemaker and caretaker. Being a homemaker is viewed as equally important as that of the breadwinner, and, for some, possesses a status that is not seen as oppressive (Lee et al., 2010). Rather, being a homemaker is seen as a safe haven for Japanese woman who typically possesses autonomy in domestic matters, such as maintaining the financial budget and decision-making relevant to child rearing practices. This has become especially prevalent in recent decades, with the father figure increasingly absent from the home due to high demands at work (Lee et al., 2010).

This notion of preserving a clear distinction between the role of the male as breadwinner and the female as homemaker in a heterosexual couple is further visible in the inequality in salary in Japan. This salary gap further demonstrates the attempt of Japanese men, who remain in most positions of power, to preserve their hegemonic status, illustrating the threat of what may happen should women abandon their expected role as homemaker for a career as breadwinner. For example, according to the National Tax Agency Japan (2016), the overall average annual income of Japanese workers in 2015 was 4,200,000 yen (approximately $38,000) before tax. The average annual income of male Japanese workers, specifically in 2015, was 5,210,000 yen (approximately $47,000). On the other hand, the average income of female Japanese workers in 2015 was only 2,760,000 yen (approximately $25,000; National Tax Agency, 2016). The annual income difference between the male and female Japanese workers in 2015 was 2,450,000 yen (approximately $22,000), clearly showing that, in general, Japanese men earn almost twice the income of Japanese women. Based on this report, it is evident that equal job opportunities between Japanese male and female workers are still far from being achieved in today's Japan. The annual income gap indicates that Japanese women are economically disadvantaged and, at a minimum, it hinders Japanese women from being financially independent. Ultimately, this income inequity is informed by gender ideology, perpetuating gender roles that serve to maintain Japanese men in the role of breadwinner and women in the role of homemaker. By preserving this status, the threat to the hegemony of men is minimized. The findings of our study reveal that these traditional roles of breadwinner and homemaker, as well as the gap in the expected income of the participants, continue to perpetuate the threat that gender equality in the work force and salary earnings would have on these traditional roles that have been steeply entrenched in Japanese history.

METHODOLOGY

The inquiry under discussion is a mixed methods study conducted at an international liberal arts university in rural Japan. Implementing a mixed methodology afforded us the ability to not only quantify the salary expectations of the students enrolled in the course with the ability to compare groups (e.g., based on on gender), but also to gain a deeper understanding as to why the students have these expectations in their future careers. The university is made up of predominantly Japanese students from a wide variety of locations throughout Japan who enter the university by following a standard entrance exam procedure. The entire curriculum is taught in English by a group of international faculty members. Additionally, all students are required to study abroad for one academic year at one of approximately 180 partner institutions around the world as a requirement for graduation. The students have a choice of two majors, global studies or global business, with the option of adding a teaching license in English.

Setting

One of the main purposes of the course is was to explore the impact issues related to global educational systems, as well as to examine the curriculum on teaching and learning that is a part of those systems. Gender in education is one of the topics covered in the course; in preparation for the discussion on this topic, the students were asked to fill out a short survey anonymously regarding the desired annual income that they would like to earn by the age of 30. The results of the survey were introduced in the class lessons on gender with the aim of examining the differences between the male and female participants' ideal annual income and how their own desires reflect Japanese society's views on the roles of men and women.

Participants

The participants of this study were 59 undergraduate university students who were enrolled in a teacher education course between 2015 and 2017. Students enrolled in this course were between 18 and 22 years old. Furthermore, they were of a mixed range of level in their program from their first year to their senior year. Although this is a teacher's licensure course, not all of the participants were planning to become teachers in the future. Some chose to take this course as an elective toward their degree. Others were pursuing licensure not with the intent to teach, but because of the advantage that possessing a teaching license provides when seeking employment in a field not related to teaching.

Data Collection Procedures

The researcher administered a short, anonymous survey to each student. The students were asked the following question: "By the age of 30, how much would you like to earn in terms of annual income (before tax)?" They had a range of annual salary options from which to choose: 3,000,000–4,000,000 yen (between approximately $27,000 and $36,000), 4,010,000–5,000,000 yen ($36,000 to $45,000), 5,010,000 to 6,000,000 yen ($45,000 to $54,000), 6,010,000–7,000,000 yen ($54,000 to $63,000), or 7,010,000 or more yen ($63,000+). They were then asked to offer an explanation as to why they chose that particular answer in an open-ended response. We collected data in the form of an anonymous survey response.

Data analysis

Descriptive statistics were used to calculate the frequency of the responses and mean average salary expectations. Qualitative analysis was used to examine the explanations that participants offered in terms of their expectations for future salaries through the lens of content analysis (CA). We adopted Neuendorf's (2011) definition of CA as "systematic" and "objective." Krippendorff (2013) adds that CA is one of the most significant methods for analyzing data in the social sciences, because such analysis affords the researcher the ability to view text from a unique perspective that other methods do not offer (p. xii). He explains that CA: (a) is "an empirically grounded method" (p. 1) that methodologically studies textual data, how individuals interpret that data, as well as the impact that such data has on society; (b) "transcends traditional notions of symbols, contents and intents" (p. 2) where texts are more than mere words, but that they contain deeper meanings and the words are simply a vehicle through which these meanings are transferred from one individual to another; and (c) gives researchers the means by which to critically examine data, no matter the outcome, through a unique analysis (pp. 1–5).

CA afforded us the ability to examine the implications in the meaning behind their words in the explanations they provided. In particular, we were interested in understanding the underlying message that is conveyed when students attempted to explain their beliefs in the worth they think they have or do not have relative to their gender. We coded the data from the open-ended question independently for themes relevant to the research question in an effort to comprehend these messages. The data were reviewed and coded following the approach of constantly comparing data throughout the analysis process (Glaser, 1992; Strauss & Corbin, 1998). In the data analysis, we first read each student's explanation three times. We then began to code each explanation, followed by comparing each of the codes and the data associated with each code, along with how this explanation related to their salary expectation. This comparison provided us with the opportunity to identify themes that emerged from commonalities across the data and how it related to the quantitative survey data. From this analysis, four themes surfaced: (a) internalization of gender inequality, (b) being under pressure to become a breadwinner, (c) women's liberation, and (d) money becomes a symbol of success for men. We discuss these themes in detail in the following section.

We also compared the average annual income of Japanese people and the participants' ideal annual income that they want to earn by the age of 30. By examining the gap, we looked closely into how much more or less the female participants in this study expect to earn compared to the actual annual income of Japanese women in order to scrutinize gender ideology that disregards the current circumstances of female workers in Japanese society.

FINDINGS

Table 2.1 shows that only 19% of the male participants expect to earn less than 5,000,000 yen per year. On the other hand, 40% of the female participants expect to earn less than 5,000,000 yen. Table 2.1 also reveals that 43% of the male participants hope to earn more than 7,010,000 yen compared to 22% of the female participants who desire to have a salary in the same range. Approximately half of the male participants (48%) prefer to earn more than 6,010,000 yen ($56,000), which is much higher than the actual average annual income of Japanese workers. Overall, Table 2.1 reveals that the male participants in general show a greater desire to earn a high annual income compared to the female participants, who, by and large, hope to

TABLE 2.1   Ideal Annual Income of University Students (by Gender)

Income Range	Males		Females	
	n	%	*n*	%
3,000,000–4,000,000 (yen)	2	9	3	8
4,010,000–5,000,000 (yen)	2	10	12	32
5,010,000–6,000,000 (yen)	7	33	10	27
6,010,000–7,000,000 (yen)	1	5	4	11
7,010,000 (yen) or more	9	43	8	22
Total	21	100	37	100

earn around the same amount as the national average annual income of Japanese workers.

The quantitative data presented in Table 2.1 provides a snapshot of the participant's salary expectations. However, to gain a deeper understanding into the participants' expected earnings, the open-ended survey data offers us the rationale behind the ideal annual income that each participant selected. We discuss in the following sections each of the themes that emerged throughout the data analysis process.

Internalization of Gender Inequality

Several of the female participants who indicated that they expect to earn less than 5,000,000 yen by the age of 30 stated that they do not anticipate gaining a high annual income since generally, women in Japan do not get paid well. One of the female participants who selected between 4,010,000–5,000,000 yen stated "I think it's enough to have 30–40 man yen for a month. For females, even 401–500 man yen is a high earner."[1] Another female participant who chose the same salary range stated, "I thought it would be enough but I don't know exactly about earning, so I decided comparing with my mother's income." For this female participant, the important role model is her own mother and her mother's income becomes the standard salary expectation that she might be able to earn in the future. One female participant who chose between 3,000,000 yen–4,000,000 yen remarked, "I am ok if I can earn 25 man yen per month." It may be her personal preference and probably money does not define her happiness, but the notion that 25 *man* yen per month is enough on which to live may be a learned or internalized perception that she has acquired as a woman. The female participants' responses suggest the continued acceptance of the gender inequality that is reflected in many women's goals and expectations. As the data suggest, the glass ceiling effect is also pervasive and it stands towering over women in Japan. Accordingly, the female participants are inclined to accept that their socioeconomic achievement will be lower than that of men in Japan once they enter the work force, and these data confirm that many young Japanese women accept this inequality.

Being Under Pressure to Become a Breadwinner

Although some female participants mentioned that they hope to earn a higher annual income for their future family, the pressure that comes from being a breadwinner became especially apparent in the male participants' open-ended responses. This pressure is particularly prevalent in reference to the idea of needing an appropriate income in order to take care of their future spouse and children, no matter whether they chose a career with an average or above-average annual salary range.

One example of this theme is illustrated in the response of a male participant who selected between 4,010,000–5,000,000 yen when he stated, "This amount of money would be enough for my family if I have a wife and two children. And maybe I can save some money for my children's future." Another male participant who chose between 5,010,000–6,000,000 yen noted, "If I can earn about 40 man yen per month, it would be enough to raise my [future] children." Another male participant who also chose the same annual salary range commented, "I don't care about money, but I want enough money to support my kids and wife." A male participant who chose more than 7,010,000 yen remarked, "I want to give my future children possibilities for their future," whereas another who selected this same salary range admitted, "I want 3 or 4 kids." Overall, nine out of 21 male participants (approximately 43%) mentioned their future family in explaining the reasons why they wanted to earn their selected annual income. In contrast, only seven out of 37 female participants (approximately 19%) stated their desire to earn the selected annual income in the interest of their marriage and future children. Interestingly, even though some of the male participants referred to their need to earn a high salary in order to support their future spouse, none of the female participants discussed the need to earn a high salary for their future spouse, supporting the continued belief of the primary role of women to serve as homemaker, not breadwinner. In contrast, based on these responses, the male participants reflect the general societal pressure to live up to the gender ideology that urges them to become a breadwinner in their future family.

As for the notion of men as a breadwinner, women play an essential role in sustaining the pressure for the male to take on this role. A female participant who selected between 3,000,000–4,000,000 yen revealed, "I don't need so much. I will find a husband who earns more." Also, one of the female participants who selected between 4,010,000–5,000,000 yen mentioned, "If I don't marry by age 30, 40–man yen [per month] is enough to live by myself. And if I marry and have children, I hope my husband will earn for it." Throughout Japan's history, men have typically been seen as the breadwinners and women were supposed to take on the role of housemaker. As the analysis of the data in this study suggests, these gender images and roles are still preveleant in the beliefs of today's Japanese youth. Therefore, for many of the male and female university students who participated in this study, the idea of men as breadwinners still remains as a major and prime expectation for men in Japan to uphold.

Women's Liberation

Based on the anecdotal evidence of in-class discussion, even though many of the participants, in particular the females, did not know the average income of Japanese workers nationwide while completing the survey, they seemed aware that women in Japan earn less money than men. During the in-class discussion regarding the gap between men and women in terms of their annual income, which took place in the following class session after the data were collected, many of the female participants displayed their disconsolate feelings toward the gap and became more aware of gender inequality entrenched in Japanese society. While acknowledging the obstacles that women in Japan need to face in order to be socioeconomically independent, some of the female participants still expressed their desire to overcome the challenges related to gender inequality.

One example of this goal to challenge the traditional career expectation of women in Japan comes from a female participant who selected between 5,010,000–6,000,000 yen as her expected annual salary range when she expressed, "If I go back to Tokyo and get opportunities to work, I would like to work not caring too much about taking care of family hopefully, because I am woman." For this female participant, developing a better working career is more desirable than fulfilling the preconceived notion of women as housemakers. A female participant who selected more than 7,010,000 yen asserted, "I want to earn as much income as possible. I don't really have a certain goal in price, but I definitely want to have the equal amount of salary men who are at the same position get." Another female participant who also selected the same salary range revealed, "Want to be rich. Want to travel around the world."

Even though some of the female participants who hope to earn a high annual income stated that they would like to earn as much money as possible to provide their future children with better educational opportunities, the data in the previous paragraph suggest that there are also several female participants who wish to challenge the preconceived gender ideology that has been entrenched in Japanese society for a long time. Despite the fact that women are still socioeconomically disadvantaged in Japan, and that many of our participants still accept these inequities, the importance of women's liberation as well as women's equal rights has slowly but steadily passed on to some of the female university students who participated in this study. The findings of this study reveal that although the view of women's role as that of homemaker is still very much present in the minds of young people who will soon move into adulthood, some students have begun to develop an understanding that the role of homemaker is not the only option for women in society.

Money Becomes a Symbol of Success for Men

Our analysis also indicated that some of the male students referred to their parents' or siblings' (often brothers) annual income as a point of reference to justify their own salary choice. A male participant who selected the annual salary range of 5,010,000–6,000,000 yen confessed, "I want to earn more money than my brother does." A male participant who selected more than 7,010,000 yen explained that this salary choice is "Due to my family income." These two male participants expressed their desire to earn more than or close to their parents' or siblings' annual income. They have both internalized some of the characteristics generally assigned to men such as competitiveness, pride, pretention, and belligerence. This was perhaps best illustrated by a male participant who selected more than 7,010,000 yen and remarked, "I need a high income to look back at all the people who made fun of me. Also you can't buy happiness; however, you need money to become happy." For some of the male participants, it would appear that obtaining a high annual income represents a symbol of being triumphant and the meaning of success is attributed to the amount of money they can receive. Our findings further demonstrate that young men today continue to have the belief that they must follow the path of their ancestors, providing for their future family as the breadwinner.

DISCUSSION

In this section, we discuss how our analysis shed light on our research question: How do issues of gender ideology entrenched in Japanese society for generations affect today's pre-service teachers' assumptions toward their tacit beliefs about their gender role in the work force? We also discuss how the survey results and our analytic findings have been utilized in the teacher education course in order to help the university students to become aware of the gender ideology that perpetuates the traditional gender roles for men and women in Japanese society.

As presented in the previous section, we found that some of the female university students who participated in this study expressed, at least to some extent, their desire to establish a career after graduating from university, a finding supported by Lee et al. (2010). Some of the female university students are motivated to take a significant role in the work force by overcoming the gender stratification that women in Japan have experienced and have been expected to comply with for generations. Additionally, some of the university female students indicated their wish to be socioeconomically independent and to emancipate themselves from the normative gender ideology that is deeply-rooted in Japanese society. These findings may suggest some progress in Japanese society relevant to gender equity, especially among those with greater education, where such attitude changes are likely to begin (Cunningham, 2008). Despite these potential changes in attitude, the majority of the female university students have internalized the traditional gender ideology of gender inequality ingrained in Japanese society, as indicated by responses to the annual income that the female university students expect to earn by the age 30, which for most is lower than that of the male participants. Therefore, the notion of men as the breadwinner has also been ingrained in the female university students. Accordingly, the traditional idea that women ascribe their happiness to finding a financially stable husband with whom to raise a new family has been passed on to many of the female university students, confirming the findings of previous research (Lee et al., 2010). Additionally, these normative roles that continue to pervade Japanese society are based on the presupposition of heterosexuality, excluding the consideration of other gender and sexual identities beyond those of the cisgender heterosexual male and female.

In addition to the influence of the gender gap on the female participants of our study, who still largely expect to have a husband who will be the breadwinner, we found that the gender stereotypes of men as a breadwinner have a strong impact on the male university students, findings that are supported by Adachi (2017). As indicated in the findings, for approximately half of the male university students, supporting their future spouse and children is one of the primary reasons why they wish to earn a higher annual income in the future. Gender ideology embedded in Japanese society places pressure upon the male university students to take on financial responsibilities as a main provider for his family. However, the excessive sociocultural pressure on the male university students to continue keeping up with their breadwinner status could be detrimental to their mental health. According to the Ministry of Health, Labor and Welfare (2017), the total number of suicide cases occurring in Japan in 2016 was 22,080 and 69.1% of the total suicide cases were of men. Regarding the causes of the suicides, the majority of the suicide cases of women in Japan were attributed to health problems (64.7%), followed by family problems (17.3%), financial problems (5.7%), and work problems (3.1%). For men, the most common causes of suicide were health problems (42.9%), followed by financial problems (20.8%), family problems (14.1%), and work problems (11.7%). The ratio of men who took their own life due to financial problems and work problems (total of 32.5%) were much higher than that of women (total of 8.8%). These data support the notion that men in Japan who are commonly placed under pressure to take on a traditional gender role as the breadwinner may be more likely to fall into a challenging and stress laden situation as they face serious financial issues or work-related problems, findings that are supported by other research (Fukuda & Hiyoshi, 2011; Wada,

Eguchi, Yoneoka, Okahisa, & Smith, 2015). The negative impact that the traditional gender ideology, deeply rooted in Japanese society, could have on the younger generations of people in Japan must be urgently examined in the education environs in order to address a context that for some may be quite literally a matter of life and death.

In order to illustrate forms of engaging students on topics relevant to gender and gender inequality/inequity, in the following we discuss how we approached such topics in our own coursework. The data of this study were collected through one of the teacher education courses offered by one of the authors of this chapter at an international liberal arts college in rural Japan, and the survey results were presented in the class lessons on gender. The university students who are enrolled in the teacher education course looked initially uncomfortable when we discussed gender as the main topic of the class session. After presenting several short video clips that perpetuate stereotypical gender images such as TV commercials and a situation comedy, followed by small group discussions to address the gender messages that are present in the clips, the university students, the female students in particular, began to feel comfortable discussing gender stereotypes by referring to their own thoughts and experiences. Based on anecdotal observation of in-class discussions, by the time the survey results accompanied by the data regarding the actual income differences between men and women were introduced, the female university students became more aware of the fact that gender inequality is still prevalent and indicated their discontentment with the inequality.

The class instructor then introduced a short clip from a documentary film called *Tough Guise: Violence, Media & the Crisis in Masculinity* (Ericsson, Talreja, & Sut, 2002) with the aim of reexamining the nature of male masculinity that could prompt violence against not only women and the LGBTQ community, but also men themselves. At the end of the lesson, we discussed the fact that the excessive gender binary which is often reinforced by the existence of unquestioned gender stereotypes ingrained in society hinders the LGBTQ community from constructing their own sociocultural identity. Overall, the survey regarding the ideal annual income that the university students expect to earn by the age of 30 and its results, play a significant role in the lessons on gender. Not only does the activity work as an essential reference for the university students to scrutinize gender inequality, but it also serves as an important practice for the university students to further broaden their perspectives on gender as a social construct.

This attitude that perpetuates "traditional" male and female roles is problematic not only for heterosexual male–female couples, but it is indicative of a much larger problem in Japanese society. The breadwinner-home-maker structure found in Japan is designed to benefit and support only heterosexual male-female couples who are legally married. Consequently, this system affects the lives of those whose identity does not lie within the male/female binary or for those who may not enter into a heterosexual relationship (or any relationship for that matter). In particular, Japan has not yet legalized same-sex marriage, so there are no legal protections for same-sex couples at the national level, and only two wards of Tokyo presently provide a very limited number of benefits to same-sex married couples in Japan (Mosbergen, 2015). Furthermore, given the inequality in pay based on gender that has been discussed in this chapter, two women in a relationship may never be able to earn the same combined salary as that of two men in today's Japan. Although Japan does not offer any benefits to same-sex couples, two men could still live a financially stable and comfortable life based on the current salary inequalities.

Another significant problem with the breadwinner-homemaker system is that it is designed for a *couple*. Although this system would not likely have a negative impact on a single male, a single woman would have a difficult time finding a position that pays enough to live on her own without financial assistance from her family, especially if she also happens to be a single mother. In fact, although legislation is underway to make changes, currently a single woman who becomes pregnant is not eligible for the same state support benefits as those who become single mothers through divorce or death ("Unmarried Single," 2017). To add insult to injury, Japanese society also places a stigma of shame on single mothers and women who have children have even greater difficulty finding a job that pays a livable wage (Fifield, 2017). As Fifield reports, many single mothers struggle to earn enough to live above the poverty line.

CONCLUSION

This chapter aims to shed light on the misconceptions of Japanese undergraduate students that reflect gender inequality in Japan and to highlight how one instructor attempted to disrupt the traditional views of gender roles that continue to be so deeply entrenched in Japanese society. Despite the more apparent improvements in Western society, in Japan the socioeconomic gap between men and women and earning expecations in relation to gender are still significant as the data in this study reveal, even among the current generation of youth who will soon be embarking on their journey into adulthood. Many of the participants' comments highlight the continued expectation for men to be the breadwinner and for women to rely on men to be the breadwinner, an attitude that is extremely challenging to change.

The status that men and women have in Japanese society has been distinctively unequal throughout history and are perpetuated even today, as evidenced in our findings. Disrupting these views in teacher education is challenging given the lack of critical thinking that takes place in Japanese education. However, as we have shown in this chapter, there are opportunities for planting seeds in the minds of youth, even in situations where learners may have never had experiences with challenging society. This project only raises awareness of the inequities that exist in Japanese society for women and the LGBTQ community, but it is our goal to open the eyes of our students so that when they go out into the "real" world and they see how their future students, co-workers, neighbors, friends, and family members are treated, that perhaps they will look for opportunities to help change society.

NOTE

1. One *man* is 10,000 yen, or about $90 (USD).

REFERENCES

Adachi, T. (2017). Work—family planning and gender role attitudes among youth. *International Journal of Adolescence and Youth, 23*(1), 52–60. Retrieved from http://dx.doi.org/10.1080/02673843.2016.1269655

Ashikari, M. (2003). Urban middle-class Japanese women and their white faces: Gender, ideology, and representation. *Ethos, 31*(1), 3–37. doi:10.1525/eth .2003.31.1.3

Cunningham, M. (2008). Changing attitudes toward the male breadwinner, female homemaker family model: Influences of women's employment and education over the lifecourse. *Social Forces, 87*(1), 299–323. https://doi.org/10.1353/ sof.0.0097

Davis, S. N., & Greenstein, T. N. (2009). Gender ideology: Components, predictors, and consequences. *Annual Review of Sociology, 35*, 87–105. https://doi. org/10.1146/annurev-soc-070308-115920

Ericsson, S. (Producer), Talreja, S. (Producer), & Sut, J. (Director). (2002). *Tough guise: Violence, media, and the crisis in masculinity* [Motion picture]. United States: Media Education Foundation.

Fifield, A. (2017, May 28). In Japan, single mothers struggle with poverty and a "culture of shame." *The Washington Post.* Retrieved from https://www.washingtonpost .com/world/asia_pacific/in-japan-single-mothers-struggle-with-poverty-and -with-shame/2017/05/26/01a9c9e0-2a92-11e7-9081-f5405f56d3e4_story .html?utm_term=.42d4f355fc52

Fukuda, Y., & Hiyoshi, A. (2011). Influences of income and employment on psychological distress and depression treatment in Japanese adults. *Environmental Health and Preventive Medicine, 17*(1), 10–17. https://doi.org/10.1007/s12199 -011-0212-3

Gender Equality Bureau Cabinet Office. (2017a). Actions for appointing women to executive positions. In *Women and men in Japan 2017.* Tokyo, Japan: Author.

Retrieved from http://www.gender.go.jp/english_contents/pr_act/pub/ pamphlet/women-and-men17/pdf/2-8.pdf

Gender Equality Bureau Cabinet Office. (2017b). Education and research fields. In *Women and men in Japan 2017*. Tokyo, Japan: Author. Retrieved from http:// www.gender.go.jp/about_danjo/whitepaper/h29/gaiyou/html/honpen/ b1_s05.html

Glaser, B. G., & Strauss, A. L. (1967). *The discovery of grounded theory: Strategies for qualitative research*. New York, NY: Aldine.

Japan's Gender Wage Gap Persists Despite Progress. (2017, Feb. 23). *Nikkei Asian Review*. Retrieved from https://asia.nikkei.com/Politics-Economy/Economy/ Japan-s-gender-wage-gap-persists-despite-progress

Krippendorff, K. (2013). *Content analysis: An introduction to its methodology* (3rd edition). Los Angeles, CA: SAGE.

Lee, K. S., Tufis, P. A., Alwin, D. F., & Teachman, J. (2010). Separate spheres or increasing equality? Changing gender beliefs in postwar Japan. *Journal of Marriage and Family, 72*(1), 184–201. doi:10.1111/j.1741-3737.2009.00691.x

Miller, P. C. (2017). Challenging the myth of homogeneity in Japan in first-year writing. In N. Araki (Ed.), *Diversity in Japanese education* (pp. 83–101). Rotterdam, The Netherlands: Sense.

Ministry of Internal Affairs and Communications Japan. (2016). *Statistical handbook of Japan 2016*. Tokyo, Japan: Author. Retrieved from http://www.stat.go.jp/ english/data/handbook/pdf/2016all.pdf#page=17

Mosbergen, D. (2015, November 5). Tokyo issues Japan's first same-sex marriage certificate. *Huffington Post*. Retrieved from http://www.huffingtonpost.com/ entry/tokyo-japan-same-sex-marriage_us_563b20e9e4b0b24aee48f8a5

National Tax Agency Japan. (2016). *Private-sector annual income actual condition survey 2017*. Retrieved from https://www.nta.go.jp/kohyo/press/press/2016/ minkan/

Neuendorf, K. A. (2011). *The content analysis guidebook* (2nd edition). Thousand Oaks, CA: SAGE.

Strauss, A., & Corbin, J. (1998). *Basics of qualitative research: Techniques and procedures for developing grounded theory* (2nd ed.). Thousand Oaks, CA: SAGE.

Unmarried Single Parents to Become Eligible for State Support. (2017, August 23). *The Japan Times*. Retrieved from https://www.japantimes.co.jp/ news/2017/08/23/national/unmarried-single-parents-become-eligible-state-support/#.WZ5TL62B1E4

Wada, K., Eguchi, H., Yoneoka, D., Okahisa, J., & Smith, D. R. (2015). Associations between psychological distress and the most concerning present personal problems among working-age men in Japan. *BMC Public Health, 15*. https:// doi.org/10.1186/s12889-015-1676-7

Zuo, J., & Tang, S. (2000). Breadwinner status and gender ideologies of men and women regarding family roles. *Sociological Perspectives, 43*(1), 29–43. https:// doi.org/10.2307/1389781

CHAPTER 3

THE HEGEMONY OF TRANSITION AND TRANSGENDER COUNTERNARRATIVES IN CHILDREN'S PICTURE BOOKS

Ashley Lauren Sullivan and Laurie Lynne Urraro

ABSTRACT

As a result of the post-gay marriage backlash, the United States has shifted its gaze to transgender children. This shift has led to increased misunderstanding, gross overgeneralizations, and an expectation that all non-cisgender children follow the same path. We call this the hegemony of transition: the belief that (among other things) all gender creative children wish to fully transition from one dichotomous gender to another and that all children can and will "pass." This dominant narrative is present in most transgender children's picture books, as problematized by young gender creative people in our research study. However, there is a recent shift to include transgender counternarra-

Exploring Gender and LGBTQ Issues in K–12 and Teacher Education, pages 29–51
Copyright © 2019 by Information Age Publishing
All rights of reproduction in any form reserved.

tives in picture books, contesting the hegemony of transition. These stories portray gender creative, gender expansive, genderqueer, etc. children who do not identify as cis or trans. These books do not conform to the rigid expectations of some of the trans storylines that have come before.

As international discourse focuses more on the issues impacting transgender persons, the result is, indubitably, increased visibility of transgender individuals. According to Phillips, "perceptions of transgender are mediated by culturally constructed images" (2006, p. 1), those visual depictions of transgender individuals that contemporary society consumes daily via television, film, and social media. In the last several years, trans characters have become commonplace in popular television programs such as *Transparent, I Am Jazz, Orange is the New Black, Pretty Little Liars, Glee,* and *The Fosters* (Funk & Funk, 2016); in film, for example, *Albert Nobbs* from 2011, *Dallas Buyers Club* from 2013, *The Danish Girl* from 2015, and on social media websites such as Facebook (where Caitlyn Jenner has 3.86 million followers as of March 2018). Likewise, international trans models Valentijn De Hingh (from Paris) and Andreja Pejić (from Australia) can be seen walking the runways of top international fashion shows. Trans individuals have also made their way into the pages of children's picture books. Books such as *10,000 Dresses* (2008), *But, I'm Not a Boy!* (2014) and *When Kayla Was Kyle* (2013) depict a variety of trans individuals. Nonetheless, the representations of the trans individuals in film, television and children's books are, unfortunately, often homologous. For example, many of the young characters in picture books are identified only as "male" or "female." These characters must often completely transition in order to be accepted (and have gender expressions that allow them to "pass" in a manner that aligns with their gender identities). The term for this problem is "transnormativity." A transnormative worldview asserts that the gender identities of trans individuals align with socially prescribed gender expressions. For example, a child who identifies as a girl will have long hair, wear dresses, play with dolls, and love the color pink. Anything other than this alignment is viewed as failure. Thus, all trans individuals seek the same path with the same outcome. Yet, in reality there are individuals who do not subscribe to such a bifurcated nomination. The trans population is composed of persons with gender identities and expressions as diverse as the shades in the rainbow. How do their stories play out in children's picture books? Our study focuses on the content of texts with transgender characters. We wish not only to problematize the homologous occurrences in children's picture books (and delve into the factors that frame this issue), but also to analyze a plethora of more expansive narratives in children's picture books that demonstrate gender identities and expressions beyond what we term transnormative.

It is nearly impossible to estimate how many individuals (both internationally and in the United States context) identify as trans. This is due to many factors. Some individuals have not come out publicly. There are inadequate or non-existent reporting techniques in certain countries or regions. In some cases, there is a deliberate exclusion of transgender persons as part of data sets. Additionally, there are a wide variety of the ways in which transgender individuals define themselves that researchers may be unaware of. In the United States, while national statistics demonstrate that transgender individuals account for 0.6% of the U.S. population (or 1.4 million adults) (Deschamps & Singer, 2017), there appears to be a paucity of data that parses out the number of individuals whom statistics paint with a broad brush as transgender, but who truly identify as more of what the Human Rights Campaign's report terms "gender expansive" (Resources on Gender-Expansive Children and Youth, 2017, What is "Gender Expansive?" section, para. 1). While transgender is "a broad term that can be used to describe people whose gender identity is different from the gender they were thought to be when they were born" (National Center for Transgender Equality, 2016, para. 2), gender expansive individuals are those who do "not identify with traditional gender roles but were otherwise not confined to one gender narrative or experience" (Resources on Gender-Expansive Children and Youth, 2017, What is "Gender Expansive?" section, para. 1). Although gender expansive can be viewed as a subset of individuals under the transgender umbrella, in this work, we differentiate the two. We have chosen to do so because many of the gender expansive individuals in our study do not identify as transgender.

Gender expansive individuals not only possess and display an identity that flows between and among categories of gender nomination (male, female, both, neither, sometimes one, sometimes another, sometimes both, etc.) but also, in terms of articulating this identity, many of these individuals do not prefer to be identified by the pronouns of only "he" or "she." Instead, some choose to utilize both, or adopt pronouns and possessive adjectives that do not exclusively fall into either masculine or feminine categories. These include, but are not limited to, "they," "their," "co," "one," "ze," "sie," "ey" and/or "hir" (University of Wisconsin-Milwaukee, n.d.). Those individuals who define as "bigender" switch between pronouns and adjectives. They may prefer several different pronouns. Other gender expansive individuals do not use any pronouns and adjectives at all, preferring to be referred to by their names every time someone refers to them. In this chapter, we employ the term gender expansive as an umbrella term referring to all non-cis and non-transgender gender identities, including gender non-conforming, bigender, genderqueer, genderfluid, and so forth. We recognize that this term is not uniformly employed. Table 3.1 provides

TABLE 3.1 Gender Expansive Gender Identity Names and Descriptions

Gender Expansive Gender Identity Name	Gender Expansive Gender Identity Description
Agender/Neutrois/ Gender Neutral/ Genderless	Neither male nor female (Weber, 2014)
Androgyne/ Androgynous	Having both male and female characteristics (Weber, 2014)
Bigender	Identifying as female and male at different times and switching between the two (Weber, 2014)
Demigender	Having a weak or partial connection to a gender identity (Gender Wiki, 2016)
Gender Creative	People (typically children) who do not conform to traditional gender norms (Sirois, 2016)
Gender Fluid/ Transfluid	Expressing both male and female characteristics at different times (Weber, 2014)
Gender Nonconforming/ Variant	Those who not act according to societal expectations for their sex (Weber, 2014)
Gender Questioning	Trying to figure out their gender identity (Weber, 2014)
Genderqueer	Umbrella term for all non-conforming gender identities (Weber, 2014)
Hijra	Belonging to a third gender, located in South Asia. Sometimes identifying as transgender or intersex as well (Khaleeli, 2014)
Intersex	Those who have sexual chromosomes, anatomy, and/or sex organs that are not defined as male or female (Weber, 2014)
Non-binary	Those who disregard the idea of male/female dichotomy or continuum with androgyny in the middle. They view gender as more of a web or three-dimensional model (Weber, 2014)
Pangender	Identifying as a third gender, with both male and female aspects (Weber, 2014)
Polygender	Experiencing multiple gender identities, either simultaneously or varying between them (Gender Wiki, 2016)
Trigender	Experiencing three gender identities, either simultaneously or varying between them. These can include male, female, and/or any non-binary identities (Gender Wiki, 2016)
Two Spirit	Term referring to gender variant Native Americans (Weber, 2014)

an extensive, but by no means exhaustive, list of the most commonly used gender expansive gender identities.

As the knowledge base regarding the spectrum of gender expansive identities expands, we must ask: What forms of societal recognition and validation are available for those individuals whose ontology of identity does not fit neatly into prescribed, frequently used, and socially common categories? As university educators in both the fields of early childhood and elementary education and Spanish, who are passionate about the field of early childhood teacher preparation, we are particularly concerned about the repercussions for young gender expansive children thrust into classrooms and schooling systems that maintain repressive, restrictive, heteronormative and transnormative expectations. In an effort to counter these stifling expectations, we investigated the manner in which gender expansive children find recognition of themselves in media such as children's books. We asked which literary portrayals offer a spectrum of identity representation. This includes those children who do not want to "pass" (e.g., a child assigned male at birth who is perceived formally and informally by society as female) or "transition," (changing one's body and/or clothing to a different gender). Such queries spurred us to initiate a research project that initially sought to locate gender expansive characters in children's picture books. In this chapter, we continue the conversation begun in that initial project as we analyze the types of narratives in children's picture books that proffer gender expansive or transgender main characters. We begin with a discussion of the theories that ground our chapter and inform our thinking and analysis. We then continue with a discussion of the types of non-cisgender narratives available in children's picture books. We explain how several of these are problematic as they instantiate the problem of transnormativity. We analyze the narrative contestations to this problem of transnormativity, what we term "transgender counternarratives," and frame this discussion within our qualitative research studies. Finally, we consider the implications of these types of storylines for teacher education and the work of early childhood educators.

QUEER THEORY, THE "HEGEMONY OF TRANSITION," THE "PROBLEM OF PASSING," AND TRANSGENDER COUNTERNARRATIVES

Our project examines the types of narratives within the corpus of children's picture books. We have used queer theory to examine what we term the problem of passing and the issues with transnormativity (specifically with regard to how both of these intersect in children's picture books). Emerging in the 1990s, queer theory gained prominence as a means to disrupt the hegemonic gender binary (the belief that that there are only two genders: male and female) and served as a means to situate both theoretical and practical explanations, representations, and validations of varied gender identities and expressions. This revolutionized scholarly insight of gender and ushered a movement away from understanding gender as a binary system.

Theorists such as Judith Butler (2006), Eve Kosofsky Sedgwick (1990), and Monique Wittig (1992), to name a few, all problematize the notion that gender is only presented as a bifurcation. They argue instead for a view of gender that both recognizes and legitimizes those "in-between zones" that lie between and spill out from the gender binary. For example, Butler (2004) theorizes that:

> Even within the field of intelligible sexuality, one finds that the binaries that anchor its operations permit for middle zones and hybrid formations... Indeed, there are middle regions, hybrid regions of legitimacy and illegitimacy that have no clear names, and where nomination itself falls into a crisis produced by the variable. (p. 108)

Thus, queer theory promotes a consideration of gendered ontologies that exceed and rework and binary, and that legitimate genders that occupy such spaces. It is precisely this consideration of this interstitial and non-binarized theory that we have applied to the analysis of the works in this chapter. We sought out children's literature that incorporates characters who do not identify as cisgender. Specifically, we searched for tales that did not follow transnormative storylines. Therefore, we build upon the already existing corpus of theory in order to recognize non-normative gender ontologies. However, we do this while also problematizing some of those same non-normative ontologies for the implicit homologous assumptions present therein.

Our criticism of some of the storylines involving trans characters in children's picture books emerges from the work of trans scholars such as Jack Halberstam (2012) and S. Bear Bergman (2009). Both Bergman and Halberstam build upon the theories of Butler, Sedgwick, and Wittig as they, too, bolster the endorsement of a more fluid approach to gender. Halberstam's (2012) particular theory of "gaga feminism" is defined as "a politics that that brings together meditations on fame and visibility with a lashing critique of the fixity of roles for males and females" (p. 5). This theoretical approach critiques the hegemonic view of gender and argues for an expanded definition. Bergman (2009) likewise advocates for legitimacy of gender expansive ontologies in stating that "genders that are unusual, nonstandard, mix-n-match, or new to us are just as valid as the ones we're more accustomed to" (p. 91). Our research project draws from the gender theories of Butler, Wittig, and Sedgwick as well as the more emergent theories of Halberstam and Bergman.

The Hegemony of Transition

Although repeated exposure to trans people in the media helps to eliminate some stereotypes, for example, that being transgender is a choice, it also works to establish new ones (Halberstam, 2012). When the general public is continually exposed to individual stories containing narratives bound by common themes, those narratives can begin to solidify as truth, as one way of being (Bergman, 2009). We theorize this phenomenon as the hegemony of transition. This hegemony of transition plays out as follows: those who are not cisgender (those whose gender identity aligns with their assigned sex at birth), are, in fact, transgender, and wish to transition from one dichotomous gender to another. They first come out, are rejected by some and supported by others. They then go to the doctor who gives them permission and guidance to transition. They change their name, hair, clothing, and interests. They then take hormones and have surgery to complete the transition. After the transition is complete, they now fit stereotypical presentations of the "new" gender and pass well in society.

We opine that the hegemony of transition is not only misguided but also can be downright dangerous. Some trans and/or gender expansive people, for a myriad of reasons as diverse as the individuals themselves, cannot or do not wish to transition. An individual may wish to transition only some aspects of themselves, but not others. For example, they may wish to change their hairstyle, name, and clothing, but may still identify as the gender they were assigned at birth. If the expectation for trans and/or gender expansive people is to appear and act as one dichotomous or new gender only, what about the individuals for whom passing is not a reality? Gender confirmation surgery is expensive, and not attainable to the many trans people living under the poverty line (Stack, 2016). For children, transition involving puberty blockers and hormones (in order to, for example, change their bodies completely from their gender assigned at birth to another) may be impossible with the lack of supportive parents (Olson, Durwood, DeMeules, & McLaughlin, 2016). Passing (when society does not question one's gender but rather automatically assumes that individual is cisgender) can be extremely difficult for persons who have endured secondary puberty and experienced body changes that are irreversible (voice depth, height, etc.) or very difficult, expensive, and/or painful to alter (facial hair, breasts, Adam's apple, body shape, etc.; Begun & Kattari, 2016). Importantly, some gender expansive persons simply do not want to be referred to as transgender. They may self-identify somewhere in the gender expansive universe, but not necessarily anchored to any one denotative fixity.

The Problem of Passing

My problem is that none of the bodies into which I would like to live in are available to me...It is your job, the word *passing* communicates, and, what's more, your solemn responsibility to create a presentation of gender that conforms well enough to the prevailing standards of whatever context you find yourself in to call forth from onlookers the gender attribution you desire...if you do not *pass*, you are a failure. If you do, you are a success. (Bergman, 2009, pp. 51, 106, 105)

This quote from queer theorist and trans-activist S. Bear Bergman instantiates the increasingly more complex and layered ways in which gender ontologies are mapped onto bodies. Concomitantly, there is the problematic expectation of transgender people to transition fully from one gender to another, to "cross" successfully, to pass effectively in order for their bodies to be legitimated and socially accepted. This explains what we call the problem of passing for those individuals in society who do not wish to pass, or transition. Passing can and does privilege the experiences, perceptions, and realities of cisgender people over trans individuals. People who are not cis regularly become subject to a normalizing gaze. When a trans person is viewed through a dichromatic cis filter, reality is obscured, and cis comfort becomes paramount. The practice of passing becomes much more about putting cis individuals at ease than it is about the ability of trans individuals to transition to a gender not assigned at birth (as some may choose to do). Passing morphs into an expectation, a requirement for all trans individuals. The problematic idea that one should strive to pass as cis reinforces a hegemonic, cisnormative, transphobic worldview. For those who do not identify as cis, existence can become a purgatorial torment, and escape is only possible via the forced prescription to a dichotomy that does not (and should not) fit all individuals.

METHODOLOGICAL APPROACHES IN OUR STUDIES

As many global communities shift to an increased understanding of the varied ways in which people identify and express their genders, the stories and narratives used in elementary classrooms must shift as well. Storytelling conveys cultural nuances, connects the listener and reader, disseminates information, and, at times, acts as a form of resistance (Klein, Manzano, Johnson, Robinson, & Yee, 2014). Storytelling has always been used as a means of challenging structural power inequities (Ashton, 1978). As such, books have been frequently banned from public and school libraries. And so, in secret or in defiance, educators resist. The telling of trans tales through published (and somewhat easily accessible) children's picture books is a recent phenomenon. Within that genre, there is the emergence of a subset of books that counter the hegemony of transition. These transgender counternarratives seek to dismantle, undermine, and reframe the manner in which we view individuals who identify as gender expansive. We now shall examine the initial study of our query into non-cisgender characters in children's picture books that began in 2015.

THE 2015 STUDY

The ability for children to see themselves represented in books is critical for identity development. Children need and want to see representations of themselves or who they desire to be in the texts they consume (Klein et al., 2014). There has been a recent shift to try to include trans narratives in books for three- to eight-year-olds. The publications of *Rough Tough Charley* (Kay, 2007) and *10,000 Dresses* (Ewert & Ray, 2008) ushered in a new wave of children's picture books, with transgender characters gracing the pages of books written for young children for the very first time. We focused our study on locating transgender storylines in books that were in English, Spanish, and/or that were bilingual (English-Spanish), as there are over 55 million Spanish-speakers in the U.S (US Census Bureau, 2017) and 4.3% of them are LGBTQ (Konnoth & Gates, 2011).

Our 2015 content analysis of children's picture books containing transgender characters identified the volume and content of these books (Sullivan & Urraro, 2017). In our study, we were unable to locate any children's picture books in English or Spanish that contained transgender characters published prior to 2007. However, there were books containing gender expansive characters that were published prior to this. We located a total of 38 books (via internet search and our university's library search engine) that contained transgender or expansive characters. It also noted trends among the books, most notably that the majority of the characters were White, able-bodied, and upper middle class. Nearly all of the books told either a transition story or were about loving, accepting, and supporting transgender children. The books conveyed a didactic message about educating cisgender people about transgender people. Also, the transgender characters were not present in story lines that did not emphasize the characters' "trans-ness."

The 2016/2017 Study

In our 2016/2017 study, we held focus groups with transgender and gender expansive individuals in order to discuss the books examined in our 2015 study. We chose three states (two in the Northeast and one in the Midwest United States). We utilized convenience sampling, contacting the facilitator of transgender community groups and asking if we were able to hold focus groups with their members. We first attended support meetings (facilitated by these groups) on several occasions prior to data collection. These support groups offered camaraderie, socialization, and a place to share common struggles and ask for or offer advice. Our intention in attending the meetings was to form relationships with the members and explain our project. We attended the public support groups as they are the primary means that these individuals meet on a regular basis. The five group member participants at site 1 consisted entirely of adults. There were four transwomen and one transman. Site 2 contained primarily children/teenagers as well as a few parents (six individuals) as participants. There were three cisgender parents present, one female trans child, one transwomen, and one gender non-conforming teenager. Site 3 was comprised of a multi-age group and included children, teens, adults, and parents (twelve individuals) as participants. There was one cisgender parent, two trans children, and eight gender expansive and/or gender queer children participants. Each of the individuals in the study chose a pseudonym by which we could identify their feedback. The participants at all three sites contained a sampling of interested individuals from the support groups. Support group members were able to opt out of the focus groups.

One hour-and-a-half long session was completed with each group. During the first thirty minutes of each session, we provided a sample of randomly assigned books containing transgender and gender expansive characters to each of the focus group members. While they read, they made notations regarding their feedback of the books. Due to the speed at which they read, some were able to read more books than others. We did not require a minimum or specify a maximum number of books that the individuals could read. While they read, the focus group participants had access to the questions we would ask them upon conclusion of the reading session. The questions were as follows: What do you think of the books? Which books resonated with you? Why? Do you prefer to see human characters or non-human characters (e.g., animals, aliens) in books with transgender characters? Is there anything missing from the books that you would like to see? If so, what?

Once the reading portion concluded, the focus group members provided feedback and/or critiques of the books during a sixty-minute-long group discussion. This discussion was guided by the questions we had provided. In addition, we collected the written reflections and notes of the participants. Lastly, we shared with them our own findings from the 2015 study and asked them to reflect on these. We asked the focus group members their views as to how aligned our findings were to their own interpretations and opinions of the books. These focus groups were audio recorded (and later transcribed). We also took notes during the discussions. The quotes included in this chapter were pulled both from the transcriptions as well as our notes.

Categorizing the Books

When referencing the types of books, we differentiate between the terms "transgender" and "gender expansive" based on the collection and analysis of our data from this most recent study. We classified the books under these categories based on the feedback gained from our focus group participants. The categorizations were made based on whether or not the focus group participants believed the characters in the books to be gender expansive or transgender. Books classified as transgender contained characters who transitioned from assigned birth gender to a different dichotomous gender identity. Books classified as gender expansive identity contained characters whose gender identity was neither exclusively male nor female, but did not align with assigned birth gender. Books classified as gender expansive expression contained characters whose external appearance did not match societal expectations for the gender to which they were assigned. These characters did not have a gender identity that was different from the gender that was assigned to them at birth. Although we did bring a sampling of gender expansive identity books to the focus groups (i.e., books that contained characters who internally identified as being gender expansive). Table 3.2 highlights the classification of the text and which texts were employed for the 2015 and 2016/2017 studies. To provide the reader with a current snapshot of the available literature, we have included additional texts in the table. Further explanation and specific examples of focus group responses to books in these categories are discussed in the following sections.

FINDINGS

Transgender (often Transnormative) Storylines

For the books that contained transgender characters, the focus group members identified 21/24 as being problematic with regard to reinforcing the hegemony of transition. In these texts, characters fully transition (typically with the support of a medical professional) and, after transition, those characters fully pass. However, 3/24 books effectively dismantle the hegemony of transition, meaning that they do not proffer transnormative storylines. The interviewed participants felt that the transnormative storylines were detrimental to young gender expansive readers who could not transition, did not wish to transition, did not conform to the binary, or did not view passing as necessary. They yearned for more books containing gender expansive characters. Although the individuals in the focus groups did not use the term transnormative, their issues with the books were related to their transnormativity. For example, the books' reinforcement of

TABLE 3.2 List of Books with Transgender and Gender Expansive Characters

Author(s)	Title	Publication Year	Character Gender	Included in the 2015 Study	Included in the 2016/2017 Focus Group Discussion
Gran Ovidio Acopán and Manuel Gutiérrez	Piratrans Carabarco	2015	Gender Expansive–Identity	X	X
J.J. Austrian	Worm Loves Worm	2016	Gender Expansive–Identity		
Brett Axel	Goblinheart, A Fairy Tale	2012	Transgender	X	X
Christine Baldacchino	Morris Micklewhite and the Tangerine Dress	2014	Gender Expansive–Expression	X	
Helga Bansch	Odd Bird Out	2011	Gender Expansive–Expression	X	
Nina Benedetto	About Chris	2015	Transgender		X
Nina Benedetto	My Favorite Color is Pink!	2015	Transgender		
Nina Benedetto	It's Me	2016	Gender Expansive–Identity		
S. Bear Bergman	Backwards Day	2012	Transgender	X	X
S. Bear Bergman	Is That For a Boy or a Girl?	2015	Gender Expansive–Expression		
S. Bear Bergman	The Adventures of Tulip, Birthday Wish Fairy	2012	Transgender	X	X
Talcott Broadhead	Meet Polkadot	2014	Gender Expansive–Identity	X	X
Jacinta Bunnell and Irit Reinheimer	Girls Will Be Boys Will Be Girls Will Be . . . A Coloring Book	2004	Gender Expansive–Expression		
Jennifer Carr	Be Who You Are	2010	Transgender	X	X
Babette Cole	Mummy Never Told Me	2003	Gender Expansive–Identity		
Monique Costa	When Leonard Lost His Spots	2012	Transgender	X	X

(continued)

TABLE 3.2   List of Books with Transgender and Gender Expansive Characters (continued)

Author(s)	Title	Publication Year	Character Gender	Included in the 2015 Study	Included in the 2016/2017 Focus Group Discussion
Kevin Diller	Hello, My Name is Octicorn	2016	Gender Expansive–Identity		
Christina Engela	Other Kids Are Almost Just Like You	2016	Transgender		
Marcus Ewert and Rex Ray	10,000 Dresses	2008	Transgender	X	X
Amy Fabrikant	When Kayla Was Kyle	2013	Transgender	X	X
Campbell Geeslin	Elena's Serenade	2004	Gender Expansive–Expression	X	
Maya Christina González	Call Me Tree/ Llámame Árbol	2014	Gender Expansive–Identity	X	X
Maya Christina González and Matthew Smith González	I am Free To Be Me. Gender Now—A Learning Adventure for Children and Adults	2010	Gender Expansive–Identity		
Louis Gould	X: A Fabulous Child's Story	1978	Gender Expansive–Identity	X	X
Dylan Greenberg	Sid Doesn't Feel Like a Boy or a Girl	2015	Genderd Expansive–Identity		X
Michael Hall	Red, A Crayon's Story	2015	Transgender	X	X
Jessica Herthel and Jazz Jennings	I Am Jazz	2014	Transgender	X	X
Jenson J. Hillenbrand	Parts and Hearts	2016	Transgender		X
Tobi Hill-Meyer	A Princess of Great Daring	2015	Transgender		
Jo Hirst	The Gender Fairy	2015	Transgender		
Sarah and Ian Hoffman	Jacob's New Dress	2014	Gender Expansive–Expression	X	
Henrick Hovland	John Jensen Feels Different	2011	Gender Expansive–Expression	X	

(continued)

TABLE 3.2 List of Books with Transgender and Gender Expansive Characters (continued)

Author(s)	Title	Publication Year	Character Gender	Included in the 2015 Study	Included in the 2016/2017 Focus Group Discussion
Karleeen Pendleton Jiménez	*Are You a Boy or a Girl?*	2000	Gender Expansive–Expression	X	X
Myles Johnson	*Large Fears*	2015	Gender Expansive–Expression		
Verla Kay	*Rough, Tough Charley*	2007	Transgender	X	X
M.F. Keene	*Bonnie Does Not Like Dresses*	2015	Gender Expansive–Expression	X	
Anna Kemp	*Dogs Don't Do Ballet*	2010	Gender Expansive–Expression	X	
Eileen Kiernan-Johnson	*Roland Humphrey is Wearing a WHAT?*	2013	Gender Expansive–Expression	X	
Cheryl Kilodavis	*My Princess Boy*	2010	Gender Expansive–Expression	X	X
Sophie Labelle	*A Girl Like Any Other*	2013	Gender Expansive–Identity		
Jessica Lam	*The Adventures of Tina and Jordan*	2013	Transgender		
Katie Leone	*But, I'm Not a Boy!*	2014	Transgender	X	X
Elizabeth Levy	*Nice Little Girls*	1974	Gender Expansive–Expression	X	
Bruce Mack	*Jesse's Dream Skirt*	1979	Gender Expansive–Expression	X	
Kyo Maclear	*Spork*	2017	Gender Expansive–Identity		
Bill Martin Jr. and John Archambault	*White Dynamite and Curly Kidd*	1986	Gender Expansive–Expression	X	
McNall Mason and Max Suarez	*Play Free*	2012	Gender Expansive–Expression	X	
Angela McAllister	*Yuck! That's Not a Monster!*	2010	Gender Expansive–Expression	X	

(continued)

TABLE 3.2 List of Books with Transgender and Gender Expansive Characters (continued)

Author(s)	Title	Publication Year	Character Gender	Included in the 2015 Study	Included in the 2016/2017 Focus Group Discussion
Lilly Mossiano	My New Daddy	2013	Transgender		
Lilly Mossiano	My New Mommy	2012	Transgender		
Willa Naylor	Truly Willa	2016	Transgender		X
Leslea Newman	Sparkle Boy	2017	Gender Expansive–Expression		
Brook Pessin-Whedbee	Who Are You? The Kid's Guide to Gender Identity	2016	Gender Expansive–Identity		
Phyllis Rothblatt	All I Want To Be Is Me	2011	Gender Expansive–Identity	X	X
Sarah Savage	Are You a Boy or Are You a Girl?	2015	Gender Expansive–Identity	X	X
Miriam Schlein	The Girl Who Would Rather Climb Trees	1975	Gender Expansive–Expression	X	
Laurie Stiller	Princess Max	2001	Gender Expansive–Expression	X	
Kai Cheng Thom	From the Stars in the Sky to the Fish in the Sea	2017	Gender Expansive–Identity		
Andrea U'Ren	Pugdog	2001	Gender Expansive–Expression	X	
Deborah van der Beek	Melinda and the Class Photograph	1991	Gender Expansive–Expression	X	
Jess Walton	Introducing Teddy	2016	Transgender		X
Wallace Wong	When Kathy is Keith	2011	Transgender	X	X

the gender binary, the book narratives' expectations that characters who transition will now only have interests associated with their "new" gender, and that the characters will pass. Excerpts of the participants' comments throughout the focus groups sessions are included to illustrate the main themes and findings.

Many of the individuals from our study self-identify as gender expansive or gender queer. As a result, the focus group participants were interested in finding themselves represented in the books. These participants were particularly critical when this did not occur and addressed the multiple deficits in the books currently on the market that they deemed transnormative. One of the books they critiqued was *Backwards Day* (Bergman, 2012). This story takes place in an alternative universe in which, on one day of the year, everything changes, including the characters' genders. The main character, who identified as a boy during the majority of the year, remained a boy on Backwards Day. The Backwardsologist (doctor) explains that "Andy was already backwards. That's why Backwards Day didn't affect him. You see? For Andy, being a girl was as backwards as backwards can be. Now he's set right. Oh, how wonderful" (Bergman, 2012, p. 7). In response to this book, a gender non-conforming youth at site 2 stated, "The characters act like one is the opposite of another; nothing is just the 'opposite.' You don't just 'become' the other binary." This person also noted, "The gender binary doesn't even describe all cis people."

Be Who You Are (Carr, 2010) was another text critiqued for its transnormativity. In this book, the main character, Nick, is truly a girl named Hope. Hope says, "I never felt like a boy inside. I have always felt like a girl" (Carr, 2010, p. 28). She states that she was, "born in the wrong body" (Carr, 2010, p. 10). A participant from site 1 explained that, "'Born in the wrong body' is the stereotype. I suspect this stereotype emphasizes the binary and the need to 'pass,'" which he cites as problematic. Like *Be Who You Are*, *I am Jazz* (Herthel, Jennings, & McNicholas, 2014) also discusses a mismatch between body and brain. *I am Jazz* is an eponymous tale about Jazz Jennings, who shares her story of overcoming obstacles in order to be accepted as a girl. Jazz, who reflects on her transition throughout the book, states, "I have a girl brain and a boy body" (Herthel et al., 2014). During the focus group at site 2, one participant asked: "Why do we always say 'boy brain and girl body'? If I have a boy brain, then I am a boy and every part of me is a boy- including my body." In reference to *I am Jazz*, a participant at site 1 critiqued, "It is okay if trans girls like some boy things and trans guys like some girl things." This participant was referring to the over-abundance of pink and feminine activities that Jazz enjoys in the text.

Parts and Hearts: A Kids' & Grown-Ups Guide to Transgender Transition (Hillenbrand, 2016), is a non-fiction text that was problematized by participants for its trans stereotypes. Rosa (site 2) critiqued that this book "uses gender norms as the deciding factor of trans. It claims that surgery is a major part of being trans." Per the focus group members, an additional example of a transnormative storyline is *Red, A Crayon's Story* (Hall, 2015). In this book, Red, a blue crayon with a red label is initially misunderstood by the other crayons in the box. The other crayons and art supplies insist that Red must indeed be the color red due to his red label. The narrator explains that "He was red but he wasn't very good at it" (Hall, 2015 pp. 1–2). Red was eventually accepted for his true "blue" nature. The consensus of many of the focus group participants was that this text was, indeed, transnormative, as it only permitted one solid color of crayon (blue or red for example).

The Value of All Transgender Narratives

It is important to note, as did many of the focus group members, that while the storylines identified as transnormative are not and should not be deemed representative of all individuals, these books do represent the experiences of some trans children. Many trans individuals do, in fact, desire to pass and transition. Thus, there is a marked value in both transnormative (21 books) and non-transnormative narratives (3 books). They both can and do effectively portray the struggles and triumphs of some transgender children. Both kinds of books were revolutionary, paving the way for other non-cis storylines, and have surely provided comfort to many transgender readers. It is not our desire for the reader to take away that these books fundamentally lack merit, just that they only provide one kind of narrative.

Several of these transgender books were highly lauded by both the trans and gender expansive focus group members. One example of such a book was *10,000 Dresses* (Ewert & Ray, 2008), whose main character Bailey possesses a talent for making (and wearing) a variety of dresses out of diverse materials (such as mirrors), commenting that the diversity of such dresses "do show us ourselves" (Ewert & Ray, 2008, p. 28). Bailey does not receive support from her family, but she does find validation in her neighbor. This transgender character neither passes nor transitions during the story. Additionally, both *A Princess of Great Daring* (Hill-Meyer, 2015) and *Other Kids are Almost Just Like You* (Engela, 2016) offered transgender counternarratives.

Gender Expansive–Identity Books

Many of the individuals in the focus groups, transgender and gender expansive alike, favorably responded to the transgender counternarrative books that actively contested the hegemony of transition. One participant from site 3 highlighted the dearth of gender expansive books, stating: "I have yet to see a children's book about gender that has stepped away from the issue of 'what girls like vs. what boys like' and simply talked about how the transgender or gender questioning character feels on the inside." Of the books we located, there were fewer books about gender expansive identity (16 books) than there were about transgender characters (24 books). Although 48/62 books were published within the past decade, the gender expansive books tend to be a bit more recent. 56.25% of the gender expansive identity books were published in the past 3 years (2015–2017) vs. 37.5% of the transgender books, perhaps due to the fact that there is more visibility of gender expansive individuals today.

An example of a gender expansive identity narrative is *Meet Polkadot* (Broadhead, 2014). This is a text that provides definitions for numerous gender terms in a story about a genderfluid individual. To quote the text, "the Gender Binary is an imperfect way for cultures to describe gender identity as it leaves out a lot of people" (Broadhead, 2014, p. 10). Focus group members appreciated this assertion. One participant from site 2 reinforced the book's message in stating that "people should not be put into boxes." The book *Piratrans Carabarco* (Acopán & Gutiérrez, 2015), written in Spanish and only available in Europe (obtained by our university library and translated into English by Laurie Urraro for the focus group participants), shows how a trans-pirate named Shipface possesses both male and female body parts. Shipface proudly responds to those who are critical of Shipface for not having what is necessary to be a pirate, retorting "I do have what one should have" (Acopán & Gutiérrez, 2015). In the text, Shipface flows between and among genders seamlessly on a daily basis.

Another transgender counternarrative that includes a gender expansive identity is *X: A Fabulous Child's Story* (Gould, 1978). This story tells of a child who was raised gender neutral in an effort by the main character's parents to allow the child to grow and develop without the restrictions of socially imposed gender norms. When asked if the baby was a boy or a girl, X's parents simply replied "It's an X" (Gould, 1978, p. 7). A participant from site 2 explained that this book is "great for gender non-conforming kids." Another participant from site 2 stated that the book, "explains the social importance of removing labels from children." Regarding this book, a parent of a trans child from site 3 stated "Can't believe this was 1978!! Where did we go wrong?," echoing the sentiment of many at the focus groups.

The focus group participants lauded these texts. This was especially true of those participants who identified as gender expansive who viewed these texts as a means by which the characters in the book (and perhaps those children reading the texts) could identify with not having only to choose a gender such as male or female. Likewise, they appreciated that the texts do not emphasize the need for characters to have to transition and pass in order to be accepted for who they are in society.

Gender Expansive–Expression Books

In addition to books about transgender characters and characters possessing a gender expansive identity, there were also transgender counternarratives containing characters who had an expansive gender expression. This expression primarily manifested in relationship to clothing, or clothing and interests, hobbies, etc. Here we located 24 books. An example of this type of storyline is found in *My Princess Boy* (Kilodavis, 2010), a story about a boy who "likes pretty things. Pink is his favorite color. He plays dress up in girly dresses. He dances like a beautiful ballerina." (Kilodavis, 2010, p. 2). The character exhibits a gender expansive expression through clothing, toy selection, and activities.

Melinda and the Class Photograph (van der Beek, 1991) is another example of a text with a character who has a gender expansive expression. In this book, the main character, a pig named Melinda, resents being forced to wear a cute, fluffy, white dress for that year's class photograph. The character states, "My name's Mel. And I don't like dresses" (van der Beek, 1991, p. 2). Similarly, another example of a gender expansive gender narrative is *Play Free* (Mason & Suarez, 2012). In this text, the focus is not on clothing so much as it is on play activities. The book suggests that children should be allowed to play freely and without limit. One of the characters, Sue, "likes to play with monster trucks and go to the zoo and feed the ducks, and drinks apple juice while eating popcorn with cheese, ask if she wants some, I bet she'll say 'please'" (Mason & Suarez, 2012, para. 20–21).

Both the gender expansive identity and the gender expansive expression books proffer an important representation of some individuals whose gender expression is multiple and varied, as they demonstrate the varied and non-transnormative gender expressions of the characters held within their pages. These counternarratives would be of particular value to early childhood educators, as it is critical to teach about the entire gender spectrum-not just cis and trans individuals. As mentioned earlier, the books represent individuals whose gender identity or expression disrupts transnormativity.

DISCUSSION

Our research over the past several years has introduced us to a myriad of different individuals, in different parts of the country and of varying ages. One of the transgender individuals who took part in our study exclaimed, "it would have been nice to have something that helped to explain what we were going through when we were young," reflecting a common opinion that more resources and supports are needed for gender expansive children. These would help gender expansive children feel less alone in the gender-binarized world that solely provides two gender options. Thus, with our project, we determined to analyze texts that not only validated transgender identities, but gender expansive identities as well.

We developed a clear and pervasive realization that further solidified with each subsequent focus group—while some individuals identify as transgender, many, in fact, do not want to be defined by the transgender label. They identify with and express a variety of different genders, each unique from the next. Gender, as we know, is much more than two perfectly square, two-dimensional check boxes (Butler, 2006). It is organic, and fluid but sometimes fixed and biological. It is restrictive yet expansive, and influential though influenced. For some individuals, gender identification can change daily. A gender expansive individual from site 2 remarked that, whenever asked "Are you a boy or a girl?", the answer they prefer to give is "People can be male, female, both, or neither. *I'm a unicorn.*" Such a reflection underscores the importance of transgender counternarratives. These contestations to the hegemony of transition, as we have seen, have surfaced in several of the children's picture books that we analyzed in our study. Early childhood educators are some of the first individuals in a child's life who can positively impact gender expansive children, and, as such, it is therefore incumbent upon early childhood educators be informed of diversity of gender identities, that not all children will identify with a gender that corresponds to their biological sex, and that a recognition and affirmation of diverse genders should be reflected in the literature children engage with.

CONCLUSION

At a time when the hegemony of transition equates trans children's lives with passing and abandonment of interests and appearance associated with the "opposite gender," it is increasingly important to educate cis adults (particularly parents, children's book authors, and teachers) about those who fall outside the binary. It is our hope that not only transgender narratives but also those we have located within the gender expansive universe find their way onto the shelves of elementary schools, bookstores, and online sites. Through this increased access to these texts, transgender and gender expansive children will experience validation and connectedness to the storylines as they recognize themselves in the narratives. Likewise, cis children will learn that not all individuals fit so neatly into the normative categories of boy or girl.

These transgender counternarratives that counter the hegemony of transition and the problems associated with passing mark a pronounced change in the ever-growing catalog of gender expansive children's picture books. They also serve to connect and humanize the experiences of gender expansive individuals. This chapter is a call for researchers to adopt queer theories as productive analytics recognizing that individuals should never be limited to one single nomination, but frequently occupy a multiplicity of loci identities (such as gender identities) across a spectrum. It is also a call to action, for the faculty who train future teachers, the authors who write children's picture books, and the educators who work with young children, to expand the dissemination of transgender counternarratives as a means to break down the problem of passing and reduce the hegemony of transition. As Halberstam articulates, "What if we actually stopped and recognized the multiple ways in which men and women, boys and girls, exceed and fall short of the definitions that give those categories heft and longevity?" (2012, p. 9).

REFERENCES

Acopán, G. O., Gutiérrez, M., & Asociación de Transexuales de Andalucía-Sylvia Rivera. (2015). *Piratrans carabarco* [Pirate shipface] (1st ed.). Málaga, Spain: La Calle.

Ashton, E. (1978). The effect of sex-role stereotyped picture books on the play behavior of three-and four-year-old children. (Unpublished doctoral dissertation). University of Massachusetts.

Begun, S., & Kattari, S. K. (2016). Conforming for survival: Associations between transgender visual conformity/passing and homelessness experiences. *Journal of Gay & Lesbian Social Services, 28*(1), 54–66. doi:10.1080/10538720.201 6.1125821

Bergman, S. B. (2012). *Backwards day.* Toronto, ON: Flamingo Rampant.

Bergman, S. B. (2009). *The nearest exit may be behind you.* Vancouver, BC: Arsenal Pulp Press.

Bornstein, K., & Bergman, S. B. (2010). *Gender outlaws: The next generation.* Berkeley, CA: Seal Press.

Broadhead, T. (2014). *Meet Polkadot.* Olympia, WA: Dangerdot Publishing.

Butler, J. (2006). *Gender trouble: Feminism and the subversion of identity.* New York, NY: Routledge.

Butler, J. (2004). *Undoing gender.* New York, NY: Routledge.

Carr, J. (2010). *Be who you are.* Bloomington, IN: AuthorHouse.

Deschamps, D., & Singer, B. L. (2017). *LGBTQ stats: Lesbian, gay, bisexual, transgender, and queer people by the numbers.* New York, NY: The New Press.

Engela, C. (2016). *Other kids are almost just like you.* Raleigh, NC: Lulu.com.

Ewert, M., & Ray, R. (2008). *10,000 dresses* (First ed.). New York, NY: Seven Stories Press.

Funk, S., & Funk, J. (2016). Transgender dispossession in transparent: Coming out as a euphemism for honesty. *Sexuality & Culture, 20*(4), 879–905. doi:10.1007/s12119-016-9363-0

Gould, L. (1978). *X, a fabulous child's story.* New York, NY: Daughters Pub.

Halberstam, J. (2012). *Gaga feminism: Sex, gender, and the end of normal.* Boston, MA: Beacon Press.

Hall, M. (2015). *Red: A crayon's story* (1st ed.). New York, NY: Greenwillow Books.

Herthel, J., Jennings, J., & McNicholas, S. (2014). *I am jazz!* New York, NY: Dial Books.

Hillenbrand, J. J., & Omahne, Q. (2016). *Parts & hearts: A kids (& grown-ups) guide to transgender transition.* Morrisville, NC: Lulu.

Hill-Meyer, T. (2015). *A princess of great daring.* Toronto, ON: Flamingo Rampant.

Kay, V. (2007). *Rough, tough Charley.* Berkeley, CA: Tricycle Press.

Khaleeli, H. (2014, April 16). Hijra: India's third gender claims its place in law. *The Guardian.* Retrieved from https://www.theguardian.com/society/2014/apr/16/india-third-gender-claims-place-in-law

Kiernan-Johnson, E. (2012). *Roland Humphrey is wearing a what?* Boulder, CO: Huntley Rahara Press.

Kilodavis, C. (2011). *My princess boy: A mom's story about a young boy who loves to dress up.* New York, NY: Aladdin.

Klein, C., Manzano, S., Johnson, V., Robinson, S., & Yee, L. (2014). *The importance of all children seeing themselves in literature.* Retrieved from https://www.scholastic.com/teachers/videos/teaching-content/importance-all-children-seeing-themselves-literature/

Konnoth, C., & Gates, G. (2011, November). Same-sex couples and immigration in the United States. Retrieved from http://williamsinstitute.law.ucla.edu/wp-content/uploads/Gates-Konnoth-Binational-Report-Nov-2011.pdf

Mack, B. (1979). *Jesse's dream skirt.* Chapel Hill, NC: Lollipop Power.

Mason, M. N., & Suarez, M. (2013). *Play free.* USA: Max N' Me Studio.

National Center for Transgender Equality. (2016, August 04). Understanding transgender people: Retrieved from https://transequality.org/issues/resources/understanding-transgender-people-the-basics

Olson, K. R., Durwood, L., DeMeules, M., & McLaughlin, K. A. (2016). Mental health of transgender children who are supported in their identities. *Pediatrics, 137*(3). doi:10.1542/peds.2015-3223

Phillips, J. (2006). *Transgender on screen.* New York, NY: Palgrave Macmillan.

Resources on Gender-Expansive Children and Youth. (2017). In *Human Rights Campaign.* Retrieved from http://www.hrc.org/resources/resources-on-gender-expansive-children-and-youth

Savage, S. (2015). *Are you a boy or are you a girl?* London, England: TQUAL Books.

Sedgwick, E. K. (1990). *Epistemology of the closet.* Berkeley: University of California Press.

Sirois, M. (2016). *Definitions.* Retrieved from https://gendercreativelife.com/definitions/

Stack, L. (2016, July 1). The challenges that remain for LGBT people after marriage ruling. *The New York Times.* Retrieved from https://www.nytimes.com/2016/07/01/us/the-challenges-that-remain-for-lgbt-people-after-marriage-ruling.html?_r=0

Sullivan, A. L., & Urraro, L. L. (2017). Missing persons' report! Where are the transgender characters in children's picture books? *Occasional Paper Series, 2017*(37).

Retrieved from https://educate.bankstreet.edu/occasional-paper-series/vol2017/iss37/4

University of Wisconsin-Milwaukee. (n.d.). *Gender pronouns*. Retrieved from https://uwm.edu/lgbtrc/support/gender-pronouns/

U.S. Census Bureau. (2017, August 31). *Facts for features: Hispanic heritage month 2017*. Retrieved from https://www.census.gov/newsroom/facts-for-features/2017/hispanic-heritage.html

Van, B. D. (1992). *Melinda and the class photograph*. Minneapolis, MN: Carolrhoda Books.

Weber, P. (2014). Confused by all the new Facebook Genders? Here's what they mean. *Slate*. Retrieved from http://www.slate.com/blogs/lexicon_valley/2014/02/21/gender_facebook_now_has_56_categories_to_choose_from_including_cisgender.html

Wittig, M. (1992). *The straight mind and other essays*. Boston, MA: Beacon Press.

CHAPTER 4

PLEASURE GAMES (OF TRUTH) IN BOYS' SCHOOLING

Interrogating Gender and Sexuality Through a Pleasure Lens

Göran Gerdin and Amanda Mooney

ABSTRACT

Despite a policy environment in the U.S. K–12 Physical Education (PE) that calls for the "full inclusion of all students," research that establish schools, PE and sport as sites of heteronormative and masculinizing practices continues to be reported. In this chapter, we adopt a Foucauldian pleasure lens to interrogate the particular games of truth/truth regimes that adolescent boys' in two specific boys' school sites in New Zealand and Australia negotiate in their experiences of PE, sport, and broader school cultures. We argue that pleasure is the glue that (re)produces heteronormative schooling cultures and existing (unequal) power relations between different identities/subjectivities. In conclusion, we suggest that interrogations of the interrelationship/s between masculinity, sexuality, and sport through a pleasure lens offers new theoretical perspectives to explore normalised cultural practices and offer potential to make visible spaces in which these can be productively disrupted.

Exploring Gender and LGBTQ Issues in K–12 and Teacher Education, pages 53–69
Copyright © 2019 by Information Age Publishing

The problematization of sport as a site that cultivates and (re)produces dominant forms of masculinities and heteronormativity has occupied much of the gender and sexuality research landscape (Aitchison, 2007). Like the United States K–12 Physical Education (PE) context, many international PE curricula calls for the full inclusion of all students. Yet, research that establishes boys' PE and sport as sites of heteronormative and masculinizing practices that potentially "damage" participants continues to be reported (Atkinson & Kehler, 2010). Notwithstanding Jackson's (1996) assertion over two decades ago that theorizing about gender, sexuality, and subjectivities has become more sophisticated, we still lack theoretical tools and nuanced accounts that provide answers to the fundamental question, "How did I/it get this way?" This we argue holds the key to conceptualizing experiences in sport and PE, and schooling more broadly, beyond a heteronormative paradigm and has potential to reveal spaces and practices that can promote more agentic and desirable expressions of gender and sexuality.

This chapter draws on data from two ethnographic studies on boys' schooling and PE in New Zealand and Australia generated through observations, video recordings, focus groups and individual interviews with teachers and boys aged 12–15. The PE curricula in both these countries emphasize students' interrogations of discourses and power relations that shape student subjectivities/identities. The New Zealand PE curriculum states that students will, "analyse the beliefs, attitudes, and practices that reinforce stereotypes and role expectations, identifying ways in which these shape people's choices at individual, group, and societal levels" (Ministry of Education, 2007, p. 17). In Australia, the Victorian PE curriculum requires students to "evaluate factors that shape identities and analyse how individuals impact the identities of others" (Victorian Curriculum & Assessment Authority, 2016, p. 73).

In this chapter we employ a pleasure lens to interrogate the particular "games of truth" that boys negotiate in their experiences of PE, sport, and broader school cultures. As Foucault (1997) argues, by playing a particular game of truth, that is engaging with the socio-historical discourses and power relations that perpetuate some ways of being, "by showing its consequences, by pointing out that there are other reasonable options, by teaching people what they don't know about their own situation, working conditions..." (pp. 295–296), we consider the role pleasure plays in preserving dominant embodied masculinities and power relations. This lens offers potential for new understandings about the intersections between gender, masculinity, sexuality, and physical performances/performativity as experienced by adolescent boys to disrupt (hyper)heteronormative cultures of boys' education that privilege "normal" student identities, at the expense of "abnormal" others. Drawing on Foucault's (1980, 1985) thinking around the workings of discourse and relations of power, and Butler's (1990) concept of performativity, this chapter seeks to examine, challenge, and hopefully disrupt understandings of embodied performances of gender and sexuality in schooling by discussing their articulations with pleasure.

IDEOLOGIES OF MASCULINITY
AND HETERONORMATIVITY

Foucault conceptualized games of truth as an evolution from his earlier theorizing on regimes of truth (Peters, 2004). In short, games of truth consider "how the human subject constitutes itself by strategically entering into such games and playing them to best advantage" (Peters, 2004, p. 57). This then implies that subjects contend and understand the "truths"—politically and socially produced through discourse-power relations—that they are required to strategically negotiate. Yet, as research suggests, these truths are differential and largely perpetuated through schooling practices that have historically (re)produced an ideology of masculinity (Mac an Ghaill, 1994; McKay, Messner, & Sabo, 2000). It is these ideologies that perpetuate the privileging of some masculine identities, often at the expense of marginalized others (including other masculinities and femininities).

In boys' schools in particular, privileged or hegemonic masculinities are largely recognizable through displays of "authority, physical and emotional toughness, superiority, sporting prowess, aggression, violence, heterosexuality and male homo-social bonding" (Bhana & Mayeza, 2016, p. 38). Despite being largely unattainable for most students (Connell, 2005), there are particular *ways of being* a boy that appear culturally valued/dominant in the context of an all-boys' school. These are identifiable in physical attributes (such as size and muscularity) and/or through specific embodied practices and behaviors that can serve as high status markers of this privilege, such as athletic physicality. Further, these privileged masculinities are continually reinforced and supported by many males/boys within the school context "because it also serves to give them power" (Bhana & Mayeza, 2016, p. 38). While an extensive body of literature exists to argue that hegemonic masculinities manifest as a culturally specific dominant ideal, these are contextually bound and produced, and many boys are required to negotiate the games of truth that make some ways of being more desirable than others in their school environment.

In this chapter, we adopt the position that gender is performative and thereby reject an essentialist conceptualization of masculinity since this can be seen to conceal gender's performative character (Butler, 1990). Through a performative lens, masculinities are (re)performed in multiple, fluid and socio-historic ways, as shaped by the workings of discourse (Foucault, 1978). However, at the same time, we acknowledge that certain forms of masculinity as produced by discourses are positioned more powerfully than others due to the workings of normalization. Foucault (1978) argues that it is through processes of normalization that subjects are produced both as individuals and as different by constituting what and who is to be seen as normal or deviant.

Being a, or performing, boy at school also requires the strategic negotiation of social markers, behaviors, or practices that align with dominant masculinities and for many, the differentiation and distancing of those that position them as "other." These performances of gender typically involve rejecting that which is considered feminine (e.g., being aggressive over passive and playing rugby instead of netball). Reaffirming male and female identities is also often linked to the pervasiveness of heteronormativity (Warner, 1993) which is based on the assumption that everyone is heterosexual and that heterosexual desire is related to girls and boys being different and opposite. For instance, in PE, heteronormativity can be seen to determine the way in which boys (and girls) feel they can appropriately engage in certain activities and still be viewed as normal (Larsson, Fagrell, & Redelius, 2009). As others have demonstrated, the heteronormative character of discourses and practices associated with PE help produce particular gendered identities and bodies (Larsson et al., 2009).

The emphasis on the physical body in PE has also been shown to be a prime site for the manifestation of heterosexism and homophobia in both the teaching and content of PE (Clarke, 2006). Changing rooms have been identified as places where boys' masculine identities and bodies are monitored among themselves in largely hidden, anxiety-producing, and ritual ways that have no ostensible (or inherent link) to the pedagogy of PE itself (Atkinson & Kehler, 2010). For boys who reject adhering to (hyper)masculine and heterosexual performances, there is a strong risk of becoming ostracized and denied the status afforded to others who do perform in this way (Epstein, 1997).

Numerous studies have shown how hierarchies of masculinities contribute to unjustified treatment of not only girls but also boys in schools and PE (Light & Kirk, 2000; Renold, 2004). Hickey (2008) demonstrates how, through the differentiation of insiders and outsiders, individuals who perform alternative masculinities are subjected to oppression and violence by those who perform hegemonic masculinities. Other studies have detailed boys' performances of masculinities as enabled and/or constrained by power structures that exist or are embedded in material contexts/locations such as gyms, parks, school yards/playgrounds, basketball courts, and PE classrooms/changing rooms (Gerdin, 2017). For instance, O'Donoghue's (2007) work provides insights into how boys' embodied performances of gender are played out in the schoolyard, entrance hall, corridors, and toilets where bullying can occur away from the surveilling gaze of the teachers.

What becomes apparent in the discussion above is the complexity surrounding boys' performances of gender (masculinities) in various school contexts—the games of truth boys are required to strategically negotiate are differential across school sites (e.g., schoolyard, classroom, and PE/sport contexts) and are identified, taken up or resisted by individuals in different ways. How then can we interrogate certain performances of gender as a means to making visible possibilities to challenge limiting practices that simultaneously privilege some boys, while marginalizing others? We believe the answer to this question lies in an interrogation of the pleasures derived through these performances and employ a Foucauldian pleasure lens to explore this below.

PLAYING GAMES OF TRUTH: PLEASURE AS A THEORETICAL LENS

Drawing on poststructuralist perspectives, our understanding of pleasure is informed by Foucault (1978) who asserts that there are no pre-existing, inherent pleasurable feelings; rather, pleasure is interpreted by people in relation to the discourses circulating in a given socio-cultural context. Foucault's (1985) interest was not in the origins, essential nature, or meanings of pleasure, but in "the ontology of force that linked together acts, pleasures, and desires" (p. 43). Connections between pleasures and desire is important since what we find pleasurable is dependent on what we desire (Aho, 1998). In this sense, pleasure can be seen as the satisfaction of a desire that is intrinsic, an inherent feeling that we all possess (Gerdin, 2017). However, desire, like pleasure, can be viewed as discursively constructed and constituted by the workings of discourse and relations of power. In this respect, Turner (2008) argues that Foucault avoids the pitfall of treating desire as a unified phenomenon because he treats desire as the product of certain socio-historic discourses.

Rose (1999) uses the term *technology of desire* as a way of understanding the mechanisms at work that create the desires we work to please. Understood through a Foucauldian lens, power can be viewed as constructive and productive, and desire as produced through power/knowledge. This view opposes other conventional philosophies and social theories, where power is seen to repress desire. From this perspective power is not necessarily negative/repressing, but instead productive: "it traverses and produces things, it induces pleasure, forms of knowledge, produces discourse" (Foucault, 1980, p. 119). Dominant understandings of the social and peer-group status attained by sporty (hyper)masculine and heterosexual boys often represent experiences/outcomes that are desirable for many boys in school. It is in this sense Foucault (1980) suggests that "power is not simply oppressive;

we are caught in its networks precisely because some aspects of the exercise and experience of power are profoundly pleasurable" (p. 34).

What we want and what we strive for are, in a Foucauldian sense, discursively constructed. We believe that exploring the constructions of pleasure can reveal the discursive practices/formations circulating in boys' schooling which shape boys' ideas about their gendered/sexualised selves and bodies. In this chapter, therefore, pleasure is conceptualized as a productive effect of power (Foucault, 1980, 1985) and as inextricably linked to the performance (Butler, 1990) of gendered and sexed bodies.

METHODOLOGY

Data generated through (visual) ethnographies conducted in two all-boys' schools in New Zealand and Australia were analyzed to inform our discussion of the ways in which performances of gender and sexuality are interwoven with pleasure(s). Following granted ethics approvals, across both school sites at Kea College (New Zealand) and St. John's College (Australia), 132 boys' PE classes were observed, video-recorded and analyzed, with selected clips drawn on in subsequent focus groups with students (four to six students in each) or individual interviews with teachers and students involved with the lesson in focus. Collectively, across the two data-sets, 84 individuals (80 students and four teachers) participated and of those, 68 participants agreed to take part in the interviews. All participants and school sites have been assigned a pseudonym. At Kea College, Year 10 boys (aged 14–15 years) and at St. John's College Year 8 and 9 boys (aged 12–15 years) were recruited to participate in the study.

The schools included were selected as they were the first two that agreed to participate in the study and also because of the researchers' background knowledge of and proximity to the schools. The principal, teachers, and boys were all sent copies of the participant information sheet, outlining the objectives of the study, and also accompanying consent forms. Since all the participating boys were younger than 16, parental consent was also required. Given that PE is not compulsory after Year 10 in New Zealand and Australia, and that continued studies in PE are self-selected, older year groups were not included. Selecting Year 8–10 PE classes therefore ensured that the research participants consisted of boys with a wide range of attitudes towards the PE subject while also having reached an age where they were able to discuss and reflect on 8–10-year experiences of schooling and PE.

The ethnographic work commenced with both researchers observing the teacher's PE classes (recorded in field notes) and the purpose of these observations was for the researchers to familiarize themselves with the context and participants. The focus groups and individual interviews attended to select themes and issues identified as a salient part of the observations and video recordings of the PE lessons. An interview guide containing open-ended prompts based on themes identified during observations and video recordings was used. Although the interviews did not progress in a linear fashion, they were typically initiated by asking the boys or teacher to talk about something that had been observed during class or recorded in the video clips. Once a topic had been introduced, the interviews then attempted to discuss/negotiate the boys' and teacher's views (in separate interview contexts), perceptions and experiences of these particular situations. The time length of each interview varied between 30–60 minutes and were digitally recorded and later transcribed verbatim. The ethnographic data consisted of observational field notes, video recordings of PE classroom activity and transcripts (from focus groups and individual interviews). All observational notes and interview transcripts were compiled and prepared for detailed analysis and video-recordings were edited/organized, with the audio from video clips identified as most relevant for the research questions transcribed.

Data was analyzed using Foucault's (1980, 1985) theoretical conceptualization of discourse/power/pleasure to understand students as gendered/sexualized subjects and to interrogate the discourse-power relations that perpetuate these subjectivities. Differing discourses produce variable forms of knowledge or truths about boys and their subjectivities. We followed Foucault's assertion that our aim as researchers was not to discover truth/s, but to understand how discursive practices/formations bring forth various truths in particular ways. In this manner, we explored how the games of truth (Foucault, 1988) associated with boys, gender/sexuality and pleasures in boys' schooling are played out.

Our analysis focused on boys' performances of gender and their articulation with, or disruption of, discourses related to masculinity, sport, fitness, and health. That is, did the boys' behavior and actions during PE align with masculine ideals of competition, aggression, and physicality, or did they focus more on participation and inclusion? How did different groups of—or individual—boys' behavior and actions vary between different games/activities, such as dodgeball and rugby, that could indicate certain discursive links between masculinity and the types of games/activities engaged in during PE?

Based on the particular focus of this chapter, we also attended to the production of pleasure, when and how boys seemed to enjoy PE and experiences of schooling more broadly. For instance, at what point during the lessons and while doing what kinds of games/activities did boys seems to enjoy PE? How did the boys' and the teacher's use of those game/activity spaces (re) produce PE as a meaningful and enjoyable space? Did the boys participation in and through PE seem to reify the importance of (hyper)masculinity and heteronormativity in PE? Presented below is selected data, analyses and discussion resonant with themes relevant to the above stated questions.

The findings reported in this chapter are partly represented in narrative form, compatible with Foucauldian approaches. Foucault (1991) acknowledged that he wanted the readers of his texts to have an experience that would challenge their thinking and "an experience that might permit an alteration, a transformation, of the relationship we have with ourselves and our cultural universe" (pp. 36–37). Foucault, however, did not want his texts to be instructive for how people should think. Rather he viewed them as invitations that allowed readers possibilities "to slip into this kind of experience" (Foucault, 1991, p. 40). In this vein, we invite the reader of our chapter to engage with our participants' experiences, challenge their thinking and invite possibilities for transformation in the heteronormative culture in boys' schooling and PE. Presented below are the findings in the form of two narratives from each of the school sites that contextualise the privileged role sport and PE can play in the construction of desirable (hegemonic) masculinities in boys' schools. Collectively they provide insight into our problematizations of these games of truth and make visible spaces where they may be disrupted.

PERPETUATING GAMES OF TRUTH ABOUT HEGEMONIC MASCULINITY: KEA COLLEGE

Above all Kea College can be seen as a school that lives and breathes for sports, evidenced by both the physical spaces and the way that the teachers talk about schooling and PE. For instance, there is a new sports complex near the perfectly groomed rugby and soccer fields named after the long-standing school principal (described in an informal conversation with one of the teaching staff "as the school's biggest rugby head"). Next to this there is a multipurpose astro-court (artificial grass) field with lines for tennis and hockey including a smaller fenced off area for basketball. Over the hill there is another sports-field used for the school's elite rugby, cricket and soccer teams. When entering the main building and reception area, you are immediately faced with a big cabinet filled with various sporting trophies. The official school website is full of upcoming events related to sports. The school prospectus talks about sporting excellence, sporting profile and enjoyment of sport—sport as the vehicle for producing well rounded healthy young men.

During an initial interview with the head of department (HOD) of PE, Mr. Whyte, he discussed the goal of PE as most boys should "find at least one sport they will continue doing later in life." Mr. Whyte also highlighted the character-building and fitness/health benefits that come with life-long sport engagement. The aim is for students to "gain a love of sport" given its (perceived) link with remaining active and healthy throughout their lives. The boys themselves describe sport as a key reason for attending school. Dominic, one of Mr. Whyte's students explained, "It's a really sporty school . . . play rugby for the school . . . it's cool playing the national sport for the school."

Sport involvement at Kea College is constructed both by the school and the students as an expected and normal masculine venture. Discourses produce certain kinds of desires as appropriate and appealing (Turner, 1997) or what Rose (1999) refers to as technologies of desire. Sport is discursively produced as an expected and desirable endeavor for boys, since it helps them reaffirm and confirm to normal masculine identities (Butler, 1997). It is seen as important due to its masculinizing abilities and the all-round development of healthy young men since it articulates with good health, social development, and competitiveness.

RE-FRAMING GAMES OF TRUTH ABOUT HEGEMONIC MASCULINITY: ST. JOHN'S COLLEGE

Like Kea College, St. John's College also has a long history of promoting and celebrating the sporting endeavors and achievements of its students. The main entrance to the school sits amidst two sporting ovals, an all-weather surface court area (with basketball, tennis and volleyball line markings) and cricket pitches and nets. Behind the main reception area looms a large gymnasium complex that houses indoor basketball courts, a weights-room, a fitness studio, change-rooms (with showers), and a large office facility for PE staff. Located on either side of this facility are two additional ovals, that are fastidiously maintained for the elite, or the upper echelons of sporting competition within the school. In addition, the link to the Old Collegians, or "old boys," is prominent throughout the reception foyer. Like Kea College, there were a number of sporting trophies in display cabinets, but positioned on easels in front of these were art sculptures, paintings and technology-controlled robots on pedestals. As Mr. Xu, the School Principal comments:

> We realized that the first thing you saw when you entered the school building was a foyer that had our history on a wall . . . there were sporting trophies from the 1940s and with all these memorabilia confronting you in your first point of contact with the school, how were we to be anything else than just a good sports school?

In conversations with other members of the school's leadership team, it became evident that there had been some significant attempts to disrupt some of the prevailing discourses around sport and masculinity within the school. For example, the Head of PE, Mr. Zanders, explained:

> When I was a student here it was an extremely macho culture, every boy was out to prove himself all the time and there were obvious pecking orders ... you had to find something you were good at and use this to get respect amongst your peers but that was when it was a real old school, boy school ... now, we have moved away from the macho sporting culture that we used to have, I mean the connections to the old boys in perpetuating that was massive.

The strategic appointment of a female Deputy Principal was considered by the Principal to be another key attempt to disrupt dominant gendered discourses within the school. While we are not advocating that it is solely the role of females employed within this school environment to do this front-line gender work, it is interesting to consider Mrs. White's reflections about the particular aspects of the school that she felt needed to be addressed initially.

> When I first came in the gate, well at the time there was no creative arts center there was a whole lot of ugly concrete downball courts ... just the physical appearance of the place which was really deceptive because when you drive around the outside of the school all you see are lush, green sporting ovals and a big sports pavilion on top of a hill ... it looks pretty impressive from a distance and leaves no doubt that the school is all about sport.

In both of these narratives we see indicators of the strong coupling between sport and its role (often unwittingly) in the provision of spaces where dominant masculinities are performed. Historically there has been a strong rhetoric around the role sport can play in creating moral characters, particularly in the context of boys' education (Messner, 1992). Further these excerpts provide evidence of its discursive materiality through the physical environment, reception foyers and sporting facilities. The historical legacy of this discourse is conveyed through links to past collegians and tradition is often drawn on to perpetuate custodial games of truth that privilege sporting masculinities. As both Mr. Whyte (Kea College) and Mr. Zanders (St. John's College) indicate, boys that display a love of sport and an ability to perform in this context are often afforded a hierarchical status not accessible for others.

Collectively, these accounts point to the contextual discourses that act to produce a range of options and constraints for the boys (and their teachers) at these schools. The discursive articulations between masculinities, fitness/health, sport, PE and the body are influential in shaping the boys' experiences of schooling and PE and the production of both heteronormative subjectivities and pleasures. Pleasures emerge within discourses and relations of power at these schools to render the boys recognizable (Butler, 2004) as, for instance, (hyper)masculine and heterosexual boys. Boys' performances of gender/sexuality and their articulations with pleasures can therefore be understood as attempts to make themselves recognizable within this game of truth.

In the next section, we will draw on two popular (and similar) ball games, to discuss how these activities and practices act as incitements for the boys to enter the game of truth related to (hegemonic) masculine pleasures in boys' PE.

PLEASURABLE GAMES: EMBODYING PRIVILEGED AND DESIRABLE MASCULINITIES IN BOYS' PE

Notwithstanding the dominant discourses circulating at the macro school level discussed above, our attention now turns to a micro-level discussion of the PE classroom. In doing so, we consider parallel pleasures derived from student participation in commonplace games that are similar in nature across the two research sites—dodgeball and battle-ball. At both schools, physical and invasion style ball games were the most popular PE activities according to our participants. At Kea College, one of the most popular ball games at the time of the study was dodgeball. Dodgeball is a game in which players on two teams try to throw balls at each other while avoiding being hit themselves. The following is an extract from the observational notes generated at Kea College.

> At the start of the lesson one of the boys asks the teacher "What are we doing today sir?" and another one yells out, "Dodgeball sir, please sir!" Mr. Whyte replies, "Yes Dodgeball" and it seems like the whole gym erupts from boys calling out "Yes!"...Mr. Whyte calls out, "You and you, you are team captains." Two of the boys then start calling out the names of the other boys to come and join their teams. The boys who get picked stand up and walk proudly with their heads up high towards their team captain with some of them high-fiving them as they walk past. By the time the last few boys get picked the other boys have already started playing with the balls...The game of dodgeball starts and the gym is filled with loud noises from balls bouncing. No one is safe, including myself and the boys who are not participating...The game continues for the whole lesson and I have no idea if anyone won the game or if scores were kept. Mr. Whyte abruptly calls, "Ok that's it for today boys!" A final burst of noise and grunts is heard and the boys rush over to the side of the gym to change into their school uniforms. As the boys leave the gym I overhear one of the boys saying "Man, I love dodgeball, we should just do that every time in PE!"

While observing during this lesson, the boys were overheard saying things like, "Get off the ground, you girl," "Get up, you pussy," or "Lick my cock, homo." At times some boys get hit in the face, and it is apparent that even though they experience pain, they try hard not to show it. At the conclusion of this lesson, some boys provided comment on their experiences of PE:

> **Göran:** So what activities and sports do you want more of in PE?
> **All:** Dodgeball!
> **Göran:** Less of anything?
> **Miles:** Yeah badminton.
> **Dominic:** Badminton is gay.
> **Miles:** Yeah dodgeball is for real boys and badminton is for wusses.
> [Laughter]

At St. John's College, one of the most popular ball games was battle-ball (a variant of dodgeball). This game is played between two teams with the distinct goal of eliminating players from the opposing team by hitting them with a foam ball, and then knocking down targets that players work to protect. In a student focus group following a lesson, we were confronted with varied perspectives of their experiences of this game.

> **Amanda:** Tell me about some of the experiences in PE that you have really enjoyed?
> **Jimmy:** Team games like battle-ball, but she [the PE Teacher] won't play it cause she is new, she doesn't know how to play it so we don't get to play it yet much ...
> **Brendan:** Yeah, like if we had battle-ball, it is good because everyone enjoys it ...
> **Craig:** I notice like the quieter people sometimes, they just keep to themselves and don't talk to people, they just have their one or two friends and that's the only people that they really talk to ... they just stand down the back of the court to avoid getting hit
> **Dale:** Yeah but you can include them in battle-ball.

In the discussion above the boys' pleasures in the game of battle-ball are made visible. Whilst the general consensus appears that this is a game that is pleasurable for everyone, Craig's comments suggest that this pleasure is differential and variable and that in fact, there are spaces within this game where boys can stand to actively avoid taking part in the game. The boys' perceptions of this are taken up in the discussion below.

> **Jimmy:** In a game like battle-ball you've got to throw a ball at someone to eliminate them, the good kids would always target the bad kids ... you would always see these kids hiding down the

back... but that still is OK because someone has to protect the cones.

Amanda: Would most students enjoy this, the concept of having a ball thrown at you?

Kyle: Absolutely, every single one, no-one wouldn't... there is different positions in battle-ball.

Matt: There are people who go up the front and throw the balls and there are people at the back that protect the cones... it's not for me... there is nothing better than hitting someone full pelt when they don't expect it.

Sebastian: Yeah, there are heaps of options in the one game.

Dale: We had a kid this year and he got hit and had blood coming out but he was still laughing.

DISCUSSION

The boys' commentary across both school sites demonstrate (dis)pleasures of how they represent and interpret different kinds of sporting activities in PE and how they engender themselves and others as gendered subjects of different kinds of sporting activities (Larsson et al., 2009). Dodgeball and battle-ball are constructed as activities for "real" boys, which can be used to reaffirm embodied privileged and desirable masculine identities.

At both schools, these activities normalize the inflicting ("there is nothing better than hitting someone full pelt when they don't expect it") and/or receiving of pain ("had blood coming out but he was still laughing") through throwing the ball at each other as an expected part of their PE experience. Not conforming to these notions about what these sporting experiences should involve means attracting comments aimed at othering the boys ("Get off the ground you girl" and "Get up you pussy"). Equally, other activities such as badminton are constructed as activities for girls, and therefore not for masculine boys. The way activities are constructed in PE provides a discursive context within which boys learn to conform to and play the game of truth related to ideals such as physical and emotional toughness and homophobia (Bhana & Mayeza, 2016). Different kinds of activities/sports, in this way, act to position individual boys and groups of boys in competing ways depending on their embodied performances—whether they are able (and willing) to play along (or not) with these truth games. The conversation from the boys at St. John's College above highlights variability in how boys choose to take up different roles and positions in the game of battle-ball. Boys who, through their performances, display a lack of self-confidence and a reluctance to appear aggressive and competitive in connection with popular ball games such as dodgeball and battle-ball, will end up representing marginalized, undesirable or "abject" (Butler, 1990) masculine identities. The pleasures derived from this game of truth are intensified by (sporty and heterosexual) boys exerting power (Bhana & Mayeza, 2016) over other boys, which reaffirms a hierarchy of masculinities which are both productive and pleasurable (Foucault, 1980).

The social norms of (hyper)masculinity and heterosexuality can be seen to act as incitements for the boys to enter into the game of truth (Markula & Pringle, 2006). What is made visible within this analysis is that the practices of the self that boys engage are agentic and driven by a desire to conform, to become normal and achieve a sense of belonging. To align with identity positions normalised by a contextually specific power/discourse nexus (Markula & Pringle, 2006), boys enter these pleasure games of truth to reaffirm certain privileged and desirable heteronormative masculinities within this context. However, those boys who are unable or unwilling to play these power games (game of truth) potentially experience school and PE more negatively. The discourses and relations of power in boys' PE that allow for particular subject positions and produce certain pleasures can at times also induce (dis)pleasures (e.g., exclusion pain, humiliation, embarrassment, harassment, bullying, homophobia). Power-induced pleasures in PE related to performances of gender and the game of truth in PE not only restricts certain pleasures, but also have negative consequences/outcomes for those boys who are unable/unwilling to live up to or perform privileged/desirable masculinities within this context.

Our analysis demonstrates how boys in these school settings are immersed in a power/discourse nexus (Markula & Pringle, 2006) which simultaneously enables/restricts performances of gender, sexuality and pleasures. What we term the pleasure games (of truth) in boys' schooling highlights how pleasures derived from discursive practices/formations operating within these school cultures can be seen as linked to performing/conforming to dominant notions of being a boy at these schools. Indeed, the boys' desire to become recognizable (Butler, 2004) is a significant act in these contexts. To choose to present themselves as someone recognizable to their peers is both related to feeling normal, and a source of pleasures. Butler argues that being recognizable is an important site of power since who becomes recognized, and by whom, is determined by social norms (discourses). Further, by choosing to be recognized (or not) within those social norms points towards the agency of individuals in the performances of gender. This idea of recognition and its connections to pleasures and power in boys' schooling is significant. There are all sorts of ways that the boys could be recognized in their performances of gender, whether conscious or not. Including pleasures in the analysis of discourses and relations of power reveal the different ways in which the boys' gendered and sexualized embodied subjectivities are performed that might otherwise go unnoticed.

We therefore argue that pleasure is the glue that (re)produces heteronormative schooling cultures and existing (unequal) power relations between different identities/subjectivities. Returning to Jackson's (1996) question about how "I/it" ended up this way, we suggest that it is pleasure as co-constitutive of performances of gender and sexuality that (re)constructs certain subjectivities as productive and privileged/desirable within schooling. In order to further challenge and disrupt gender and sexuality in education we need to interrogate the schooling pleasures (bound to these performances). Any real attempt to challenge the (hyper)heteronormative culture of schooling needs to challenge dominant forms of pleasures as well. Interrogations of the interrelationship/s between masculinity, sexuality and sport through a pleasure lens offers new theoretical perspectives to explore normalized cultural practices and offer potential to make visible spaces in which these can be productively disrupted.

CONCLUSION

In conclusion, boys enter these games of truth for the pleasures they derive from the activities and practices delivered through boys PE, so we want to assert that teachers need to teach from the full spectrum of the current curriculum and design PE lessons where activities and practices facilitate boys learning about and constructing their bodies and masculine identities in diverse ways. PE lessons should help boys question and challenge hyper masculine and heteronormative bodies in PE. This should, in particular, focus on how the ongoing normalization of privileged and marginalized bodies and identities in PE and the broader physical culture reproduces inequalities in terms of physical activity and health outcomes.

The challenge, we contend, is in supporting teachers to be reflective about the ways in which various activities and sports employed within their classes are embedded with discursive meanings about sport, fitness and health as associated with masculinity, bodies and sexuality (amongst other identity markers) that (re)construct those meanings for their students. It is often the taken-for-granted practices of everyday PE, left unchallenged and uncritically adopted, that present the most significant barriers to achieving more inclusive pedagogies—this we argue, is a key imperative for teacher education and professional learning programs. Coupled with this is a need for more research into school cultures, educational policies and PE practices as they connect with boys' (and girls') development of healthy, well-educated and physically active identities that can contribute to equality and social justice in our society.

REFERENCES

Aho, J. (1998). *The things of the world: A social phenomenology.* London, England: Praeger.

Aitchison, C. (Ed.). (2007). *Sport and gender identities: Masculinities, femininities and sexualities.* London, England: Routledge.

Atkinson, M., & Kehler, M. (2010). Boys, gyms, locker rooms and heterotopia. In M. Kehler & M. Atkinson (Eds.), *Boys' bodies: Speaking the unspoken* (pp. 73–90). New York, NY: Peter Lang.

Bhana, D., & Mayeza, E. (2016). We don't play with gays, they're not real boys . . . they can't fight: Hegemonic masculinity and (homophobic) violence in the primary years of schooling. *International Journal of Educational Development, 51,* 36–42. doi:10.1016/j.ijedudev.2016.08.002

Butler, J. (1990). *Gender trouble: Feminism and the subversion of identity.* London, England: Routledge.

Butler, J. (1997). *Excitable speech: A politics of the performative.* New York, NY: Routledge.

Clarke, G. (2006). Sexuality and physical education. In D. Kirk, D. Macdonald, & M. O'Sullivan (Eds.), *The handbook of physical education* (pp. 723–739). London, England: Routledge.

Connell, R. W. (2005). *Masculinities* (2nd ed.). Cambridge, England: Polity Press.

Epstein, D. (1997). Boyz' own stories: Masculinities and sexualities in schools. *Gender and Education, 9*(1), 105–115. doi:10.1080/09540259721484

Foucault, M. (1978). *The history of sexuality, volume one: An introduction.* Harmondsworth, England: Penguin.

Foucault, M. (1980). *Power/knowledge: Selected interviews and other writings 1972–1977* (C. Gordon, L. Marshall, J. Mepham, & K. Soper, Trans.). In C. Gordon (Ed.). New York, NY: Pantheon Books.

Foucault, M. (1985). *The use of pleasure: The history of sexuality, volume two.* London, England: Penguin.

Foucault, M. (1988). Technologies of the self. In L. Martin, H. Gutman, & P. Hutton (Eds.), *Technologies of the self: A seminar with Michel Foucault* (pp. 16–49). Amherst: University of Massachusetts Press.

Foucault, M. (1997). *Ethics: Subjectivity and truth.* New York, NY: The New Press.

Gerdin, G. (2017). *Boys, bodies and physical education: Problematizing identity, schooling and power relations through a pleasure lens.* Milton Park, England: Routledge.

Hickey, C. (2008). Physical education, sport and hyper-masculinity in schools. *Sport, Education and Society, 13*(2), 147–161. doi:10.1080/13573320801957061

Jackson, S. (1996). Heterosexuality as a problem for feminist theory. In L. Adkins & V. Merchant (Eds.), *Sexualising the social: Power and the organisation of sexuality* (pp. 15–34). London, England: Macmillan.

Larsson, H., Fagrell, B., & Redelius, K. (2009). Queering physical education: Between benevolence towards girls and a tribute to masculinity. *Physical Education and Sport Pedagogy, 14*(1), 1–17. doi:10.1080/17408980701345832

Light, R., & Kirk, D. (2000). High school rugby, the body and the reproduction of hegemonic masculinity. *Sport, Education and Society, 5*(2), 163–176. doi:10.1080/713696032

Mac an Ghaill, M. (1994). *The making of men: Masculinities, sexualities and schooling.* Buckingham, England: Open University Press.

Markula, P., & Pringle, R. (2006). *Foucault, sport and exercise: Power, knowledge and transforming the self.* New York, NY: Routledge.

McKay, J., Messner, M., & Sabo, D. (2000). *Masculinities, gender relations and sport.* Thousand Oaks, CA: SAGE.

Messner, M. (1992). *Power at play: Sports and the problem of masculinity.* Boston, MA: Beacon Press.

Ministry of Education. (2007). *The New Zealand curriculum: Achievement objectives by learning area.* Wellington, New Zealand: Learning Media Limited.

O'Donoghue, D. (2007). 'James always hangs out here': Making space for place in studying masculinities at school. *Visual Studies, 22*(1), 62–73. doi:10.1080/14725860601167218

Peters, M. (2004). Educational research: "Games of truth" and the ethics of subjectivity. *Journal of Educational Enquiry, 5*(2), 50–63.

Renold, E. (2004). Other' boys: Negotiating non-hegemonic masculinities in the primary school. *Gender and Education, 16*(2), 247–266. doi:10.1080/09540250310001690609

Rose, N. (1999). *Powers of freedom: Reframing political thought.* Cambridge, England: Cambridge University Press.

Turner, B. (1997). From governmentality to risk: Some reflections on Foucault's contribution to medical sociology. In A. Petersen & R. Bunton (Eds.), *Foucault, health and medicine* (pp. xi–xxi). London, England: Routledge.

Turner, B. (2008). *The body and society* (3rd ed.). London, England: SAGE.

Victorian Curriculum and Assessment Authority. (2016). *The Victorian curriculum: Health and physical education.* Retrieved from http://victoriancurriculum.vcaa.vic.edu.au/

Warner, M. (1993). *Fear of a queer planet : Queer politics and social theory.* Minneapolis: University of Minnesota Press.

SECTION II

EXPLORING LGBTQ ISSUES IN K–12 SCHOOLS

CHAPTER 5

USING LITERACY TO EXPLORE HETERONORMATIVITY WITH SECOND-GRADERS

Paul Hartman

ABSTRACT

Although there has been a growing amount of research exploring lesbian, gay, bisexual, transgender, and queer (LGBTQ) related issues in schools, the context of most of this research is middle and high schools, leaving a gap in understanding the ways these issues surface and operate within primary classrooms. This teacher action research project examines data from an after-school literacy club with six second-graders. Drawing from queer theory, this project offers a critical analysis of literature discussions of children's books containing themes of non-heterosexuality and/or non-normative gender expression/identities to understand the ways the children reified, challenged, and disrupted heteronormativity through their discussions. The findings highlight both the problematic and promising possibilities of using LGBTQ-themed texts with young children and encourage teachers and teacher-educators to think through how they might engage young students in grappling with the complexity of the process of privileging and othering, particularly regarding gender and sexual identity.

Exploring Gender and LGBTQ Issues in K–12 and Teacher Education, pages 73–94

Talking about gender and sexual identity with children in primary classrooms is complicated. As Fine (2006) reminds us, the "discourse of desire"—the discourse that provides crucial knowledges and understandings to children regarding gender and sexuality—is absent, even at the same time statistics overwhelmingly document the harmful effects of homophobia and heterosexism in U.S. public schools, including lower attendance rates, lower grade point averages, strong links to depression, substance abuse, and suicidal thoughts (Hong & Espelage, 2012).

Most of the current research that highlights explicit attempts at combatting homophobia/heterosexism in schools utilize the high school classroom as its context (Blackburn, 2012; Blackburn & Clark, 2011). Though, in a recent survey of kindergarten through grade six teachers (Kull, Kosciw, & Greytak, 2015), 46% of elementary teachers always or sometimes hear others make comments like "that's so gay," contributing to hostile and unwelcoming environments for (perceived) LGBTQ identified students and students with non-normative expressions of gender, even in primary grades. And although scholars have highlighted the agency of young children and their active construction—and sometimes rejection—of gender norms and of heteronormativity within primary and elementary classrooms (Blaise, 2005, 2009; Thorne, 1993), there remains a large gap in understanding how heteronormativity might be challenged or disrupted in the primary classroom.

This project highlights my attempt as a teacher-researcher to use literacy to confront LGBTQ and gender-related issues with a diverse group of six second-graders in an after-school literacy club in which I was the teacher. In this chapter, I critically analyze the discussions of children's literature that I read aloud to the students that contain LGBTQ and gender creative-related themes. The findings expose both the promises and problematic elements that such work produces and can better equip other teachers and teacher-educators as they attempt to engage young learners in similar kinds of critical thinking and exploration.

THEORETICAL FRAMEWORK

Queer theory helps me to develop a perspective that aims to make my teaching and classroom more inclusive for all students—especially those who have been marginalized because of their creative gender expression and/or (perceived) sexual orientation (Blaise & Taylor, 2012). The term "queer" is often used as an identifier to capture gender and sexual expressions of identities that fall outside of heterosexual and gender norms, like lesbian, gay, bisexual, and transgender, among others. Queer theory also disrupts essentialist understandings of gender and sexual identity (e.g., "boys will be boys") and helps understand the multiple possibilities each individual has to express their gender and sexual identities. From this perspective, I understand queer theory and queer identities as multiple and shifting (Jagose, 1996).

Queer theory is also helpful to understand the ways in which heteronormativity (i.e., the assumption that everyone is heterosexual and that masculine acting men desire feminine acting women and vice versa, casting all other expressions of gender and sexual identities to the margins) is structured and maintained—even within primary classrooms. Butler (1990) discussed such structures as the "heterosexual matrix," the tacit rules that govern and reify dichotomous and narrow understandings of male and female, and that rely on the understanding that desire is only (or most) acceptable, when experienced between biological men and biological women who express their genders in the most socially desirable (and powerful) ways (Connell, 1987). By locating and recognizing queer gender/sexual identities (or subjectivities) that are cast to the margins (i.e., non-heterosexuals and non-normative expressions of gender) within the heterosexual matrix (or heteronormativity), queer theory enables a disruption of identities and expressions considered normal. For teacher researchers and teachers, Blaise's explorations (2005, 2009, 2012) of the ways young children reify the heterosexual matrix reminds us that queer theory is "queer" because it questions the assumption there is any "normal" expression of gender" (2012, p. 88) and encourages educators (and more specifically, early childhood teachers) to cultivate and adapt a queer lens with the aim of engaging their students in such thinking. I use queer theory as described above as I approach literacy teaching, understand identity, and understand the ways in which some expressions of gender and sexual identity are praised, while others are not.

RESEARCH CONTEXT AND PARTICIPANTS

As a gay, White, cis-male and a teacher of twelve years, I have a deep commitment to transformative teaching practices. Through my years as a classroom teacher, as well as my own experiences in school as a feminine acting boy and a member of the LGBTQ community, I have had the unfortunate opportunity to observe and experience the ways in which some young children are marginalized in classrooms because of their non-normative gender expressions and/or (perceived) non-heterosexuality. This recognition has promoted my resolve to develop a pedagogy to work against such marginalization.

I designed this study to be able to formally analyze the ways in which LGBTQ themed children's books might be used as a tool to engage children in thinking about gender norms with the aim of developing more inclusive and nuanced understandings of gender and sexual identity amongst my students. Additionally, as a doctoral student studying literacy education, I thought such a project would function as an important and interesting dissertation study.

The project—a fifteen week after-school literacy club—took place in the winter and spring of 2015, at which time I took a leave of absence from my job as an elementary teacher. I took the leave of absence mostly because the district in which I taught did not allow teachers to conduct research within their own classrooms. Therefore, in order to conduct such a study in which I was the teacher, taking the leave of absence, and conducting the project outside of school hours and outside of the school district (the literacy club met at a nearby community center) were the only way for this project to commence.

All students in the class were eligible to participate and I selected the first three boys/girls to get permission from their parents/guardians to participate. Once the six children were identified, I explained the nature of the study in more depth and gave an overview of the kinds of activities with which the children would engage. I then formally obtained parental permission and child assent using IRB-approved permission/assent forms.

The children were all seven or eight-years-old during the course of the study and they all attended a large, kindergarten through grade eight school in a diverse urban neighborhood. Over fifty languages were spoken by the students in the school, over 90% of students qualified for free or reduced lunch, most of the students were first or second-generation Americans and about 50% were classified as English Learners. The six children in this study reflect these school demographics. None of the students in the study had LGBTQ identified parents, and none of the children expressed having LGBTQ identified family members. Refer to Table 5.1 for more specific information regarding the children. Pseudonyms are used for all child-participants.

TABLE 5.1 Child Participants			
Name	Gender	Race/Ethnicity	Language Spoken in addition to Standard English
Sara	Female	First-generation Mexican American	Spanish
Tariq	Male	First-generation Senegalese American	Wolof
Myra	Female	Emigrated from Somalia when she was 3	Somali
Javon	Male	African American	African American English
Aliya	Female	Father is Nigerian immigrant; Mother is African American	Yoruba; African American English
Donald	Male	First-generation Nicaraguan American	Spanish

Each of the fifteen weekly literacy club sessions was ninety minutes in length. Much of that time was devoted to engaging the students with interactive read alouds, while the remainder of the sessions emphasized writing about the books we had read, snack time, independent reading, and small art projects. During each of the fifteen sessions, I read aloud a picture book and engaged the children in a literature discussion. I chose a multicultural selection of fifteen picture books to read with the children. The selection of books provided positive and affirming representations of cultures, books that won literary awards, and books that I thought would be of interest to this group of students (information I gathered from both my interactions with the children and through a survey I administered at the onset of the literacy club meetings). Of the fifteen sessions, five focused on children's literature that contained themes of LGBTQ identities and/or gender creativity. Those sessions and the discussions therein were audio-recorded, transcribed, and analyzed for this study. Table 5.2 gives a brief description of these focal texts.

I decided to disperse these five focal texts throughout the fifteen weeks and read them respectively in sessions three, five, eight, ten, and twelve. With these texts, as well as the other ten texts, I pre-read the books several times, developed comprehension, analytic, and critical thinking questions, and anticipated moments in each text I thought would be ripe for engaging and critical discussion. During the read aloud discussions, I remained flexible and attempted to allow the children's comments and interactions to drive the discussion.

TABLE 5.2 LGBTQ & Gender Creative-themed Children's Books Used for Literature Discussions

Title of Book	Theme/Short Description	LGBTQ Representation?
King and King	The story of the marriage of two adult male princes.	Yes, gay male identity, though not explicitly stated.
10,000 Dresses	Main character (middle childhood age) is assigned male gender at birth, but identifies as a girl.	Yes, transgender female identity, though not explicitly stated.
Sissy Duckling	Main character, a boy duckling, faces struggles because of his stereotypical feminine qualities.	No, though gender non-conformity (i.e., "sissy" identity) is a major theme of the book.
Elena's Serenade	Main character is a young girl who wants to partake in a male-dominated profession/art (glassblowing) and challenges gender norms to achieve her goal.	No, though gender norms and stereotypes are major themes.
Jacob's New Dress	A kindergarten-aged boy faces struggles as he follows through with his desire to wear a dress to school.	No, though gender norms and stereotypes are major themes.

Framing and Data Collection/Analysis

As a teacher action research project, I employ Cochran-Smith and Lytle's (2009) concept that teacher action research and inquiry may be enacted as a stance. This stance values teachers' ways of knowing and understands it as "a larger epistemological stance, or a way of knowing about teaching, learning, and schooling that is neither topic- nor project-dependent" (p. 44). I tap into my "way of knowing" as a teacher and of young children as I planned each after-school session and as I analyzed the collected data.

As stated earlier, during this project I had been a teacher for twelve years. Given my commitment to elementary teaching and my desire to make my classroom and teaching more inclusive, it was important for me to conduct such an action research project. I have first-hand experience with my voice—and the voices of my teacher-colleagues—being silenced, marginalized, or devalued when it comes to making school and classroom-wide instructional decisions. Traditional educational research tends to be conducted by outsiders who seek to increase their own knowledge. Though the intention of such research is usually to directly benefit the teacher/ students being researched, this is rarely the outcome. Teacher action research, on the other hand, can lead to immediate improvement in teaching and learning. Zeni (1998) refers to this daily process of reflection and good teaching as the "zone of accepted practice." Indeed, this project and the time I took to formally analyze the data had a direct positive impact on the teaching and learning processes in my classroom.

Data was in the form of audio recordings of the five read alouds and literature discussions of LGBTQ and gender creative themed children's books. The initial data analysis was ongoing while I simultaneously collected more data (audio recordings of read alouds) as I led more literature discussions with the after-school literacy club. Between each weekly literacy club meeting, I listened to the audio recording of the literature discussion that transpired the week prior, reflected, and recorded notes. This process allowed me to shape the project—namely by choosing the order of the books we read and discussed as a group—and to remain focused throughout the process (Glesne & Peshkin, 1992). The audio recordings were then transcribed, coded, and critically analyzed as a whole after the completion of the project.

I sought to analyze the kinds of discourse that emerged when young children engaged with topics explicitly related to LGBTQ identities. I carefully attended to the ways in which the heterosexual matrix was either reified, challenged, or disrupted in the discussions. To do this, I employed Rymes' (2009) concept of the dimensions of "language in use" when analyzing the literature discussion transcripts. Rymes' framing of discourse attends to the complex dimensions of the ways language is used: how social factors outside the immediate interaction influence how words function, how the patterns of talk within an interaction influence what can and cannot be said, and the influence an individual has on how words are used and interpreted in an interaction. In the following section, I discuss the findings of this project and provide excerpts from the literature discussions that serve as illustrative examples of how language was used by the students, by specifically paying careful attention to the ways in which the children reified, challenged, or disrupted the norms that uphold the heterosexual matrix. In this sense, I brought my understanding of queer theory to my analysis and tried to locate the ways in which power was embedded in the children's talk.

FINDINGS: LOCATING POWER IN THE LITERATURE DISCUSSIONS

During my initial analysis of the data, I noticed the complexity and conflicting nature of the discourse that emerged. In this first round of analysis, the two most obvious and broadest categories of discourse were coded as *rejections* (of LGBTQ identity and/or non-normative expressions of gender) and what initially appeared to be *disruptions* (of heteronormativity). This is represented in Figure 5.1. The numbers on the left-hand side in Figure 5.1 represent each round of analysis, while the circles on the right represent the categories and subcategories in which the data was coded during each round of analysis. The arrows connecting the circles represent the ways in which the discourse categories relate to one another. The broadest

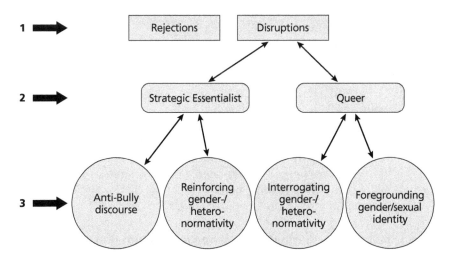

Figure 5.1 Rounds of analysis and discourse categories

categories appear in round one of analysis, become more precise in round two, and even more precise in round three of analysis.

After my initial analysis I was interested in looking more closely at the ways in which the discourse coded as disruptions operated. I further analyzed the discourse coded as disruptions and found two sub-categories, one characterized as *strategic essentialist* and the other as *queer*. In the third round of analysis, I more precisely categorized the data into the four categories. Emerging from the *strategic essentialist* category were the *anti-bully discourse* and *reinforcing gender/heteronormativity* subcategories. Emerging from the *queer* category were the *interrogating gender/heteronormativity* and *foregrounding gender/sexual identity* subcategories. These separate rounds of analysis allowed me to more precisely understand the ways in which the children's words reified, challenged, or disrupted heteronormativity. In the sections below, I provide examples from the data exemplifying the respective (sub)categories represented in Figure 5.1.

Rejections of Non-heterosexuality and/or Non-Normative Gender Expression

Rejections were moments in which gender/heteronormativity was reified and any expressions or identities that fell outside of these normative understandings of gender/sexuality were explicitly rejected. This example is from our third club meeting during the discussion of *King and King*.

> **Hartman:** "The two princes are now called king and king. The queen finally has some time to herself and everyone lives happily ever after."
>
> **Myra:** Really? Oh no! <several students talking and yelling over each other>
>
> **Hartman:** Okay, remember we want everyone to be heard, so raise your hand. Don't yell.
>
> **Javon:** That's it? This book is short!
>
> **Aliya:** I don't like this book.
>
> **Hartman:** I get the feeling some people had some problems. If you do, tell why. And try to think about the other books we read too and how people were treated, and all the things we talked about when reading books.
>
> **Myra:** I don't like those boys marrying.

Myra expresses her explicit dislike of the idea of the two male characters getting married and in turn, reinforces heteronormativity by shutting down any other option.

Martino (2009) warns that the simple inclusivity of LGBTQ themes can reinforce the dominant normalization of heteronormativity in schools. The excerpt below is an example of how an explicit rejection of non-heterosexuality/non-normative gender expression/identity did just that. From our twelfth meeting, and during the discussion of the book *Jacob's New Dress*, Jacob, the main character has made the decision to wear a dress to school. I asked the children to think about what that experience might be like as illustrated in the following.

> **Hartman:** What if this happened in real life and you saw a boy student who came to school in a dress? I want you to think about it.
> **Myra:** I can't imagine that happening.
> **Tariq:** I would get a yardstick and whack his head off.
> **Students:** <Laughing loudly>

It is clear that at this point, Tariq rejects the non-normative gender expression (a boy choosing to wear a dress) by the main character, Jacob—even suggesting that Jacob be physically harmed because of his gender expression. The response of loud laughter of the students very clearly and explicitly reinforces this rejection and hence, reifies heteronormativity to an extreme and violent degree.

The common thread that ties together discourse coded as rejections is that the heterosexual matrix is reified, and identities and expressions that fall outside of these norms are rendered wrong, unacceptable, and at times, even worthy of physical harm. During such moments, it was difficult and painful to hear these kinds of comments. Throughout the course of the project I thought deeply about the ways in which I could help to cultivate a more inclusive and affirming understanding of gender and sexual identities among my students and had to process the painful comments that sometimes ensued. Luckily, there were many redeeming moments in the discussions when other students challenged such negative comments. It was through such dialogue that I hoped for a more expansive and affirming understanding of identity would emerge amongst the entire group.

Challenges and Disruptions of the Heterosexual Matrix

Discourse categorized as disruptions are moments in which gender/heteronormativity was challenged, disrupted, or interrogated. The ways in which this happened varied greatly though, necessitating sub-categories to represent the ways language operated in the discussion: *strategic essentialist* and *queer*. Below, I provide explanations and examples of discourse coded as *strategic essentialist* and *queer*.

Strategic Essentialist Discourse

An essentialist view of identity "ascribes a fundamental nature of biological determinism to humans" (Leistyna, Woodrum, & Sherblom, 1996, p. 336). This view of identity conceives of gender and sexuality as aspects of identity with which individuals are born and that remain fixed throughout one's lifetime. Essentialist understandings of identity may become "strategic" when issues of power emerge and are addressed (Spivak, 1988). Though essentialist notions of gender and sexuality run counter to a queer perspective, strategic essentialist work may bring up power issues related to identity in an oversimplified manner, but that can initiate a discussion that can later become more nuanced and complicated.

Discourse that falls under this category may seem to challenge the heterosexual matrix on the surface, but with closer examination, may also reinforce and privilege norms associated with gender and sexual identity. To help understand how language can function in such a contradictory manner, two further discourse subcategories were identified in the data: *anti-bully discourse* and discourse that *reinforces gender/heteronormativity*. Even though these two subcategories of discourse ultimately reinforce heteronormativity, it is critical to consider the ways in which this discourse initially appears to challenge/disrupt heteronormativity.

Anti-Bully Discourse

Discourse identified as anti-bully might proclaim that it is wrong for an individual to be treated unfairly because of their gender expression and/or sexual identity. However, these proclamations stop short of advocating for more fluidity in understanding gender/sexual identity, or of an interrogation of the underlying causes of gender and/or sexual identity-based bullying. In the following excerpt from our eighth meeting and during the discussion of *The Sissy Duckling*, Myra's responses embody the characteristics of the anti-bullying discourse category. In the section of the text discussed by the students, Elmer, the main character, reclaims the label "sissy."

> **Hartman:** Right. What about being a sissy? What do you think about sissies? And that word sissy? I mean . . . that word is in the title so it's kind of important in the story.
>
> **Donald:** Well, that word's mean cuz they made fun of him. It was bullying that they did.
>
> **Myra:** Yea, that is rude!
>
> **Hartman:** Right, right. But, remember at the end and Elmer said, "I am a big sissy and proud of it!"? Remember? Did he think that word was mean then?
>
> **Javon:** No! He thought that word was cool . . . like, he like . . . He was proud and happy.

> **Sara:** Yes. He liked doing . . . wearing the girl things. Like hearts and things like that.
> **Hartman:** Ah. Okay. So that word can be used in different ways, hmmm. That's kind of interesting. What about being a sissy? Elmer calls himself a sissy. Is it okay to be a sissy?
> **Sara:** Yes, yes. I think he liked it. He can be like that. Boys can like hearts and things.
> **Donald:** <Yelling> Well that's weird. That's just weird!
> **Myra:** Well, it's not nice to make fun of sissies.
> **Hartman:** Well, what about being a sissy? We know it's not nice to make fun of sissies. What about being a sissy? What do you think about a boy being a sissy?
> **Myra:** No, no! That's kinda funny I think. I don't like it. <laughing>
> **Sara:** I think it's okay. Yea. I think Elmer was nice.

Myra explains that it is rude to call Elmer a sissy, and that it is not nice to make fun of sissies, but in her comment that follows, she explains that she thinks it is funny for a boy to be a sissy and that she does not like it. Though Myra expresses displeasure with the mistreatment of Elmer, she does not like that he is a sissy. Myra does not think it is okay to bully others but does not address the underlying cause of the bullying—the expectation that girls and boys should express their genders in particular ways. Again, queer theory helps to understand how this kind of thinking reifies heteronormativity and casts non-normative expressions of gender as wrong.

Reinforcing Gender/Heteronormativity

At times, the children seemed to police the ways in which they thought gender should be expressed—in a manner that reinforced heteronormativity. One example of this was during the discussion of *The Sissy Duckling*. I asked students to predict what would happen at the end of the story, once the members of Elmer's flock realize he survived the winter in the forest and that he saved his father. The following is what transpired.

> **Hartman:** "Elmer took a deep breath and spoke to the ducks." What do you think he's going to say?
> **Myra:** I have no idea.
> **Sara:** That he's a sissy?
> **Myra:** I think he's gonna say that . . . "Last time you guys all thought that I was a sissy, but now I'm not." I dunno.
> **Hartman:** This is what he said: "I want to make one thing perfectly clear . . ."
> **Tariq:** <interrupting> Oh I know! He wants a celebration?

> **Hartman:** Maybe . . . Let's read. "I am the same duck I have always been.
> I have not changed. I am a big sissy and I'm proud of it."
> <gasps from students>
> **Donald:** Oh dang!

During the winter when Elmer nursed his father back to health in his house, and after Elmer's father apologized to Elmer for mistreating him because of his gender expression, it became evident that Elmer's "sissy" qualities were appreciated by his father, and that it was Elmer's father, not Elmer, who needed to change. Even after the students acknowledged and discussed this, Myra's comment implies that Elmer should still conform to traditional gender norms which reinforces gender/heteronormativity.

Another example that is characteristic of this category comes from our tenth meeting during the discussion of *Elena's Serenade*. Elena, the main character, disguised herself so that she could pass as a boy and learn to be a glassblower. At the beginning of the story, when Elena first relates this interest, most of the children thought her choice to disguise herself as a boy was a bad one. But, at the conclusion, the children's opinions changed. They realized that the only way Elena was going to learn to be a glassblower was if she did indeed disguise herself as a boy.

> **Hartman:** Ah, ok. But remember at the beginning of the story, you
> thought it was a bad idea for her to disguise herself as a boy?
> Everyone except Sara. Why do you think it's a good idea now?
> **Myra:** Nope, it's a good idea. A little bad of a idea too. She's a
> girl so she shouldn't wear that clothes like a boy. But she
> couldn't do it. Be a glass blower. Like what she wants to do if
> she didn't dress like a boy.

Myra acknowledges that Elena had no other choice but to dress as a boy so she could learn to be a glassblower, but at the same time she expresses disapproval with Elena's choice to "wear that clothes like a boy." With this comment, Myra was willing to make space for Elena's subversive clothing choice, but only because without it, she would be prevented from partaking in an activity that was meaningful to her.

Queer Language

The other sub-category within the disruption/challenge category is *queer*. Discourse that falls under the queer subcategory explicitly interrogates gender/hetero-normativity and disrupts the norms that uphold the heterosexual, and/or the norms that govern what is appropriate/acceptable to discuss in school. This happened in one of two ways: *interrogating gender/heteronormativity* or *foregrounding gender/sexual identity*.

Interrogating Gender/Heteronormativity

In particular instances, participants broadened their understanding of gender/sexual identity and attempted to expand the boundaries of what they understood it means to be a boy or girl. During the final part of the literature discussion of *Jacob's New Dress*, the students discussed what lesson a reader may take away from reading the story.

> **Hartman:** Why do you think the author wrote this story? Do you think the reader can learn something from this story? Like, did you learn anything from reading it?
>
> **Myra:** Oh, I don't think anything.
>
> **Javon:** Thinking, thinking.
>
> **Sara:** Don't tell someone how they have to be. You're not the boss of them.
>
> **Hartman:** Anyone think something else?
>
> **Sara:** Oh yea also, like, there's more than one ways to be a girl or a boy?
>
> **Hartman:** Yea. I think that's a good lesson. Yea, there's lots of ways to be a boy or a girl.
>
> **Javon:** There's a million thousand, million thousand ways.

It is clear that both Sara and Javon have a broad understanding of what it means to be a boy or a girl, which in turn, disrupts the discourse of heteronormativity. Their comments push back against the norms that undergird the gender norms that uphold the heterosexual matrix. During another similar excerpt from our fifth meeting, and during the discussion of *10,000 Dresses*, the students discussed the possible lesson that could be learned from having read the story. One issue they grappled with was to understand the way in which Bailey, the main character, identified.

> **Hartman:** Okay, well the parents told Bailey that she is a boy, but she didn't feel like a boy. So how did Bailey overcome this problem? What happened? Remember, Bailey went to her parents, then her brother...
>
> **Sara:** That girl, Laurel, helped her make a dress. And it makes her feel good.
>
> **Hartman:** Why do you think that made Bailey feel good?
>
> **Aliya:** Cuz he liked dresses.
>
> **Sara:** Yea, and she wants to be a she so Laurel helped her be a she too.
>
> **Donald:** What?! Well...
>
> **Tariq:** But Bailey is a boy.

Sara: But Bailey said she felt like a girl though. So, maybe Bailey is really a girl, I think.

Hartman: Hmmm. Yes exactly. It was important for Bailey that other people saw her as a girl too. Okay. Well, what about a lesson? Do you think anyone learned a lesson in this story? Or can anyone reading this story learn a lesson maybe? Did you learn anything from reading this?

Myra: Nope. I didn't.

Tariq: No, nobody really learned a lesson.

Myra: Oh. Maybe?

Donald: Bailey did?

Hartman: Ok. What lesson did Bailey learn?

Sara: Uhm, I think that, that dresses aren't only made for girls.

Hartman: So, dresses are made for anybody? Ah, ok. What do you all think?

Donald: Disagree. Well, maybe if Bailey said she was a girl, so dresses are for girls. So, it's ok.

In this excerpt, Sara advocates for the self-identification of Bailey, while other students insist that other individuals in Bailey's life can and should make that choice for Bailey. Sara explains that a lesson from the story is that dresses can be worn by anyone. This illustrates a break from traditional gender roles and modes of expression. Also, Donald's response (although seemingly unintentional) reinforces gender normativity. Nonetheless, he seemingly accepts the fact that Bailey does not "feel like a boy," and polices Bailey's gender expression, justifying her desire to wear dresses "if Bailey said she was a girl."

Another instance that illustrates breaks with heteronormativity took place during the discussion of *King and King* when it is revealed that the two princes got married.

Hartman: Well, let's read ... "The wedding was very special. The queen even shed a tear or two." So, you're right, they did get married.

Tariq: <screaming, as if shocked> Ah!

Myra: Yea, but it shows two boys ...

Donald: There is a husband marrying a husband?

Teacher: Yes, look. That's what we just read.

Sara: Ah! Oh no!

Tariq: Is it allowed to marry a man? Like a man to marry a man?

Myra: That is illegal!

Hartman: You can do that in our state. It is not illegal.

Javon: Yea, because my friend's mom. My friend's mom, like married another woman.

Myra: Uhm, when you marry another man, does it mean that… you are allowed to marry another man, or another woman? Can you marry another man or another woman in our city?

Hartman: Yes, you can.

Aliya: Some men marry cuz my mom just drives downtown sometimes, and because she sees men kissing other men. And that she said… that is disgusting.
<multiple laughs>

Javon: That's actually gay. That's actually called being gay.
<laughing and screaming from students>

The concept of gay marriage is discussed because Javon explains that he knows two women who are married to one another, clarifying that the identity of individuals in same sex relationships for the other children, "That's actually called being gay," disrupts the discourse of heteronormativity on marriage and relationships as solely occurring between individuals of the opposite sex.

Foregrounding Gender/Sexual Identity

The very act of discussing these usually hidden and taboo topics related to non-normative gender and non-heterosexual identities with young children may act as a kind of queering discourse because the act of discussing these topics challenges the norms of what should and should not be discussed in the classroom (Martino, 2009). Therefore, also falling under the queer category is discourse that incorporates discussions among the students that illustrate grappling with issues related to non-normative gender and/or sexual identities, but that does not explicitly reject these non-normative expressions/identities. Because discussions surrounding issues related to non-normative gender and/or sexual identities, particularly among young children, are commonly considered taboo and inappropriate, such discussions can act in a queering manner—disrupting the normative regulations of what is/should and what is not/should not be not talked about with and among children. I refer to such discourse as *foregrounded in gender/sexual identity*. One example of this is from the discussion of *King and King*, when I reach the portion of the narrative when the two princes appear to be in a church, about to be married. I asked the children to examine the illustration and to predict what would happen next in the story before I continued to read the text.

Javon: So like… what's happening is that they are at the bride place. And then he's sayin' <pointing to what looks like a

> priest or minister> "Do you take him as your wife? And do you take him as your husband?" And then they say, "Yes," and then I think they gonna kiss.
>
> **Students:** Eww!
> **Hartman:** Yep, that's what it looks like, right?
> **Javon:** Yes, I think those men are gay. That is gay.
> **Hartman:** Well, let's read... "The wedding was very special. The queen even shed a tear or two." So, you're right, they did get married.
> **Tariq:** Ah!
> **Myra:** Yea, but it shows two boys...

From this excerpt, the children try to make sense of the marriage of the two princes. Javon's background knowledge assists the students in coming to understand what is happening in the story. This is also the first time in which an explicit non-heterosexual identity/theme was brought into the read aloud discussion of the group. The insertion of this topic promoted a lively interaction among the students as they worked to make sense of the story.

Another example of this kind of discourse occurred during the discussion of the beginning of *The Sissy Duckling*. As we read the first pages of the story, the students grappled with understanding the gender of the main character, Elmer, as he is presented on the cover carrying a pink backpack with flowers, and wearing pink, heart-shaped sunglasses.

> **Hartman:** "Yes, Elmer was one happy duckling doing all the things he loved to do."
> **Aliya:** Is it a she or a he?
> **Hartman:** Well, what does it say?
> **Aliya:** He?
> **Hartman:** Yep.
> **Myra:** Huh? But why does he have a heart glasses, like a girl?
> **Hartman:** Well, why do you think?
> **Myra:** I think he's a girl.
> **Hartman:** But it says 'he' though.
> **Donald:** Yea, he!
> **Myra:** Oh, maybe he likes pink?
> **Sara:** I think the other ducks are gonna make fun of him. Cuz he's wearing those glasses, and like hearts.
> **Myra:** Yea girl things. I think they're gonna be making fun of him because he has girl stuff <laughing>.

Even after we confirmed that the pronoun "he" was used to refer to Elmer, Myra still insists that Elmer must be a girl because of the way he expresses his gender. At this point, a "sissy" identity is not a valid possibility for her.

And though Elmer is usually a name associated with boys, I do not think many of the students were familiar with that name.

Another example of discourse that is *foregrounded in gender/sexual identity* is from the discussion of *10,000 Dresses*. The children express confusion in the fact that Bailey, the main character, referred to herself as a girl, but that everyone else referred to her as a boy:

> **Hartman:** "'But I don't feel like a boy,' she said. 'Well, you are one, and that's that. Now go away and don't mention dresses again.' Bailey went to her room. Now she would never have a dress made of lilies and roses and honeysuckle sleeves." So what's going on here? Bailey is still shifting because she uses "she" and other people use "he."
>
> **Donald:** This is just confusing.
>
> **Aliya:** I think that she is actually a girl. But her parents don't like dresses, so they are saying that she is a boy.
>
> **Hartman:** Ok. Interesting.
>
> **Javon:** Well I think she thinks she's a girl though. But not other people. Like her dad thinks she's a boy.
>
> **Hartman:** Ah. Ok. Ya, it seems like Bailey feels like she's a girl. Let's keep on reading.

In this excerpt, the children are given the opportunity to make sense of the dilemma in which Bailey is confronted. The children's understanding of Bailey's gender identity/expression shifts as they talk with one another, and as the story unfolds. Again, this excerpt can be understood as a queering discourse, as the children are grappling with topics that are usually silenced and absent from primary literacy classrooms.

DISCUSSION

In this analysis of classroom discussion from five literature discussions of children's books with themes of nonheterosexuality and/or non-normative gender expression/identity, I explored how the inclusion of such texts enables a multitude of possibilities in the classroom discourse that may not have otherwise been present. However, as Martino (2009) warns, the simple inclusion of such themes and topics in the classroom can have un-intended consequences, such as the entry of hateful and marginalizing discourse. Indeed, these were difficult moments, particularly from my posi-tion as a gay teacher, and for students who have LGBTQ identified family members or who may have non-normative expressions of gender and/or identify as LGBTQ.

Rymes (2009) posits that new student identities are constructed through talk and by examining the ways students and teachers interact. Some students, like Sara, consistently advocated for a more inclusive and expansive understanding of gender and sexual identity. Other students, like Javon, brought words like "gay" into the group discussion—a word and identity that is commonly avoided in primary classrooms. The entry of such language has the potential to reshape students' identities (Gee, 1996), and may give the impression to students that it is acceptable and good to identify as LGBTQ or to have non-normative expressions of gender within the classroom and perhaps beyond. Additionally, comments that were common of Sara and Javon often times served as disruptions to the normative and marginalizing comments that were characteristic of Myra.

By analyzing these literature discussions, I was able to reflect on the ways in which this group of children thought about gender/sexual identity, and how I might adapt future teaching endeavors based on what I found in this study. Indeed, this reflection and direct change is at the heart of teacher action research. The findings of this study can enable teachers and teacher-educators to consider how they might incorporate such literacy-related activities in their classrooms and respond to moments when well-intentioned pedagogical initiatives create such unintended consequences. In addition, reflection on the findings provide teachers and teacher-educators an opportunity to consider ways to support young students to "queer" their thinking, (i.e., to encourage them to think about the process of privileging and othering on the basis of normative gender and sexual identity expressions).

The five books used in this study are nowhere close to an exhaustive list of children's books containing themes related to LGBTQ related themes, and the ways in which issues of non-heterosexuality and/or non-normative gender expression/identities surface within such texts is varied and complex. Other scholars have examined heteronormativity (Stafford, 2009) and homonormativity (Lester, 2014) in LGBTQ-themed children's books. For instance, in *King and King*, there are numerous examples in which power hierarchies related to race and class are recreated to normalize (white, cis-male) homosexuality.

This project demonstrates that young children already possesses conceptions about LGBTQ identities and non-normative gender expression. Such a recognition highlights how the literacy curriculum acts as an ideological filter (Dyson, 2015) and can potentially cast non-normative expressions of gender/sexual identity as either invisible, taboo, strange, or wrong, especially if these identities are missing and erased from classrooms. Teachers of young children should acknowledge that their students are already grappling with complicated issues related to identity and power, and that the literacy classroom should be a space where children can further explore these issues in an affirmative, supporting context.

Limitations and Implications

Part of this project's aim was to cultivate a more expansive and inclusive perspective of gender and sexual identity among the child-participants. However, there were moments when the opposite occurred. Though I did plan questions and anticipate moments in each book that would be fruitful for engaging interactions, upon reflection, a more systematic approach could have been useful and more productive, such as from a critical literacy perspective. Vasquez (2017) posits that "critical literacy should not be an add-on but a frame through which to participate in the world" (p. 3). Additionally, Hermann-Wilmarth and Ryan (2015) offer suggestions for teachers to address LGBTQ topics through the language arts curricula by using strategies such as reading "straight" books through a queer lens. These refinements to my teaching approach could have been productive as I engaged the children in this project in developing a critical lens as they approach literature. In fact, since the completion of this project I integrated a critical literacy perspective in my second-grade classroom teaching, and as I currently teach pre-service teachers.

Though the analysis of gender and sexual identities was privileged in this study, further exploration is needed to understand the ways in which other facets of identity (i.e., race, ethnicity, language, socioeconomic status, etc.) intersect with gender and sexual identities. Given the cultural diversity of this group of students, it would be fruitful to understand the ways these other facets of their identities may have shaped their perspectives on gender and sexuality, something I plan to pursue as I continue to reflect on this project.

Even throughout difficult moments as a gay teacher in this study—namely during moments when homophobic and heterosexist statements surfaced in discussions—I recognized my position of power not only as the teacher, but as a White, middle-class, cis-male. As such, it is imperative to assume an intersectional approach when thinking through ways to address homophobia and heterosexism in the classroom. Therefore, to explore the complex and interlocking nature of oppressions, it is crucial to mesh insights gleaned from queer teaching approaches with insights gleaned from culturally relevant (Ladson-Billings, 2014) and culturally sustaining (Paris & Alim, 2014) pedagogies.

CONCLUSION

Dyson (2015) calls upon primary-grades educators to challenge "deficit discourses" that are pervasive in primary classrooms (i.e., discourses and practices that render the lives of children from non-dominant backgrounds as invisible or in need of correction). Though she explicitly references discourses surrounding race, ethnicity, and language, I wish to encourage educators to similarly challenge deficit and harmful discourses surrounding LGBTQ identities. I found it helpful to approach such work with a perspective of gender and sexual identity informed by queer theory and I encourage other teachers and teacher-educators to explore the possibilities that such a perspective can promote. I also encourage practicing classroom teachers to document and share their anti-homophobic and counter-heteronormative work to support the learning of other educators and teacher-educators and to better understand the complexity and importance of such work within their own pedagogical contexts.

Throughout the course of this project and my time teaching young children, I have reflected deeply about the ways in which heteronormativity regulates the classroom environment. The large gap in research on gender and sexuality in primary schools can be filled by exploring the ways in which children think about and grapple with the process of privileging and othering and how literacy might be used as a tool to disrupt such norms. As educators, we must continually reflect on our practice and ask, *who or what is being left out?* As Ayers, Kumashiro, Meiners, Quinn, and Stovall (2017) remind us, we must acknowledge and embrace that "there is no simple technique or linear path that will take us where we need to go...There is no promised land in teaching, just the aching and persistent tension between reality and possibility" (p. 18). It is through the sharing of our attempts to disrupt marginalizing practices that help us explore these tensions so our classrooms might become more inclusive spaces for our students.

REFERENCES

Ayers, W., Kumashiro, K., Meiners, E., Quinn, T., & Stovall, D. (2017). *Teaching toward democracy: Educators as agents of change.* New York, NY: Routledge.

Blackburn, M. (2012). *Interrupting hate: Homophobia in schools and what literacy can do about it.* New York, NY: Teachers College Press.

Blackburn, M. V., & Clark, C. T. (2011). Analyzing talk in a long-term literature discussion group: LGBT-inclusive and queer discourses. *Reading Research Quarterly, 46*(3), 222–248. doi:10.1598/RRQ.46.3.2

Blaise, M. (2005). *Playing it straight: Uncovering gender discourses in the early childhood classroom.* New York, NY: Routledge.

Blaise, M. (2009). "What a girl wants, what a girl needs": Responding to sex, gender, and sexuality in the early childhood classroom. *Journal of Research in Childhood Education, 23*(4), 450–460. doi:10.1080/02568540909594673

Blaise, M., & Taylor, A. (2012). Using queer theory to rethink gender equity in early childhood education. *Young Children, 67*(1), 88–97. Retrieved from https://www.naeyc.org/resources/pubs/yc

Butler, J. (1990). *Gender trouble: Feminisms and the subversion of identity.* New York, NY: Routledge.

Cochran-Smith, M., & Lytle, S. L. (2009). Teacher researcher as stance. In S. E. Noffke & B. Somekh (Eds.), *The SAGE handbook of educational action research* (pp. 39–49). Thousand Oaks, CA: SAGE.

Connell, R. W. (1987). *Gender and power.* Stanford, CA: Stanford University Press.

Dyson, A. H. (2015). The search for inclusion: Deficit discourse and the erasure of childhoods. *Language Arts, 92*(3), 199–207. Retrieved from http://www2 .ncte.org/resources/journals/language-arts/

Fine, M. (2006). Sexuality education and desire: Still missing after all these years. *Harvard Educational Review, 76*(3), 297–338. doi:10.17763/haer.76.3 .w5042g23122n6703

Gee, J. (1996). *Social linguistics and literacies: Ideology in discourse.* London, England: Taylor & Francis.

Glesne, C., & Peshkin, A. (1992). *Becoming qualitative researchers: An introduction.* White Plains, NY: Longman.

Hermann-Wilmarth, J. M., & Ryan, C. L. (2015). Doing what you can: Considering ways to address LGBT topics in language arts curricula. *Language Arts, 92*(6), 436–443. Retrieved from http://www2.ncte.org/resources/journals/ language-arts/

Hong, J. S., & Espelage, D. L. (2012). A review of research on bullying and peer victimization in school: An ecological system analysis. *Aggression and Violent Behavior, 17,* 311–322. doi:10.1016/j.avb.2012.03.003

Jagose, A. (1996). *Queer theory: An introduction.* New York, NY: New York University Press.

Kull, R. M., Kosciw, J. G., & Greytak, E. A. (2015). *From statehouse to schoolhouse: Anti-bullying policy efforts in U.S. states and school districts.* New York, NY: GLESN.

Ladson-Billings, G. (2014). Culturally relevant pedagogy 2.0: A.K.A. the remix. *Harvard Educational Review, 84*(1), 74–85. doi:10.17763/haer.84.1.p2rj131485484751

Leistyna, P., Woodrum, A., & Sherblom, S. A. (1996). *Breaking free: The transformative power of critical pedagogy.* Cambridge, MA: Harvard Educational Review.

Lester, J. Z. (2014). Homonormativity in children's literature: An intersectional analysis of queer-themed picture books. *Journal of LGBT Youth, 11*(3), 244–275. doi:10.1080/19361653.2013.879465

Martino, W. (2009). Literacy issues and GLBTQ youth: Queer interventions in English education. In L. Christenbury, R. Bomer, & P. Smagorinsky (Eds.), *Handbook of adolescent research* (pp. 386–399). New York, NY: Guilford Press.

Paris, D., & Alim, H. S. (2014). What are we seeking to sustain through culturally sustaining pedagogy? A loving critique forward. *Harvard Educational Review, 84*(1), 85–100. doi:10.17763/haer.84.1.9821873k2ht16m77

Rymes, B. (2009). *Classroom discourse analysis: A tool for critical reflection.* Creskill, England: Hampton Press.

Spivak, G. C. (1988). *In other worlds: Essays in cultural politics.* New York, NY: Routledge.

Stafford, A. (2009). Beyond normalization: An analysis of heteronormativity in children's picture books. In R. Epstein (Ed.), *"Who's your daddy?" and other writings on queer parenting* (pp. 169–178). Toronto, ON: Sumach Press.

Thorne, B. (1993). *Gender play: Girls and boys in school.* New Brunswick, NJ: Rutgers University Press.

Vasquez, V. M. (2017). *Critical literacy across the k–6 curriculum.* New York, NY: Routledge.

Zeni, J. (1998). A guide to ethical issues and action research. *Educational Action Research, 6*(1), 9–19. doi:10.1080/09650799800200053

CHAPTER 6

"I WANT THEM [TEACHERS] TO TREAT US LIKE HUMAN BEINGS"

Educational Experiences of Black Gay Youth

Michael D. Bartone

ABSTRACT

A study of Black gay males' life histories, with a focus on their educational experiences, demonstrated how they have come to understand, embrace, and love their intersecting identities. Of relevance to educators is the value gained from the insight of these educational experiences to confront, combat, and dismantle racist and heteronormative facets of schooling. From an analysis and interpretation of the data of Black gay males' educational experiences, educators can begin to challenge their understanding of this community, understand what Black gay males encounter and how they navigate through schools, and find ways to best support Black gay males and create inclusive lessons for all students to understand, know, and value the Black gay community.

Exploring Gender and LGBTQ Issues in K–12 and Teacher Education, pages 95–109
95

Being Black and gay is to exist in two socially constructed liminal categories. Not only do such individuals and others who possess marginalized racial and sexual intersecting identities face social, political, and economic systems that devalues their existence (Ingraham, 1994; King, 2011), they must also navigate through schooling systems that are often hostile, especially to LGBTQ+ youth of color. Entering into a classroom, few things may be as evident as one's racial and gender categorization. Whether or not students identify with normative gender/sexual identity categorizations should be respected by teachers who should be conscious to not mis-gender (i.e., assume how a student identifies in relation to gender) or label a student with a particular racial or ethnic identification (i.e., perceive someone to be of one ethnic identity when they identify with another). In order to promote an inclusive classroom setting, simply being aware of racial, gender, and sexual categorizations is insufficient, particularly for teachers who teach students with diverse identities. Being conscious of and ultimately affirming the social categories students claim, and how identification with these social categories functions to mitigate learning, is imperative for working with students of diverse cultural, linguistic, and sexual identity backgrounds.

The purpose of this study is to investigate narratives from males who identify as Black and gay and have self-possession, meaning an acceptance, appreciation, and love of their intersecting racial and sexual identities. The narratives focus on how their schooling experiences connected with the understanding of their intersecting racial and sexual identities. Given little is understood about the experiences of Black gay youth in schools (Bartone, 2015; McCready, 2010), the educational narratives of the participants provide insight of what schooling experiences may be like for many LGBTQ+ youth of color, and more specifically, how Black gay males navigate and negotiate through school cultures characterized by racism and heteronormativity. Further, this work provides evidence of ways educators can support students embodying racial and sexual intersecting identities. In the following sections I discuss racism and heteronormativity as constructs that informed the educational experience of the research participants. I then relate the theoretical frameworks and methodological approach followed with the study's findings. I conclude with a discussion of this inquiry with implications for teaching and research.

RACISM

Racism has been defined as a system, a project providing for political, social, and economic policies, that, in the context of North America and Europe, priveleges the White race (Omi & Winant, 1994). This project of race and the ideologies that encompass and make up racism allow for structural and institutional forces to benefit White individuals, oppressing and marginalizing individuals and communities of other racial backgrounds (Omi & Winant, 1994). The discussion Omi and Winant (1994) provide of racism and how racism functions and is entrenched in the fabric of society "link[s] racial formation to the evolution of hegemony, the way in which society is organized and ruled" (p. 56). Leonardo (2009) notes the discourse of "'Whiteness is grounded in the belief White is normal and universal where 'the white race speak[s] for the human race'" (p. 263). Many teachers lack critical awareness of racism and its privileging of Whiteness, and in turn Amer-Eurocentricity which "is based on White supremacist notions whose purposes are to protect White privilege and advantage in education, economics, politics, and so forth" (Asante, 1991, pp. 170–171), and how these inform education and systems of schooling. Unfortunatley, this serves to perpetuate the acceptance, normalization, and employment of a colorblind ideology in pedagogical practices to the detriment of students' educative experiences, especially those from marginalized backgrounds. A privileging of Amer-Eurocentric thinking enables the potential for the mis-education not just of Black students and other students of color (Woodson, 2000), but for White students as well. King (1991) suggests that this dysconcious racism possessed by many teachers (preservice and inservice), is an "uncritical habit of mind that justifies inequity and exploitation by accepting the existing order of things" (p. 135). Such an uncritical habit of mind compounds the challenges experienced by students who possess intersecting, marginalized identities, such as Black gay youth. Similar to racism, heteronormativity also permeates society (and systems of schooling).

HETERONORMATIVITY

Chrys Ingraham (1994) links heteronormativity with socially acceptable institutional norms maintaining, "the view that institutionalized heterosexuality constitutes the standard for legitimate and prescriptive sociosexual arrangement" (p. 204). This belief and its accompanying social practices and discourses pervade society, situating heterosexuality as a norm that all individuals are expected/assumed to identify with. It is critical for teachers to recongize how heteronormativity functions in their classrooms. Particularly, teachers should be aware that not all students identify as heterosexual, and many identify or will identify in ways not conforming to the standards of heteronormativity. Thus, teachers need to engage in a pedagogy wherein students are not "othered" and heteronormativity is not perpetuated.

To be sure, it is not only within the in-service context that challenges relevant to heteronormativity surface. In teacher preparation programs, issues affecting LGBTQ+ are often overlooked or addressed in a cursory manner with, "[preservice] teachers largely...not being prepared to recognize homophobic bias, much less subvert heteronormativity" (Gorski, Davis, & Reiter, 2013, p. 225). This lack of attention to heteronormativity in teacher education programs and critical awareness among preservice teachers contributes to an inability to understand, much less recognize, how heteronormativity functions within schools and society. Such a context enables the reproduction and reinforcement of heteronormative discourses, practices, and beliefs in systems of schooling, perpetuating the marginalization of non-heterosexual individuals. Given identities are intersectional, I take up a discussion of race and sexuality in the following section, attentive to the intersection of being Black and gay.

INTERSECTIONS OF RACE AND SEXUALITY

While the empirical literature is sparse, there are some published studies attending to schooling and the lived experiences of Black gay youth and adults (e.g., Boykin, 2012; Johnson, 2005; McCready, 2010). Given Black gay youth possess socially marginalized racial and sexual identities (Dubé & Savin-Williams, 1999), it is imperative to extend and build upon this literature to better support these students in today's schools. Often, Black gay youth learn about their racial identity through family members and peers, and their sexual identity from the internet and/or community-based organizations (Jamil, Harper, Fernandez, & Adolescent Trials Network for HIV/AIDS Prevention, 2009). Yet, what about Black gay youth and their experiences in school? What effect does heteronormativity and racialized ideologies have on understanding their intersecting identities?

Black gay youth face a hostile educational system (Kosciw, Greytak, Palmer, & Boesen, 2014), a system that has disinvested in the education of Black youth (Ladson-Billings, 2006); insight on their experiences navigating through these spaces would aid in understanding how teachers can affirmatively include Black gay students and other LGBTQ+ students in their classrooms. It would support policymakers to advance agendas working to dismantle educational inequities rooted in racism and heteronormativity. Data from GLSEN'S 2013 Climate Survey show hostile heteronormative environments affect more than the social and emotional lives of LGBTQ+ youth; these environments affect their academic performance as well (Kosciw et al., 2014). Students facing sexual orientation and/or gender expression discrimination are at a greater likelihood to have increased absenteeism, lower grade point averages, and higher levels of depression (Kosciw et al., 2014, p. xviii).

Black males face schools where negative perceptions of and institutional policies toward Black youth have helped create the school-to-prison pipeline, often through unjust disciplinary actions (Ferguson, 2001). Within the school to prison pipeline are Black LGBTQ+ youth, who are disproportionately punished for breaking school polices relevant to gender non-conformativity and pushing against heteronormativity, such as boys wearing dresses or high heels or girls wearing men's suits, students engaging in performativity that challenges and goes against soceity's traditional understandings of how boys and girls should dress and act (Mitchum & Moodie-Mills, 2014). Concurrently, schools often deny "queer youth, and queer youth of color in particular, equal opportunity for a rewarding education in an environment that is safe and supportive of their various struggles for identity" (Grady, Marquez, & McLaren, 2012, p. 984). Thus, it is vital for all educators to consider how racism and heteronormativity influence their pedagogy, the classroom and school environment, and the educative experiences of their students.

THEORETICAL FRAMEWORKS

In this study I employed critical race theory and quare theory (Johnson, 2005; Taylor, 2009). These theories challenge deficit perspectives of Blackness (Howard, 2013) and gayness (Johnson, 2005) and place race (critical race theory) and queerness (quare theory) at the forefront of the study's design, questions asked of participants and data analysis and interpretation. Critical race theorists argue racism is endemic to society and cannot be divorced from one's experiences, the nation's laws, nor daily workings of society (Taylor, 2009). It illuminates how race is salient in one's schooling experiences structurally, ideologically, and pedagogically.

I employed quare theory in conjunction with critical race theory to inform my thinking of sexual identities. Johnson (2005) argues that quare theory "is a theory for gays and lesbians of color" (p. 127) and focuses on performativity and is a "theory in the flesh" (Johnson, 2001, p. 9). Quare theory provides one with the foundation of analzysis in which "the discursive process of mediated identification and subjectivity in a political praxis [that] speaks to the material existence of "colored bodies" (Johns, 2001, p. 10). In this study, it enabled me to consider how the participants understood themselves according to or in opposition to politically informed and dominant narratives of being Black and/or gay. The two frames of critical race theory and quare theory provided for an analysis of the narratives in ways that illuminated the interconnected workings of racism and heteronormativity from the participants' schooling experiences.

METHODOLOGY

This study is part of a larger study that explored the experiences of Black gay men in the metro-Atlanta area (Bartone, 2015). Using narrative inquiry (Polkinghone, 1995), five participants aged 19–24 were interviewed to obtain their life histories. Four of the participants were known or referred to me via my personal network. The other pariticipant was met through my professional network. Criteria for inclusion was: (a) identifying as Black and gay; and (b) having self-possession, acceptance, and love of their intersecting identities; participants had to express that they loved and accepted being Black and gay, had no reservations or hatred toward either of these identities. Three semi-structured interviews (Kvale & Brinkmann, 2009) took place over the summer of 2014 and focused on two phases of their lives with attention on their schooling experiences: (a) birth-middle school and (b) high-school to present. The focus was on participants' understanding of their intersecting racial and sexual identities based on lived experiences, with emphasis on their educational experiences. Polkinghorne (1988) situates narratives within the realm of meaning, viewing narratives as a means for people to create an understanding of their experiences and the significance of the experiences. In this chapter, I focus on the narratives of two of the participants, Tae and Zion (pseudonyms).

In conjunction with presenting the life histories in narrative form, thematic analysis was utilized, which keeps each participant's narrative "intact," yet when analyzed collectively, enables the identification of themes across narrations (Riessman, 2008). I analyzed the narratives that surfaced among these two participants' educational experiences in relation to race and sexuality attentive to the framining of critical race theory and quare theory. For these participants, telling their life stories was not always the most pleasant experience. Nonetheless, having brought up memories they had forgotten but now were reflecting upon, they commented on the productiveness of the experience and what they were able to accomplish throughout their schooling years despite the challenges they faced as they grappled with understanding their intersecting identities.

Presented here are representative narratives of Tae's and Zion's educational experiences. I decided to focus on Tae and Zion from among the five participants because their experiences mirror each other's and highlight the challenges faced and successes each had in understanding, embracing, and loving his intersecting identities. Both grew up in different counties in metro-Atlanta, but their neighborhoods and schools were demographically similar. Both indicated they were shy and often teased in elementary school, had a teacher who acted as a surrogate parent, and struggled to understand their racial identity in relation to their sexuality. Key events are discussed next.

EDUCATIONAL EXPERIENCES

Tae's and Zion's intersecting identities have been influenced by their social location growing up in metro Atlanta, living in middle-class majority Black neighborhoods, in solidly majority White conservative counties, while attending racially diverse schools up until high school, which was majority black. Tae's experiences are discussed first, then Zion's.

> She [the middle school teacher] was encouraging me to not give up and fight harder and do your [my] best, don't give up and be like the rest of the kids who gave up or who care about the now. She saw a lot in me, she cared for me. (Tae)

The above excerpt from Tae's first interview highlights his experience with Ms. Harper, a middle school teacher who believed in him as a student and demonstrated an ethic of care. Yet, this was not typically the case for him. School was never easy, especially in elementary school. Tae sometimes felt different than most of the other students, in part because he was shy, did not play sports, and because he felt he "was dumb" or "didn't understand what was going on." In short, he was not enacting the identity of a Black male as would be socially anticipated and expected. Compounding this situation, Tae was often instructed by teachers who did not address Blackness and the positive influence and contributions of Black Americans and Africans in the United States and abroad.

Nonetheless, it became evident Tae was learning implicitly and explicitly about the Black community, and sometimes in ways countering Eurocentric ideologies. In one account, Ms. Harper engaged in teaching practices and lessons that ran counter to the dominant Amer-Eurocentric discourses and illuminated the many contributions people of African descent have made to civilization, adamant that students like Tae should be proud of these. However, Ms. Harper did not introduce issues or topics pertinent to LGBTQ+ individuals or communities. Unfortunately, during this time, Tae had numerous encounters with homophobic peers and was frequently the target of bullies. For Tae, the internet began serving as an influence in his understanding of self and the eventual identification as being both Black and being gay. The middle school experience of being the target of peers (most of whom were also Black) contributed to a belief that the the Black community was largely homophobic. Tae's quiet nature and non-athletic disposition reinforced the perception among such peers that he was gay. During interview one, Tae stated of his middle school experience, "I'm being singled out because I'm not one of the cool kids and I could be gay, and I'm singled out [by society] now because I'm Black. I'm starting to realize I'm singled out in more than one way. I can't get away from it."

Grappling with and trying to understand his intersecting identities, Tae met other Black gay males either online or secretly at school. Those students who were openly gay knew Tae was grappling with his sexual identity and respected his desire for discretion. Tae's propensity and affinity to use online communication to meet other gay males may have been a consequence of the school's lack of attention to issues of sexuality via curricula and failure to acknowledge LGBTQ+ individuals such as himself. Further, with African and Black history relegated to the margins of the curriculum, Tae also sought to better understand himself as Black by connecting with other Black gay youth. Nonetheless, despite having several Black males as friends in high school, Tae believed those that identified as straight were homophobic and was scared to share his sexual identity. Having been caught in a lie about where he had been when he was supposed to be with his friends after school, Tae was forced to confront his friends and share the truth of his whereabouts and his sexuality: having lunch and meeting up with a gay student from school rather than being at step practice. When his close group of Black male friends told him they were friends regardless, Tae understood the meaning of support and friendship:

> I said "Yo, I didn't think you all would be this open or cool with it." They said "You know we don't care because you still our dude at the end of the day." I said "I didn't know what to tell y'all, I didn't know how to feel because I thought y'all's gonna stop being my friends." They said "Nah, Tae you our homie for life, you're really our best friend for life, so there's nothing about it can really push us away." They started laughing and clowning. That's when I came out to them. After that I felt so much better.

Not having a present father, Tae turned to his step coach in high school as a father figure who, like some of his peers, provided much needed support of his sexual identity. Tae's coach built a relationship where he and Tae would have open discussions on multiple topics, especially Tae's developing sense of being gay:

> He knew about me but was completely supportive. He didn't care, he was very calm and said "Ok." That was the support I needed. He's like a father figure to me...whenever I had a relationship going on, I would tell him "Yeah, I got this little issue with this guy I'm dating." He would say "We'll talk about it." It would be very brief, and he probably make [sic] a joke and we'll [sic] laugh then we'd go onto something else. Being with him would be so cool I forgot about what's going on.

Like Ms. Harper, Tae's coach was an exception given that most of his teachers either ignored issues of sexuality and sexual diveristy. These narrative excerpts illustrate Tae's ability to navigate his educational experiences with support from particular educators and peers with whom he could be both Black and gay without judgement. This promoted a positive sense of self-worth, having a group of peers who did not abandon him because he was gay, and a coach in whom he could confide and have the support of through the often challenging schooling experiences that largely ignored or demeaned his identities as Black and gay. Potentially, such supports enabled his ability to embrace and ultimately love his intersecting identities.

> Teachers, I didn't really snitch about it [racial and sexual teasing], whatever happened to me I dealt with. I've always been like that. (Zion)

For Zion, elementary school was a place where he felt different than the other kids, as he stated during his first interview, "I think I felt less of a person." As Zion recalls, his elementary school was a likely an equal mix of White and Black students. He remembers being name called by some White students and experiencing inner conflict because, at the time, he wanted to be friends with these boys. Throughout the interviews, he reflected upon this and realized that it may very well have been that he had a crush on some of them at that time. Being one of a very few Black students in his class, Zion's racial identity as Black (and being teased by White boys) and burgeoning understanding that he was somehow different from the other boys challenged his ability to understand the complexities of his intersecting identities.

In his accounts of middle school, the teasing Zion experienced had shifted from being called "sissy" to being labeled as "gay," by both his Black and White peers. For Zion, the term gay had no meaning; he was unaware of its definition and did not understand why people called him gay. While his peers continued to tease him on his perceived sexuality, Zion was also navigating his racial identity. Unlike the elementary school context where the White boys were teasing him, Black peers were now mocking his actions and calling him gay. While he had a small group of White friends in sixth grade, he had a hard time connecting with his Black peers. However, during the seventh grade, Zion joined an art club wherein he met Black peers whom he befriended. This group of friends shared a similar interest in art and "were really chill." By now, Zion had confided in a friend about his questioning of his own sexuality, yet was largely keeping these feelings to himself. In eighth grade Zion changed schools and found himself among other Black peers who accepted him for being introverted and not presenting as an overly masculine teenager. It was the support of peers and having a father who sought to instill pride in Zion's Black identity that he began to understand his racial identity in an affirmative light even if ignored by most teachers and the formal school curricula.

As with Tae, LGBTQ+ issues were not formally discussed in school and Zion utilized the internet as a medium to meet gay males. Despite this and the support of some peers, Zion continued to experience bullying and name calling in school. During his second interview, he recalled how in high school he had enough of a male peer calling him faggot. Demonstrating his strength, resilience, and acceptance of his identities Zion confronted the male peer:

> I'm a faggot, ok... It was a very large crowd I did it in front of. No one could say anything because he knows now what? I'm not ugly. I'm not stupid, so what else can you say? I'm not fat. The only thing you have on me is gay, what next? My hair's better than yours. My shoes are better than yours. My clothes are better than yours. It was like, ok, now that we have this one, I guess disadvantage, out of the way, what next?

Yet Zion also experienced challenges at home with a father who was disgusted by his son's sexuality and let Zion know he was a disgrace to all of the Black men in his family who fought for his freedom. It was the support of his art teacher, Mr. Karl, that fostered Zion's positive sense of self. Mr. Karl, a White man, became a surrogate parent to Zion in much the way Irvine (2003) notes Black teachers become "Other Mothers" to their Black students. In one poignant moment, Zion remembers how Mr. Karl's small action had a major influence on his self-esteem:

> My birthday was coming up and I told Mr. Karl I was bummed about it. I didn't think I was gonna do anything because I was in trouble for something, I'm pretty sure it had to do with the gay thing...Something happened to where it was just not a good situation in my house... I didn't have anything planned...On the day of my birthday, I walk[ed] into the arts room and everyone's gathered around this one table and they all look[ed] like they're looking at something. I thought, I don't know what's going on. I sit down in my usual spot and don't even look down, just put down my stuff. I look and there's this big ass cookie cake that says "Happy Birthday Zion" and it had a rainbow on the whole cookie. Mr. Karl said "Do you like your rainbow?" I said "Thank you." I started crying because why is this man that I just met, maybe didn't even know him for two months, buying me a cake? He threw a party for me, a surprise party in the classroom. I was emotionally touched that day I didn't even know what to do with myself. I just started calling him dad from that point on, and he responded to it.

Since Mr. Karl affirmed Zion and did not view his sexuality (or LGBTQ+ identities in general) as something to be "othered," he had a profound influence on the way Zion felt about himself. Such care and attention to Zion's life suggest what actions like those of Mr. Karl can do to counter the effects of heteronormativity.

DISCUSSION

The experiences of Tae and Zion provide teachers and education research-ers insight on how two Black gay males have navigated and negotiated through racialized and heteronormative schooling contexts. Such a context contributed to educative experiences where the experiences of African, Af-rican American, and members of the Black diaspora were rarely taught or discussed beyond institutional enslavement in the United States, position-ing Blackness and the Black community via a deficit lens. As gay males, they were often ridiculed for their perceived sexuality or made conscious of their sexuality as being different or "other" by both their Black and White peers, and at times Tae and Zion employed "racial shelving," bracketing race in majority-Black environments to contend with sexual identity; there is possibly an element of ridicule because their classmates might have be-lieved a Black *man* cannot be gay or being Black *and* gay is wrong. The point here is one of tension: while their racial identity is always present, often they believed they were targeted for their sexual identity and to lesser extent for their racial identity.

Tae and Zion never disavowed their Blackness, but grappled with what it meant to Black. Being Black meant they had family members who discussed what it means to be Black in a White world and could speak openly with them or with their Black peers about being Black. Yet this was untrue for being gay and understanding their sexuality and may have contributed to the use of online communication to meet other gay people. For example, when an instructor of Tae's confronted him about his sexuality in a negative manner, he was taken aback. Tae believed his presentation of self-mirrored his sexual majority peers, yet the negative, homophobic ideology of gay-ness was what he interpretted from the instructor's confrontation. For Zion, the ridicule he endured from his peers laughing at his perceived sexuality demonstrates how deeply entrenched and internalized heteronormativity is, even among younger students.

Teachers should be aware of why students like Zion would be upset. His confrontation of his peer could be read as a fight. Yet his reaction was not a result of an isolated incident or because he was a bad student. The school environment allowed for Zion's taunting (similar to the taunting and bul-lying of other LGBTQ+ students) to occur with no repercussion. Critical race theory illuminates how structurally, the schools ignored the identities of the Black students (lack of representation in the curriculum and a lack of affirming these identities through school programs or functions). Qua-re theory similarly informs how schools and members of the school com-munity failed to consider non-heterosexual identities among the student body and, as with the identities of Black students, affirm these to promote a positive-self image. Tae and Zion took it upon themselves to find ways to navigate through their school settings (seeking what supports they could find within the school and supports outside of the school via the internet) to understand and define for themselves what it means to be Black *and* gay; their schools failed to aid in this process in any substantitve manner with the exception of a few isolated inividuals.

These cases demonstrate the significance and unique challenges experienced by those who possess multiple marginalized identities, and how school environments contribute towards their "othering." This surfaced in how Tae and Zion differed from their sexual majority peers, and were viewed by some as not performing these identities the way their peers believed Black males should. Students like Zion and Tae confront schooling situations where Blackness and being LGBTQ+ collide. The representative events discussed in this chapter highlight how these encounters and others were informed both by race and sexuality and how the intersection of these mitigated their academic and social experiences at school.

CONCLUSION

The findings of this study are productive for teachers in numerous ways. To begin, educators can promote an inclusive classroom context by making the Black gay community relevant and integral to curricula and classroom discussions. Thus, this should be extended to include LGBTQ+ people of color through lessons about LGBTQ+ communities of color and their histories. Students like Tae and Zion would have benefited had they engaged with novels by Black gay males and of the Black gay experience or been introduced to Black gay mathematicians and scientists. Ultimately, this kind of content and affirmative pedagogy is of benefit to all students and may serve to diminish the heteronormative and racists discourses and practices of schooling. Such a pedagogy can enable members of the school community to be aware of the Black gay community and other LGBTQ+ communities of color, their successes and the challenges they face. This kind of teaching may further not just awareness, but insight on the intersection of racism and homonegativity LGBTQ+ people of color encounter.

An implication of this work is that educators collaborate with community organizations working with LGBTQ+ groups, and more specifically, those who attend to the unique needs of LGBTQ+ people of color. Engagement with LGBTQ+ community activists may help educators better understand these communities and how to support not only Black gay youth, but potentially LGBTQ+ youth at large. Further, the involvement of such community members can facilitate their integration as part of the school community, demonstrating to students, particularly Black gay youth and other LGBTQ+

youth, being Black (or a member of any marginalized group) and gay are valued and supported by others in the community.

A limitation of this research was the sole inclusion of Black gay males and the focus on their educative experience. Future studies can include teachers of diverse LGBTQ+ youth to gain insight on how they attend to such students in their classrooms. Interviews with teachers like Tae's coach and Mr. Karl could advance scholarship on LBGTQ+ inclusive classroom contexts, possibly supporting an understanding on ways to dismantle racist and heteronormative school environments. Of significance is insight on how teachers, who largely teach in institutions characterized by racism and heteronormativity, pereservere and adopt such a social justice, equity-oriented disposition for LGBTQ+ students.

The present context continues to oppress LGBTQ+ youth of color and the hostile school environments they navigate (Mitchum & Moodie-Mills, 2014). If educators assume the responsibility to become aware of their students' experiences and the possibility of intersecting racial and sexual/gender identities, oppressive, normative beliefs of sexuality and race may begin to diminish. Doing this work is not an easy task, requiring educators to move beyond a normative way of understanding of how racism and heteronormativity function. Yet, if members of the school community are committed to equity and social justice for all, then it is imperative such work be adopted not by a few with a commitment to supporting LGBTQ+ youth of color (and more specifically, as expressed in this chapter, Black gay youth), but the teaching force at large.

REFERENCES

Asante, M. K. (1991). The Afrocentric idea in education. *The Journal of Negro Education, 60*(2), 170–180. doi:10.2307/2295608

Bartone, M. D. (2015). *Navigating and negotiating identity in the Black gay mecca: Educational and institutional influences that positively impact the life histories of Black hay male youth in Atlanta* (Doctoral dissertation). Georgia State University, Atlanta, GA.

Blumenfeld, W. J. (1997). Homophobia and anti-Semitism: Making the links. In J. T. Sears & W. L. Williams (Eds.), *Overcoming heterosexism and homophobia: Strategies that work* (pp. 131–140). New York, NY: Columbia University Press.

Boykin, K. (2012). Introduction. In K. Boykin (Ed.) *For colored boys who have ever considered suicide when the rainbow is still not enough* (pp. xi–xv). New York, NY: Magnus Books.

Dubé, E., & Savin-Williams, R. C. (1999). Sexual identity development among ethnic sexual-minority youths. *Developmental Psychology, 35*(6), 1389–1398. doi:10.1037/0012-1649.35.6.1389

Ferguson, A. A. (2001). *Bad boys: Public schools in the making of Black masculinity.* Ann Arbor: The University of Michigan Press.

Freire, P. (2000). *Pedagogy of the oppressed.* New York, NY: Continuum.

Gorski, P. C., Davis, S. N., & Reiter, A. (2013). An examination of the (in)visibility of sexual orientation, heterosexism, homophobia, and other LGBTQ concerns in U.S. multicultural teacher education coursework. *Journal of LGBT Youth, 10*(3), 224–248. doi:10.1080/19361653.2013.798986

Grady, J., Marquez, R., & McLaren, P. (2012). A critique of neoliberalism with fierceness: Queer youth of color creating dialogues of resistance. *Journal of Homosexuality, 59*(7), 982–1004. doi:10.1080/00918369.2012.699839

Howard, T. C. (2013). How does it feel to be a problem? Black male students, schools, and learning in enhancing the knowledge base to disrupt deficit frameworks. *Review of Research in Education, 37*(1), 54–86. doi:10.3102/0091732X12462985

Ingraham, C. (1994). The heterosexual imaginary: Feminist sociology and theories of gender. *Sociological Theory, 12*(2), 203–219. doi:10.10.2307/201865

Irvine, J. (2003). *Educating teachers for diversity: Seeing with a cultural eye.* New York, NY: Teacher's College Press.

It Gets Better Project. (n.d.). *What is the It Gets Better Project?* Retrieved from http://www.itgetsbetter.org/pages/about-it-gets-better-project/

Jamil, O. B., Harper, G. W., Fernandez, M. I., & Adolescent Trials Network for HIV/AIDS Prevention. (2009). Sexual and ethnic identity development among gay-bisexual-questioning (GBQ) male ethnic minority adolescents. *Cultural, Diversity, and Ethnic Minority Psychology 15*(3), 203–214. doi:10.1037/a0014795

Johnson, E. P. (2001). "Quare" studies, or (almost) everything I learned about queer studies I learned from my grandmother. *Text and Perfromance Quarterly, 21*(1), 1–25.

Johnson, E. P. (2005). "Quare" studies, or (almost) everything I know about queer studies I learned from my grandmother. In E. P. Johnson & M. G. Henderson (Eds.), *Black queer studies* (pp. 124–157). Durham, NC: Duke University Press. doi:10.1080/10462930128119

King, J. E. (1991). Dysconcious racism: Ideology, identity, and the miseducation of teachers. *Journal of Negro Education, 60*(2), 133–146. doi:10.2307/2295605

King, J. E. (2011). Who dat say (we) "too depraved to be saved"?: Re-membering Katrina/Haiti (and beyond): Critical studyin' for human freedom. *Harvard Educational Review, 81*(2), 343–371.

Kosciw, J. G., Greytak, E. A., Boesen, M. J., & Palmer, N. A. (2014). *The 2013 National School Climate Survey: The experiences of lesbian, gay, bisexual and transgender youth in our nation's schools.* Retrieved from: https://www.glsen.org/sites/default/files/2013%20National%20School%20Climate%20Survey%20Full%20Report_0.pdf

Kvale, S., & Brinkmann, S. (2009). *Interviews: Learning the craft of qualitative research interviewing* (2nd ed.). Los Angeles, CA: SAGE.

Ladson-Billings, G. (2006). From the achievement gap to the education debt: Understanding achievement in U.S. schools. *Educational Researcher, 35*(7), 3–12. https://doi.org/10.3102/0013189X035007003

Leonardo, Z. (2009). The color of supremacy: Beyond the discourse of "White privilege." In E. Taylor, D. Gillborn, & G. Ladson-Billings (Eds.), *Foundations of critical race theory in education* (pp. 261–276). New York, NY: Routledge.

McCready, L. (2010). *Making space for diverse masculinities: Difference, intersectionality, and engagement in an urban high school.* New York, NY: Peter Lang.

Mitchum, P., & Moodie-Mills, A. C. (2014). *Beyond bullying: How hostile school climate perpetuates the school-to-prison pipeline for LGBT youth.* Retrieved from https://www.americanprogress.org/wpcontent/uploads/2014/02/BeyondBullying.pdf

National Center for Educational Statistics. (n.d.). *Table 209.10: Number and percentage distribution of teachers in public and private elementary and secondary schools, by selected teacher characteristics: Selected years, 1987–88 through 2011–12* [Table]. Retrieved from http://nces.ed.gov/programs/digest/d13/tables/dt13_209.10.asp

Omi, M., & Winant, H. (1994). *Racial formation in the United States: From the 1960s to the 1990s* (2nd ed.). New York, NY: Routledge.

Polkinghorne, D. E. (1988). *Narrative knowing and the human sciences.* Albany: State University of New York Press.

Polkinghorne, D. E. (1995). Narrative configuration in qualitative analysis. In J. A. Hatch & R. Wisniewski (Eds.), *Life history and narrative* (pp. 5–23). London, England: RoutledgeFalmer.

Riessman, C. K. (2008). *Narrative methods for the human sciences.* Los Angeles, CA: SAGE.

Taylor, E. (2009). The foundations of critical race theory in education: An introduction. In E. Taylor, D. Gillborn, & G. Ladson-Billings (Eds.), *Foundations of critical race theory in education* (pp. 1–13). New York, NY: Routledge.

Woodson, C. G. (2000). *The mis-education of the negro.* Sauk Village, IL.: African American Images.

CHAPTER 7

BEYOND THE BINARY IN ELEMENTARY SCHOOL

Lynn Bravewomon

ABSTRACT

This chapter discusses queered professional development (PD) for elementary school teachers. Engaging in the professional development resulted in increasing teachers' capacity to use LGBTQ inclusive instruction, to begin and continue to develop the practice of de-centering heteronormativity, and to normalize the presence of LGBTQ people through curriculum and instruction. Drawing on results from a student perception bullying survey, which highlighted pervasive experiences of homophobic and gender-biased bullying in schools, this study describes the creation and implementation of professional learning to increase staff and student knowledge about non-binary pluralities of Sexual Orientation and Gender Identification/Expression (SOGIE). The PD was informed by elements of culturally sustaining pedagogies and queer theory for explanations of heteronormativity, heterosexism and the limitation of binary identity categories. Such learning enabled professional contexts for integrating LGBTQ-inclusive practices in teachers' pedagogies. Ultimately, each school discussed in this study initiated and sustained school wide implementation of queered curriculum and instruction that continues to evolve to present day.

Exploring Gender and LGBTQ Issues in K–12 and Teacher Education, pages 111–126
Copyright © 2019 by Information Age Publishing

Researchers are beginning to shift away from a solitary concern with ensuring the safety of Lesbian, Gay, Bisexual, Transgender, Queer, and Questioning (LGBTQ) students and move toward focusing on school practices that counter discourses perpetuating hate-based behavior. One means of promoting this focus is the implementation of specific pedagogies and curricula that de-center (i.e., expand the understanding of sexuality beyond) heteronormativity and normalize the presence and contributions of LGBTQ people in school environments (Kissen, 2002; Rodriguez & Pinar, 2007), particularly at the elementary school level. In fact, the need for such pedagogies and curricula has been recently highlighted by the American Educational Research Association (AERA), who argued that scholars must attend to the needs of LGBTQ students and families in their work (Wimberly, 2015).

In this self-study, I reflect on a professional development (PD) sequence with elementary teachers in the Western United States. The PD sequence, which employed a student survey of perceived bullying as a PD tool, aimed to promote teachers' use of LGBTQ curriculum and instruction in their classrooms. The purpose of this qualitative self-study was to analyze my professional practice as the facilitator of a professional development sequence focused on LGBTQ inclusiveness with elementary teachers. Ultimately, I found a connection between the guided teacher discussion in the PD about the survey results and their subsequent use of instructional materials with positive images, language and themes representative of the LGBTQ community.

In the sections that follow, I begin with an overview of the literature regarding the need for teachers to disrupt heteronormativity in their practices and the general lack of knowledge most teachers possess on these issues. I then explain the key conceptual frameworks that informed this work. I continue with a discussion about the process of the professional development and its outcomes, specifically regarding increasing the use of LGBTQ inclusive curriculum. Finally, I discuss challenges that arose and detail how these were addressed.

TROUBLING HETERONORMATIVE LOGIC
WITH NEW PARADIGMS FOR LGBTQ YOUTH

Most teachers with whom I have worked have reported that they lack the opportunity to receive professional opportunities to learn about the evaluative nature (Caraballo, 2016) of LGBTQ and cisgender normative language and practices, and thus perpetuated them. For example, common phrases they described using in school included "lining up in a boys and girls line." They heard student refrains of "boy colors" and "girl colors," "boy games and toys," and "girl games and toys." All of these reflect society's general lack of knowledge about how paradigms such as heteronormativity, or the privileging of heterosexuality as normal, reinforce binaries about social relationships, including pervasive gender binaries (Zacko-Smith & Smith, 2010).

Likewise, most of the teachers I have worked with have not had the opportunity to learn the value of using an inclusive pedagogy to support the reality of a world that is free from fixed and static notions of identity (Caraballo, 2016). Further, most heterosexual/cisgender elementary school teachers with whom I have spoken have little-to-no connection with the LGBTQ community, and so they struggle to understand the critical impact their daily language, routines and practices have on both LGBT people as well as (the "Q"), gender queer/gender fluid, gender fabulous youth, and their cisgender peers. In my work with teachers, I have witnessed that heteronormative paradigms are so deeply instilled and reproduced at schools that, before they can change their practices, teachers must first learn to see beyond their comfort zones. For teachers who are integrating mental schema on sexuality necessary to create LGBTQ-inclusive practices, repeated and scaffolded opportunities to internalize what healthy gender exploration looks like for all students, and how to support cisgender students as gender-fluid accepting peers, are necessary.

Since 2001, as coordinator of my school district's Safe and Inclusive Schools Program (SISP), I have developed and facilitated PD sessions to promote LGBTQ inclusiveness in our schools. To develop the sessions, I drew from GLSEN National Climate Survey recommendations regarding the need for instruction with positive LGBTQ-inclusive content (Kosciw & Diaz, 2006; Kosciw, Diaz, & Greytak, 2008). Because the original survey primarily focused on the high school level, I modified it for elementary and middle school teachers. In addition, I developed a survey to gauge elementary students' perceptions on bullying, particularly LGBTQ related bullying, which I would also use as a PD tool to facilitate elementary teachers' use of LGBTQ-inclusive instruction. I used this survey at Lilac Elementary and Cedar Elementary (pseudonyms) during the 2010–2011 school year. My aim was to use the PD to introduce a fluid understanding of LGBTQ identities as a way to illuminate the heteronormative logic that reinforces fixed gender binaries and sexual orientation categories not just in normative discourse, but also in the materials and curricula that are used with students. In addition to discussing these topics and the results of the survey with the teachers during the PD, I also shared the survey results with students in collaboratively presented or modeled lessons that demonstrated the ability of students to engage in thoughtful reflection about identity and being allies to one another across the differences they perceive in one another.

CONCEPTUAL FRAMES

The two conceptual frameworks that undergird this study are queer theory and culturally sustaining pedagogy. By employing these as guiding frames, I identified means to shift instructional practices away from neutrality and/or deficit perspectives of heterosexism and heteronormativity, and instead move toward engaging in an explicit countering of these as forces of oppression.

Although not specifically a pedagogical approach, elements of queer theory (DePalma & Atkinson, 2009; Robinson & Ferfolja, 2008; Sumara & Davis, 1999; Sykes, 2011; Zacko-Smith & Smith, 2010) offer important insights for teachers regarding the relevance of deconstructing binary paradigms in educational settings. Queer theory delineates a knowledge base about Sexual Orientation and Gender Identity/Expression (SOGIE) related to the limitations of heterosexism and heteronormativity. Heterosexism, the belief that heterosexuals are superior to any other sexual identity (Robinson & Ferfolja, 2008), produces and sustains homophobia (beliefs and acts of hatred of a sexuality other than heterosexuality) with external and internal expressions. Externally, homophobia is expressed through hate-based behavior, but it is also internalized by LGBTQ people who express and exemplify it as self-devaluation and negative self-beliefs (Sumara & Davis, 1999; Watson, 2005).

Another key concept from queer theory includes heteronormativity, a social construct that describes the complex ways heterosexual culture is the norm against which all other identities are measured, and, if they do not measure up, "others" and diminishes other identities of SOGIE (Robinson & Ferfolja, 2008). Through the multiple daily ways beliefs and attitudes about heterosexuality are performed in social interactions and practice, heterosexuality is reinforced as normal and reifies binary concepts of SOGIE. Through these heteronormative paradigms of SOGIE, non-heterosexual people are pathologized and devalued, and people who are (or are perceived as) Lesbian, Gay, Bisexual, Transgender and Queer are positioned as invisible, deviant, taboo, unacceptable, and abnormal (DePalma & Atkinson, 2009; Robinson & Ferfolja, 2007; Sumara & Davis, 1999; Watson, 2005; Zacko-Smith & Smith, 2010).

Culturally sustaining pedagogy (Paris, 2012; Paris & Alim, 2017) focuses on teacher practices supporting students of color in the embodiment of their cultural expression in school. As a key piece of this pedagogy, teachers must engage in ongoing self-education about youth culture, avoid replicating oppressive culture practices (such as reproduction of homophobic behavior), and help students develop affirming practices (Paris, 2012). Caraballo (2016) describes the "figured world" of schooling as the daily conscious and unconscious routines and language that transmit values of dominant social paradigms such as racism, and particular to this study, heterosexism and heteronormativity. Within this figured world, teachers are key agents in students' experiences of their culture and identities and affect how these are valued in school settings (Caraballo, 2016). Although culturally sustaining pedagogy was originally created to address the needs of students of color, I argue that the elements noted above can also help teachers attend to the needs of students related to sexuality and gender identity/expression.

Collectively, these ideas from queer theory and culturally sustaining pedagogy informed my understanding of the powerful impact that using LGBTQ-inclusive instructional practices can have on the daily experience of students and on elementary teachers learning. LGBTQ-inclusive instruction, as I define it here, challenges and interrupts discourses of societal binaries to end the exclusion of LGBTQ people and of other marginalized and vulnerable groups of people through a human rights lens (Sykes, 2011). I argue that such a pedagogy, informed by queer theory and culturally sustaining pedagogy, can augment the dismantling of binary categories, expanding ways for teacher to validate students' identity and family culture at school. An LGBTQ-inclusive pedagogy can create space for students to enact a broader interpretation of self as they "practice" fluid and developing identities, rather than being forced into fixed identity categories (Caraballo, 2016).

METHODS

This study utilizes critical self-study (Laboskey, 2004) to identify themes and productive pedagogical strategies that emerged from the PD to promote awareness of LGBTQ inclusiveness and the use of LGBTQ-inclusive instructional materials. As such, this study draws from core values of equity and social justice with the aim of improving one's professional practice and professional outcomes, not just for myself, but also for the teacher PD participants (Laboskey, 2004). In this work, I sought to investigate how teachers responded to the PD sessions and in turn, improve my own pedagogical practice as the session facilitator. A key aim was to shed light on how the PD contributed to the teachers' meaning making of LGBTQ issues and how the PD sessions impacted teachers' learning and practices.

Context and Professional Development Sessions

Cedar and Lilac Elementary Schools are located on the west coast of the United States in a metropolitan area of a major city. Cedar Elementary serves approximately 775 students per year, while Lilac Elementary serves approximately 500 students. The two schools have the same student demographics: approximately 50–60% Hispanic, 10% African American/Black, and 10% White. Likewise, approximately 60% of families of both schools participate in the National School Lunch Program.

I administered the voluntary and anonymous quantitative student perception survey to 364 students from 2nd to 6th grade at the two schools. Lilac Elementary surveyed 2–6th grade and Cedar Elementary surveyed 4–6th grade. The survey was completed during 20 minutes of class time, during which students who chose to complete the survey circled or checked the type of language they heard at school that they perceived as bullying/hurtful language. With the help of teacher volunteers, I collected the forms and hand-tallied the student data, engaging in informal discussion and observation of the results as we tallied the responses. I then compiled the data. As a self-study, the analysis of this work is my own meaning-making of my experience with the PD sessions and use of the survey.

I facilitated two strands of professional development with staff from each of the two school sites. The first strand involved ongoing annual PD for teacher leadership teams. The session topics for this strand included learning and practicing grade-level appropriate language about LGBTQ people to use with students, as well as reviewing and practicing reading aloud from storybooks with positive images of LGBTQ people. The sessions also included identifying anticipated questions site staff might have about LGBTQ-inclusive instruction. We discussed responses to these potential questions and PD participants practiced them through roleplay simulations.

The second strand consisted of two 45-minute PD sessions at Cedar Elementary and Lilac Elementary, taking place during staff meetings. In the first session, we reviewed the responsibility for all staff to interrupt homophobic and gender-biased bullying as indicated by our district's board resolutions and enumerated anti-harassment policies, as well as state legislation about creating safe learning environments for LGBTQ students. Additionally, teaching staff reviewed storybooks with positive LGBTQ images, language and themes, and practiced reading them aloud. The second session occurred after the student survey was conducted, and I provided the results to participants and discussed them. The leader teachers, the principal and I collaboratively explained individual site plans for ways to conduct student instruction with the survey results. Each site then conducted a variety of activities in which teaching staff could observe me and/or the site administrator present instruction using the survey results with students. Teacher leaders also helped teachers use these resources and activities in their classrooms.

Data Sources and Analysis

Data sources included teacher feedback evaluations I collected at the close of each elementary LGBTQ-inclusive PD session I facilitated, journals that document my experiences with the PD session, and my reflections about the process and outcomes of this work. These data sources enabled me to reflect upon and consider my engagement, as facilitator, with the teachers; reflections and observations of how teachers responded to the sessions; and my own meaning-making of the feedback evaluations provided by the teachers. The journal, which I maintained throughout the course of the PD session sequence and through the data analysis for this study, served as a primary data source.

To analyze the data, I completed a two-step process to unpack the impact of the student survey results relevant to the PD sessions, my work with the teachers, and my subsequent experiences working with the teachers in their classrooms to implement teaching practices or approaches that emerged from the PD. First, I conducted initial and thematic coding (Saldana, 2015) of my journal entries in conjunction with the feedback and other data sources to critically investigate how LGBTQ-inclusive instruction and teaching strategies for such inclusion were being constructed. Second, I revisited these codes through secondary reading of all the data sources and considered how the emergent themes surfaced across the data. As I continued to write in my researcher journal, these subsequent entries supported my understanding of the evaluative context of schooling and possibilities for the countering heteronormative practices to guide future PD not just for the schools in this study, but for others who may seek to take up similar work.

FINDINGS

In this section, I present the salient themes that emerged from the analysis of the PD sequence. I begin by discussing the analysis of my work with the teachers who linked the need for LGBTQ-inclusive instruction having discussed the results of the student survey about the prevalence of harmful anti-gay language at school. Second, I discuss how my facilitating the PD enabled the teachers to engage with an exploration of how homophobia is sustained in schools (in part) through the absence of positive images, languages and themes in teaching and learning. Third, I discuss my work on providing opportunities for teachers to practice using appropriate LGBTQ related language in their classrooms as a result of the PD.

Discussing the Survey: Anti-Gay Language and the Need for LGBTQ-Inclusive Instruction

The student bullying perception survey was a platform for direct discussion with teachers about the need for LGBTQ-inclusive instruction. Conversations about the survey, or "data talks," were integrated into ongoing forms of professional development opportunities specific to each site. The survey also provided a way to offer multiple exposures to concepts, language, and instructional strategies to prepare teachers to use LGBTQ-inclusive language across settings at school.

The survey results communicated the percentage of student respondents who had experienced or witnessed different types of bullying language at their schools. The four top categories across schools were negative language regarding anti-gay language, race, perceived intelligence, and body size. Students at both schools identified that they heard anti-gay bullying language the most. As shown in Table 7.1, the percentages from highest to lowest for Lilac Elementary was anti-gay language (83%), body size (72%), race (68%) and perceived intelligence (62%). For Cedar Elementary, the order was anti-gay language (84.5%), body size (72.9%), perceived intelligence (71.8) and race (65.7%).

The school specific information was received as a wake-up call to staff. At a basic level, the data refuted the argument that "anti-gay language doesn't happen in our school." For most teachers, it was the first time that student data painted a clear picture of the anti-gay bullying occurring at their sites. A silence was broken as teachers interpreted the results of the survey. They saw evidence that students described anti-gay language, provided the examples of it, and understood that it was harmful to others. They drew connections that applied to all students, LGBTQ and non-LGBTQ alike. For example, teachers saw and described how students perform binary gender identities through "acceptable" recess choices in elementary classes, and recognized that young students also use words such as "gay" in a derogatory way. These data talks provided teachers with the opportunity to

TABLE 7.1 Results of 2010 Elementary Student Bullying Perception Survey		
Identity Category Targeted by Bullying	Lilac Elementary *N* = 183	Cedar Elementary *N* = 181
Anti-gay	83%	84.5%
Body Size	72%	72.9%
Race	68%	65.7%
Perceived Intelligence	62%	71.8%

have peer-to-peer conversations and to begin to experience both adult and student-appropriate language they could use in instruction with students.

Discussions about the results of the student survey with the teachers during the professional development served as a platform for connecting the concepts of heterosexism and homophobia, as well as de-centering heteronormativity (DePalma & Atkinson, 2009; Sumara & Davis, 1999), in connection to the anti-gay and gender-biased language and behavior that surfaced in the survey results. Building upon my introduction of teachers' professional responsibility to respond to homo-trans-phobic and gender biased bullying, I emphasized the importance of proactively disrupting the "figured world" (Caraballo, 2016, p. 8) of heterosexism and heteronormativity, and instead, creating a classroom culture in which students can enact their "identities in practice" (p. 5) and "selves in practice" (p. 8) by being able to express LGBTQ identities and other aspects of themselves as they desired (Caraballo, 2016).

During the data talks, many teachers were uncomfortable using the words lesbian, gay, bisexual, transgender, queer, and questioning. A majority had only a rudimentary understanding of "LGBTQ," of how sexuality and gender are connected and different from one another, and of how uninterrupted heteronormativity becomes the default norm against which other lived forms of SOGIE are subjugated. During both the data talks and evaluations of the PD session, many teachers reiterated the need for more opportunities to learn about how to talk about LGBTQ focused bullying behavior before leading students in discussion about gender and sexual orientation arising from LGBTQ-inclusive instruction.

Professional Development Facilitation Strategies

As mentioned earlier, I used a process we called "data talks" during the staff meeting PD sessions at each elementary school. The data talks process, which follows a protocol I describe next, had multiple purposes for teachers and students alike. For teachers, the data talk protocol began with honoring the importance of direct evidence from students about bullying, which centered student authority about conditions they experience in schools. Next, we established norms for self-managing (both adult and student) reactions to openly discussing LGBTQ identities. Additionally, I discussed countering heteronormativity as a bullying intervention and prevention strategy in the context of the interconnectedness of abuse of power in all forms of bullying, as well as empowerment from using healthy forms of self-enacted power. This design provided a common language and common process for teacher analysis of data, coupled with developing next steps in terms of their goals for developing ally behavior throughout their schools.

To help teachers shape and construct their responses to the survey data, we used strategies such as pair-share and guided group discussion. For each survey category of bullying language/behavior, I prompted participants to brainstorm images students might see in media, popular culture and curriculum material that could be intentionally or unintentionally reinforcing that language or behavior. I also asked participants to "embody" the data by using their bodies to illustrate percentages. For example, 90% was represented by 9 people lining up with cards from 10–90%, and one person standing apart from them. The bodily representation added a visual impact to the number of student "bodies" affected by homophobic and gender-based bullying. From these activities, I facilitated further discussion about stereotyping, heterosexism, and homophobia through inquiry processing. Specifically, I asked questions that led teachers to draw connections about how curriculum might reinforce the "othering" of students by their peers (see Figure 7.1).

From this professional development, I concluded that the strength of data talks is that the *data talks*. Not only does it communicate a powerful message about the language and behavior to which elementary students were exposed on a daily basis, but it also centered the discussion on students' lived experience in each school, rather than focusing on staff-generated supposition and beliefs.

What are examples of the sources from which students learn to target others by ___ (for example, race)?

Where might students learn how society positions people by these different categories in the survey? Whose images do they see? Who do they not see? Who are treated well and believed? Who are not?

What are some stereotypes of this category? Stereotype beliefs? behaviors?

What might be ways curriculum and routines in school reinforce stereotypes?

What patterns and trends do you draw from reviewing answers to these questions about each different category in the survey?

What social emotional dispositions could counter the need to use bullying across these categories?

What information do you as teachers need to model positive behavior, language about ___ (for example LGBTQ people, SOGIE)

Figure 7.1 Data talk question prompts.

From PD to the Classroom: Using LGBTQ-Inclusive Language

When asked, teachers who observed or co-led the survey process with students shared comments such as, "the students were excited to complete the survey," "there were a few giggles when 'anti-gay language' was explained, but students did not act out," and "they took it seriously and really wanted to see the results." The following examples demonstrate two successful and different ways the survey was a springboard for positive momentum at each school. At both schools, the student bullying survey data helped teachers recognize not only the need for intervention when anti-gay bullying language was used, but also raised awareness of the implicit heteronormativity in their lessons. In future professional development, we reviewed the data and connected it to ways in which their current instruction inadvertently reinforced stereotypes about gender and sexual orientation.

Using Survey Results to Increase LGBTQ-Inclusive Instruction

The initial professional development using the survey data talks at each site laid the groundwork for continued reflective discussion about heterosexism and heteronormativity, as well as encouraged site administrators and teacher leaders' efforts to increase the use of LGBTQ-inclusive instruction with teachers at their sites. The following section describes the impact of using a survey highlighting student voice to call out the need to address homophobic and gender-biased language in elementary schools.

One Survey, Multiple Contexts for Professional Learning and Instruction

At each school, the introduction of the student survey resulted in multiple opportunities for staff to practice the use of concepts and elementary-level academic language with LGBTQ-inclusive instruction. Each activity provided learning opportunities for teachers to reflect about how LGBTQ-inclusive instruction can counter heterosexism and heteronormative practices that sustain LGBTQ bullying and marginalization. Each school used this conceptual content in discussions about lesson planning with different LGBTQ-inclusive books. Additionally, each site integrated a variety of ways teachers could observe LGBTQ-inclusive instruction with students. Lilac Elementary followed the student survey data talk process with classroom based "student workshops" and K–2 and 4–6 "Ally Assemblies." The student workshops blended the survey data talk with an instructional read-aloud using one of 10 LGBGTQ-inclusive storybooks provided by the district to all elementary schools. The principal of Lilac and I also co-led the assemblies in which students discussed appropriate "ally language" to use when they talked about LGBTQ people and gender identity/expression. Parallel to these activities, students and teachers worked together to practice a common language to use to intervene when homophobic/gender biased bullying language was heard.

At Cedar Elementary, I worked with their Equity Team (ET), a site based committee of teachers, to collaboratively design and facilitate short staff meeting modules on practicing language skills for LGBTQ-inclusive instruction. The ET continued to use survey data and LGBTQ-inclusive storybooks with critical literacy questioning skills to expand the notion of a "normal" family with staff and students. These critical literacy questions asked students to identify whose voice was present and/or missing in a variety of stories with and without LGBTQ themes, people and/or characters. The ET also increased teacher and student participation in instructional discussions about LGBTQ people and breaking gender stereotypes by conducting an ally march, where classes travelled to different stations displaying illustrations from books containing positive images of diverse families and gender expressions. At each station, students and teachers discussed how people expressed their varied identities and shared examples of ways students understood the experience of oppression because of these perceived and real differences.

Collaborative Leadership and LGBTQ-Inclusive Instruction

At both schools, the principals, teacher leaders, and I worked together to support teachers as they became ready to use LGBTQ-inclusive materials. Each site carried forward the collaborative approach we used in class workshops, staff modules, and school-wide activities such as assemblies, holding ally weeks, and school marches. At both schools, as a first step, teachers were invited to co-teach lessons with a grade level peer as a way to build their confidence with the activities and materials. In these initial lessons, teachers used the survey data and read an LGBTQ-inclusive story. As a closure activity, students generated posters and artwork that contributed to the school community's education and role as allies to LGBTQ people.

One common role each principal played was providing support and leadership for the activities that arose based from use of the survey. Each school's principal and teacher leadership team demonstrated a commitment to support increased use of survey data, associated concepts, and LGBTQ-inclusive instruction. In Lilac Elementary, for example, the principal was the first to teach LGBTQ-inclusive lessons, with teachers observing.

At Cedar Elementary, the principal provided leadership by prioritizing the LGBTQ community's presence throughout the school and creating empowering spaces for students to express their authentic selves. For instance, the administrator introduced the importance of staff meeting modules that the ET and I led on LGBTQ-inclusive language. These were implemented prior to expanded ally week activities that Cedar Elementary's ET created. For example, during the Cedar Elementary ally march, each class travelled to numerous stations throughout the school with images from books and themes such as lesbian moms, gay dads, adoptive families, interracial families, and gay pride flags. In this way, teachers and students discussed how to be allies related to the diversity in the school's community. One ET member also worked with 6th grade students in an ally club designed to read LGBTQ-inclusive books to younger students.

At Lilac Elementary, students clamored to engage in school-based activism. The principal and I led a student ally club in which students prepared activities to teach their peers about the family diversity, including LGBTQ people. They used the survey data for educational posters, ally week pledge card activities and a self-illustrated book affirming all families. Over time, teachers assumed the leadership of the club.

DISCUSSION

The hostile conditions in our nation's schools caused by unchecked homophobic and gender biased behavior, which are prolifically described in scholarly research (Kosciw & Diaz, 2006; Kosciw, Diaz, & Greytak, 2008), are sustained, in part, due to the absence of LGBTQ-inclusive instruction and intervention on the part of teachers in our schools. In my district, the range of teachers' responses to integrating LGBTQ-inclusive instruction into their pedagogy reflects a similar pattern to what researchers such have described (Robinson & Ferfolja, 2008; Zacko-Smith & Smith, 2010). Many teachers are willing to change their instruction, but they report being underprepared to do so, especially in terms of talking effectively with their elementary students about LGBTQ people, sexual orientation, and an expansive perspective of gender identity/expression. Many teachers have requested professional development support to understand, review and practice positive LGBTQ themed instruction.

Using the results of the student bullying survey as a reflective tool with elementary teachers regarding their students' daily experience in their school was a successful strategy to center teachers in students' experiences and introduce important LGBTQ concepts. As a result of the data talks, the teachers began to recognize that students were being exposed to and taunted with homophobic and gender biased bullying language. The teachers collectively reflected that they failed to accept this social reality prior to the survey, and expressed a need for strategies to respond to anti-gay bullying language with LGBTQ-inclusive instruction. In this way, the professional development sessions used the survey data as a bridge to provide information about social forces that sustains heteronormative practices and homophobic behavior. For example, the bullying survey data was used to facilitate discussions with teachers about the power of heterosexism and heteronormative discourses. Teachers drew connections between these social forces and their impact on maintaining the status quo and a practice of avoiding the use of LGBTQ-inclusive curriculum and instruction. Teachers also negotiated their personal reactions to discussing SOGIE, including their areas of open-mindedness and, likewise, areas of resistance. Many grappled with how their professional responsibilities aligned with personal values and sensibilities towards LGBTQ inclusion.

The professional development work supported teachers' focused and intentional practice of instruction with the surveys in their own classrooms. In a variety of ways developed by each school, teachers had frequent opportunities to observe and practice using the results from the bullying survey, appropriate LGBTQ language, and implement instructional strategies that countered of heteronormative practices. Further, teacher leaders, administrators and I supported lesson planning, instructional modeling and co-teaching to increase teacher confidence and efficacy to lead students with survey data talks and instructional read-alouds with positive images and themes about LGBTQ people. Each of these experiences strengthened the schools' use of LGBTQ-inclusive instruction with K–6th grade students.

This model of professional development addressed many needs regarding the growth of teachers' pedagogical thinking, decision-making, and ultimately, the use of LGBTQ-inclusive instruction at the elementary school level. In particular, this study shows that the same content and professional development strategies can be adapted to the needs and current practices at different schools, and adapted to the responses of both teachers and students.

CONCLUSION

This study illustrated a variety of successful professional development processes and content resulting in the use of LGBTQ-inclusive curriculum and instruction in elementary schools. Using the results of a student perception survey of bullying language at two schools as a tool, the professional development provided teachers with grounding in the knowledge and language skills to understand heterosexism and heteronormativity as social forces that sustain LGBTQ marginalization in schools. The survey offered a platform for discussions informing teachers' understanding of the need for positive images, language and themes about LGBTQ people.

This study points to the need for ongoing professional development to undergird strategies to counter paradigms of heterosexism and rigid concepts of the gender binary. Further, the findings contribute to the research base that incorporating LGBTQ-inclusive instruction can be a productive approach to dealing with LGBTQ-focused bullying. When elementary school teachers are supported with the appropriate professional learning opportunities, they can integrate empowering pedagogies that respect the range of ways students understand, respond to, and ultimately enact their SOGIE, as well as honor students who live in queer/non-heteronormative family configurations.

As the professional development facilitator, my research continues to inform the content and strategies that move teachers toward understandings of the ways dominant social paradigms reinforce both intentional and unintentional teacher instructional practices, and recognition of resultant staff and student social behavior that marginalizes and devalues students and their families based upon their SOGIE. As more and more teachers are supported throughout their careers through professional development grounding them with the skills and agency to engage in LGBTQ-inclusive instruction, the daily experience of students in school will become more LGBTQ affirmative. Their stories will not be of struggle, fear, and isolation. Instead, their stories will reflect not only empowerment of their self-expression, parity of acceptance, and solidarity across the spectrum of sexual orientation and gender expression, but also parity of achievement and success throughout their education.

REFERENCES

Caraballo, L. (2016). Students' critical meta-awareness in a figured world of achievement: Toward a culturally sustaining stance in curriculum, pedagogy and research. *Urban Education, 52*(5), 585–609. doi:10.1177/0042085915623344

Depalma, R., & Atkinson, E. (2009). "No Outsiders": Moving beyond a discourse of tolerance to challenge heteronormativity in primary schools. *British Educational Research Journal, 35*(6), 837–855. doi:10.1080/01411920802688705

Kosciw, J., & Diaz, E. (2006). *National school climate survey: The experience of lesbian, gay, and transgender youth in our nation's school.* New York, NY: GLSEN. Retrieved from https://www.glsen.org/learn/research/nscs-archive

Kosciw, J., Diaz, E., & Greytak, E. (2008). *National school climate survey: The experiences of lesbian, gay, and transgender youth in our nation's schools.* New York, NY: GLSEN. Retrieved from https://www.glsen.org/learn/research/nscs-archive

Kissen, R. M. (2002). *Getting ready for Benjamin: Preparing teachers for sexual diversity in the classroom.* Lanham, MD: Rowan and Littlefield.

LaBoskey, V. K. (2004). The methodology of self-study and its theoretical under-pinnings. In J. J. Loughran, M. L. Hamilton, V. K. LaBoskey, & T. Russell (Eds.), *International handbook of self-study of teaching and teacher education practices* (pp. 817–869). Dordrecht, Netherlands: Springer.

Paris, D. (2012). Culturally sustaining pedagogy. *Educational Researcher, 41*(3), 93–97. doi:10.3102/0013189x12441244

Paris, D., & Alim, H. S. (Eds.). (2017). *Culturally sustaining pedagogies: Teaching and learning for justice in a changing world.* New York, NY: Teachers College Press.

Robinson, K. H., & Ferfolja, T. (2008). Playing it up, playing it down, playing it safe: Queering teacher education. *Teaching and Teacher Education, 24*(4), 846–858. doi:10.1016/j.tate.2007.11.004

Rodriguez, N. M., & Pinar, W. F. (2007). *Queering straight teachers: Discourse and identity in education.* New York, NY: Peter Lang.

Saldana, J. (2015). *The coding manual for qualitative research.* Los Angeles, CA: SAGE.

Sumara, D., & Davis, B. (1999). Interrupting heteronormativity: Toward a queer curriculum theory. *Curriculum Inquiry, 29*(2), 191–208. doi:10.1111/0362-6784.00121

Sykes, H. (2011). Hetero- and homo-normativity: Critical literacy, citizenship education and queer theory. *Curriculum Inquiry, 41*(4), 419–432. doi:10.1111/j.1467-873x.2011.00561.x

Watson, K. (2005). Queer theory. *Group Analysis, 38*(1), 67–81. doi:10.1177/0533316405049369

Wimberly, G. L. (2015). *LGBTQ issues in education advancing a research agenda.* Washington, DC: American Educational Research Association.

Zacko-Smith, J. D., & Smith, G. (2010). Recognizing and utilizing queer pedagogy. *Multicultural Perspectives, 8*(2), 2–9.

SECTION III

EXPLORING LGBTQ ISSUES IN TEACHER EDUCATION

CHAPTER 8

FORGING ALLIANCES, BECOMING-ALLY

In Pursuit of Pedagogical Virtualities

Kathryn Strom

ABSTRACT

In this critically reflective essay I draw on critical posthuman concepts as I narrate an experience teaching a class on identity and social justice in a summer leadership program. After locating myself historically and politically, and introducing posthumanism, I then share about my learning-with the students: in coming into composition with them and their experiences, I realized that they were interested in learning about LGBTQ issues, which I had not included in my syllabus. This encounter forced me to confront my own heteronormative gaze and the way it informed my syllabus and my expectations of the students. I modified the course and, in forging an alliance with them around issues that were central to who they were becoming, produced new modes of subjectivity—a becoming-ally. This experience also opened up new understandings of "a pedagogy of virtualities," a pedagogy that allows for the actualization of students' and teachers' potentialities through joint activity.

Exploring Gender and LGBTQ Issues in K–12 and Teacher Education, pages 129–146
Copyright © 2019 by Information Age Publishing
129

In this reflective essay, I discuss a critical incident on my journey to understanding social justice as a multi-faceted and intersectional issue that includes issues of gender diversity and LGBTQ identities. Drawing on concepts from posthuman thinkers (Braidotti, 2013; Deleuze & Guattari, 1987), I narrate an experience teaching a class on social justice in a summer leadership program for young women in high school that served as a learning and subjectivity-making catalyst. I discuss my meaning-making of this experience through a posthuman lens, the processes through which I identified as an LGBTQ ally, and implications for other educators and teacher educators. In the sections that follow, I first locate myself historically and politically, then offer an overview of the conceptual framework for posthumanism. I then provide a reflective narration of learning with a group of students regarding LGBTQ issues and discuss our sympoiesis, or "making-with" (Haraway, 2016), a co-development that produced new modes of subjectivity for both the students and me as well as opened up new understandings of teaching and curriculum—what I call a pedagogy of virtualities.

LOCATING MYSELF

As a White, cisgender, straight, able-bodied, native-English speaking faculty member with a PhD, my knapsack is full to brimming with unearned privilege (McIntosh, 1988). My work and commitments to working toward an intersectionally-just educational system requires that I engage daily with this privilege—and use it to strategically dismantle structures that perpetuate the multiple and multi-layered forms of oppression that students face. As scholars such as Freire (1970) have noted, the work of developing a critical consciousness always in process—especially for those of us who benefit from the status quo and the unearned privileges described above. For example, the recently coined term "woke" is never actually an achievable state—perhaps one can be more or less "woke," but it is really an ongoing process of *becoming-woke* that is never finished. Because we exist in a world that conditions us, with cues both subtle and in-your-face, to uphold White supremacist heteropatriarchy, we are constantly learning and unlearning, always resisting while creating alternatives.

For me, I acknowledge both my constantly-under-construction state as well as the non-linear and nomadic path that I've traveled as I continue to develop critical consciousness. Interestingly, I became conscious of certain oppressions before others—specifically, I first recognized issues of race and class, and later language and ethnicity, but these developed prior to an awareness about inequalities connected to gender, gender expression, sexuality, and LGBTQ identities. This was likely due to my childhood experiences and those from the early days of my career in education. My upbringing in Montgomery, Alabama highlighted the entanglement of issues of race and poverty, as well as the disconnect between public narratives of the Civil Rights movement as having "solved" racial issues and the deeply entrenched, culturally-sanctioned racism I witnessed as a matter of daily life. Later, as a teacher working mainly with immigrant students near the U.S.-Mexico border in California, I also came to understand that issues of ethnicity and language were bound up with poverty and differential access to power. It was with these frames that I commenced my doctoral studies in teacher education, where I focused on preparing teachers to be linguistically and culturally responsive, and using complex, non-linear perspectives to investigate the ways that teachers "translated" their understandings into classroom practice (Strom & Martin, 2017).

As a doctoral student, I embraced critical theoretical perspectives, which helped to explain, for instance, why racism is such an enduring part of the fabric of U.S. life (Ladson-Billings & Tate, 1995), and offered insight into how schools contain structures, like tracking, that maintain and expand racial and income inequality (Oakes, 2005). Over time, I recognized that, while helpful for understanding fundamental issues of social justice in schools, these theories did not really help explain the persistence of "banking" (Freire, 1970), or transmission-based pedagogy, despite a large body of scholarship arguing for more culturally and linguistically responsive and sustaining teaching practices (e.g., Ladson-Billings, 1994; Lucas, Villegas, & Freedson-Gonzalez, 2008; Paris & Alim, 2017; Villegas & Lucas, 2002). These theories also failed to address the reductionist, binary thinking that perpetuates ideologies, such as Whiteness and heteronormativity, which are harmful to all members of society. To address this dilemma in my research, I turned to complex socio-materialist theories, like critical posthumanism (Braidotti, 2013), which I explain next.

CRITICAL POSTHUMANISM

Dominant understandings in teaching are informed by rational humanist logic, which has specific rules: there is one universal reality that is stable, is governed by discoverable and unchanging laws, and is able to be reduced to simple essences and one-to-one correspondences. From this view, the world is constructed in binaries (e.g., mind/body, self/other, human/animal, man/woman, gay/straight), and to be human means to have complete agency, free will, and the ability to reason (St. Pierre, 2000). Over time, this way of thinking has become so commonsense in the Western world that the notion that it is a *particular way of thinking* has become invisible— instead it is regarded as universal and transcendent of location and culture (Haraway, 1988). In this way, those it benefits can claim it as the only correct way of thinking and being. However, this false narrative of universality obscures that it comes from a specific place (Europe) and time (the Enlightenment), and represents the thinking of a particular group (White heterosexual Christian men; Braidotti, 2013). Thus, via rational humanist logic, we perpetuate Whiteness, heteropatriarchy, and other oppressive status quos through our very thinking patterns.

Posthumanism offers an ontological shift to radical immanence and vital materialism (Braidotti, 2013). Immanence is the idea that the world does not exist as separate categories and entities, nor is it populated by bounded individuals with agency and free will. Instead, it is one connected mass of matter that is constantly differentiating into connected multiplicities (Deleuze, 1988; Deleuze & Guattari, 1987). There is no above or below, nothing transcendent, just everything together in a middle. This is not to say that this matter is the same—as Braidotti (2017) notes, it is a matter of "we-are-in-*this*-together-but-we-are-*not*-one-and-the-same" (p. 23, emphasis in original). In fact, difference is the prevailing condition of a posthuman world, since all matter is vital, or alive and intelligent, and as multiplicities form and work together they produce qualitatively different conditions and multiplicities. Moreover, an immanent paradigm implies a simultaneous reality of the actual and the virtual—what is currently happening in the present (the actual), and the potentiality of what that present can produce (the virtual). Put another way, "to do justice to the complexity of our times, we need to think of the posthuman present as *both* the record of *what we are ceasing to be*... and the seed of *what we are in the process of becoming*" (Braidotti, 2017, p. 10, emphasis original).

In a vital materialist, radically immanent perspective, difference is not marked out by binaries, or by separations, but rather, by degrees of difference (Deleuze & Guattari, 1987). Binaries are flattened into planes or continuums. For instance, from a posthumanist perspective, the divide of nature/culture—that which is naturally occurring and that which is constructed by the sociocultural—becomes the nature-culture continuum (Braidotti, 2013), with each bound up with and shaping the other, and recognizable not by inherent characteristics or identifiers but degrees of difference and diverse modes of being. The same goes for the material and discursive—the physical world and that which represents it are entangled and co-constitutive (Barad, 2007). This idea firmly anchors the idea of the material as a key part of any posthuman analysis. In a non-transcendent paradigm, nothing is extractable from its material conditions, since material and discursive elements *make each other*—that is, they are sympoietic (Haraway, 2016).

This material analysis also extends to subjectivity. The myth of the "man of reason" (Lloyd, 2002), or the humanist subject, is that he can rise above the particular (in terms of place, body, time, culture, etc.) and use reason to come to universally true understandings. However, that's not possible: we are "embodied and embedded" in particular places, and we are connected up to specific relations of power that very much matter in the knowledge we produce (Braidotti, 2013). As I pointed out earlier, the false belief of universal transcendence is how heteronormative patriarchy comes to be seen as normal and correct—the only acceptable way to be is straight or acceptable to the straight (male) gaze. To tackle heteronormativity and other discourses that reify oppressive status quos, we have to locate ourselves within geo-political space-time as both a way to practice ethics and accountability and to expose the harm of the cultural hegemony of humanist onto-epistemology.

Finally, the posthuman subject is not a bounded individual, but a multiplicity connected with other multiplicities. We are not created as stable entities, but instead are subjectivized by apparatuses of capture. These apparatuses are molar lines, or forces/structures that bind subjects to the status quo (Deleuze & Guattari, 1987). Any category or label we are forced to occupy—man/woman, straight/gay, and so on—entraps us, overcodes us. Yet, because life is vital and intelligent, the world is always in flux, always becoming-different, and thus "there is always something that flows or flees, that escapes the binary organization, the resonance apparatus, and the overcoding machine; things that are attributed to a 'change in values,' the youth, women, the mad, etc." (Deleuze & Guattari, 1987, p. 216). These are lines of flight, or temporary breaks from status quo. Lines of flight are lines of *becoming,* or micro-transformations, that produce mutations within normative systems (socio-political, institutional, psychological, etc.). These becomings are always minoritarian—they work to subvert dominant narratives (such as heteropatriarchy) and states of affairs. Yet, how does one go about creating lines of flight? Sometimes they occur consciously, but more often, it is the collective production of an assemblage that creates the line of becoming—an act of distributed agency. In my case, the line of becoming-ally was not a self-conscious ontological identification; it was most definitely the collective enunciation of an alliance, formed into an assemblage of me/my learning, my students, and the context of the Empowered Youth Leadership Program (EYLP).

DISRUPTING (MY) HETERONORMATIVE CURRICULUM

The spring of the second year of my doctoral studies, I learned about the Empowered Youth Leadership Program (EYLP; a pseudonym), a program that cultivates feminism, leadership and activism among young women—mainly low-income women of color—in two urban "sister cities" in the Northeastern United States. The EYLP provides learning opportunities that help young women explore their own life experiences, use those experiences as frameworks for understanding the world and issues of social justice, and harness these insights to become agents of change. EYLP's Summer Leadership Institute, which offered six weeks of courses, workshops, trips, and other learning opportunities for young women regarding leadership, feminism/social justice, and activism, was advertising for faculty to teach academic or creative courses on these topics. I came across the advertisement and my interest was piqued immediately.

Throughout my doctoral program, I experienced an intensive awakening to issues of social justice in schools from a critical theoretical perspective and problematized my previously held beliefs and pedagogical practices. In particular, I recognized that I had played into a "White savior" role with the mostly Black and Brown seventh and eighth graders I taught during my years as a middle school teacher. I also regretted not knowing enough about ideas like the reproductive nature of schooling to have explored them with my students at that time. The EYLP seemed like an ideal opportunity to put some of my learning about issues of social justice into practice with young people who, socio-culturally, economically, and linguistically, were like my former students. I got the position to serve as faculty during the Summer Leadership Institute and proposed a course I entitled "Identity and Issues of Social Justice in School" for the young women in the program. The course description I wrote aimed to provide opportunities for students in the program to explore issues of social justice in schools while simultaneously unpacking their own experiences on these topics.

I was ecstatic when my course proposal was accepted, and I found out that I would be teaching alongside classes that would provide opportunities for the young women to explore oppression through photography and songwriting, examine race and racism through a historical lens, and collaboratively deconstruct issues like identity, power, and privilege. Given the course would run for six weeks, I structured the class sessions along what at the time I perceived as four "main" dimensions of social justice—racism, classism, sexism, and language discrimination—with the introductory and final weeks focused on sharing and synthesizing our learning. I allocated the first two classes for community building, norming, and exploratory writing on identity. I planned to use the students' exploratory writing to ground a group discussion on the first day that would surface students' own interests in relation to social justice, which I would then use to modify my lesson plans accordingly.

During the first week of class, as planned, I facilitated some initial community-building activities to get to know one another, and I engaged the students in independent writing. From their narratives, we segued into a discussion in which students shared about their background experiences and stories of oppression. Although some of these stories fell along the lines of the four dimensions of social justice that I had initially identified, another emergent theme that surfaced was connected with negative experiences in schools related to issues of sexuality and gender identity/expression. Although these issues had not been included as part of my original syllabus, the stories of these young women made clear that these issues were at the forefront of their consciousness. Several students, first in independent writing and then sharing out with their peers as we sat together in a large circle, identified themselves in different locations on the LGBTQ spectrum. Some of the students also spontaneously described horrific acts of homophobia, including homophobic language, they had experienced. For example, one student, who identified as a lesbian, drew gasps from around the circle as she calmly told us that a nun at her Catholic school had informed her entire class that "being gay was the same thing as being retarded." Clearly, the lives of these young women (and other women like them) were not just affected by racism, classicism, sexism, and language discrimination. Heterosexism, heteronormativity, and homophobia also served as forces of oppression that mitigated their educational and life experiences.

At the end of the first week, I was forced to reflect on the glaring gap in my syllabus regarding homophobia and heterosexism in schools, a topic that clearly was of importance to my new students. At this point in my doctoral studies, I had only minimally confronted my own straight privilege and hadn't begun to truly problematize the way my thinking and gaze were structured by heteronormativity. Nor had I spent time considering how society as a whole, and many of our everyday actions, construct heterosexuality as normal and natural, and casts any exceeding or differing types of sexuality/gender expression as abnormal/deviant and unnatural. I realized that my syllabus and course design sent a message to my new students: the oppressions that are valid struggles are those involving race, class, gender, and language. I had also invisibilized the LGBTQ oppression and struggles that many of these students confronted. While I could certainly say that I couldn't help what I didn't know, or that six weeks wouldn't allow me to cover every *ism* that exists, it simply did not change the fact that I was complicit in perpetuating heterosexism through a syllabus that failed to engage with these issues. This growing acknowledgement compelled me to rethink and revise one week of the course lessons, sparking a "becoming-ally"—a transformation of subjectivity in relation to my students, their experiences, and their storying of those experiences.

To become-ally, I had to begin to learn about, interrogate, and disrupt some internalized ideas about LGBTQ issues and identities. One was to become aware of the way that, because of my own heteronormative gaze, I made particular assumptions about these young women. I had not considered the issue of homophobia and heterosexism among the other social justice issues because, as a straight cis woman, I didn't "see" it in my own daily experience. Moreover, I was surprised to discover that several of the students self-identified as LGBTQ. Heteronormativity imposes straightness as the default setting—much like Whiteness—and as a result I had *assumed* them to be straight until I was told otherwise. As a teacher with particular power over these students as long as they were in my class, I was complicit in the larger societal disciplining of these students' bodies into the only acceptable category—hetero/cisgender. As another consideration, I had to confront the notion of sexual orientation/expression as a taboo subject when related to schooling. I had long believed that, for instance, teaching abstinence-only education was harmful, but hadn't ever taught about themes regarding sexual identity/expression. If I was a proponent of teaching students about their bodies in schools, why, then, would I regard sexuality and gender expression as taboo topics? Surfacing these contradictions in my thinking and beginning to work through them, a development which had been sparked by interactions with students, was one mutation in a becoming-ally process.

A FIRST ATTEMPT AT ALLY WORK

Upon realizing that I needed to attend to LGBTQ issues in my course, I spent the next several days researching ways to develop a plan for working through issues of homophobia and heteronormativity in schools with my students. I found some of the activities online, and others I adapted from Theater of the Oppressed games (Boal, 2005). The next week, as I walked into the building and entered the classroom to implement these newly devised lessons, I was terribly nervous and worried that students would believe that I didn't know enough to be able to guide them in any meaningful way. In the following sections I describe my engagement with students as we participated in these activities, my understanding of self as becoming-ally, and how this work as a teacher has informed my understanding of the work of teacher educators to promote their own students' ally-becomings.

Day One: Gender-less and Theater of the Oppressed

To get the day started, we played a game called "Gender-less." The object of the game was to talk to a neighbor about the last time they went on a social outing, but without using any kind of gender identifiers about the person or people that were involved in the outing—no he, him, his, boy, boyfriend, guy, and so on; no she, her, hers, woman, girl, girlfriend, chick, and so on. If any gender identifiers were used, the person was "out." After a few rounds of the game, I called time and we debriefed the experience.

Students commented on what a frustrating experience it was to try to discuss the people in their lives without assigning a gender to them, and discussed how they might feel if they had to initiate this conversation with someone about a friend or significant other who was non-gender binary or not cis-gendered.

I then facilitated a conversation about how conventional ideas about gender are embedded in our language—and how language is one tool by which we are forced into particular gender roles and expectations (or, in Deleuzian terms, are captured by molar subject-making apparatuses of gender). This led us into a conversation about homophobia and heteronormativity, and why the latter is often more difficult to raise awareness about, since it often isn't as "in your face" as homophobic language or acts of violence are. Instead, it is materialized through our everyday talk and through expectations of ourselves and others, which in turn are reinforced by society's expectations, norms, and practices.

All of the students were able to anchor their understandings in their own experiences, as all of them had, at a minimum, witnessed some kind of discrimination against LGBTQ youth. Several candidly shared that they themselves identified as LGBTQ, questioning, or gender non-binary and had experienced some form of injustice at school or in their communities. Some of the girls told the group that their parents disapproved of their self-identification, ignored it, denied it, or were confused. Many others admitted that they hadn't felt brave enough to come out to their families, or just weren't sure how to even begin to broach the conversation about being LGBTQ with their parents or caretakers. The majority of my students were African-American, and several also shared culturally-related tensions that further complexified their situation: for example, religion plays a large part in the African American community, and for many, the Christian faith deems homosexuality to be a sin. Such perspectives and beliefs produced internal conflict for these students who wanted to be open about their LGBTQ identities, but felt unable to do so because of cultural norms, religious beliefs, or the social norms and practices of the communities that they lived in and were part of.

After discussing personal stories, I asked students to synthesize what we had talked about by identifying the issues at the heart of their stories—the ways that their schools, or society, promoted LGBTQ inequities or heteronormativity. I introduced a new activity to support envisioning empowering solutions based upon a game from "Theater of the Oppressed" (Boal, 2005). In groups, students chose an issue relating to LGBTQ rights at school and acted it out in two parts. First, they created a skit to identify a problem related to LGBTQ rights and equity in school. Then, they would discuss a solution and perform a second skit to present that possible solution. In the skits that followed, students performed scenarios that included schools barring same-sex dates from the prom; refusing to sanction a Gay-Straight Alliance (GSA) club; not allowing same-sex couples to hold hands in the hall; and letting classroom bullying to continue unchecked by adults. After each group presented their problem and solution skits, we continued with a whole class discussion to brainstorm other suggestions about how we might approach each of these scenarios in our school settings, and students engaged in lively dialogue, enthused by the alternatives they had generated, reimaginings that pointed to different potential futures.

For the last activity of the day, we reviewed the American Civil Liberties Union (ACLU)'s website, which enumerates the rights of LGBTQ youth at school. Using these rights, and their working knowledge of the issues facing LGBTQ youth in their own schools, I asked students to break into small groups and make recommendations to their local public school district's advisory board. These recommendations needed to address both how to better protect the rights of LGBTQ youth, and also how to make schools more inclusive and welcoming to students no matter their orientation or gender expression. One group created a poster that outlined a proposal to create gender-neutral bathrooms for students who identified as non-gender conforming or who might feel uncomfortable using them for any reason (several students shared that bullying often took place in the bathrooms, away from the eyes of teachers). Another group suggested professional development for teachers specifically around the needs of LGBTQ youth. Others recommended adding explicit language to school codes of conduct regarding the bullying of LGBTQ youth and determined that school-wide educative assemblies on LGBTQ youth and discrimination would be beneficial. These, again, simultaneously addressed current injustices in the present—"the record of what is ceasing to be"—while mapping out more just alternatives—"the seed of what we are in the process of becoming" (Braidotti, 2017, p. 10).

Day Two: Public Service Announcements

On the second day, I brought a Sony digital video recorder for us to create our own Public Service Announcements (PSAs). The PSAs were meant to both provide a way to turn our learning together into concrete action, to connect ideas about gender identity/expression to material realities. It was also another way to explore the actual and virtual—to juxtapose what is currently with what might become (Deleuze & Guattari, 1987) by providing a creative space for students to grapple with the harm of heterosexism while imagining ways to be otherwise. After discussing what PSAs generally are meant to do, I turned to several YouTube videos that were PSAs for various LGBTQ-related issues. One clip included a re-imagining of Cinderella as "Cinderfella," and a second offered a humorous take on why NOT to use the term "gay" as a derogatory word. A final video had been created by students in Massachusetts, who provided information about LGBTQ rights in their state. As we watched the videos, I asked the students to identify the strategies that were used to get the audience's attention and to convey information. After debriefing, students split into three teams to plan, write, direct, and film their own videos. To help them include statistics and demographic information to inform their work, we searched the internet and located data, some of which provided estimates for homelessness, suicide rates, and bullying victims among LGBTQ youth. My students and I found the information to be staggering and clear evidence of the need to better support and attend to LGBTQ affirmative and inclusive schools.

The first group opted for a skit that presented a "tables are turned" situation that explored the bullying that students who identify as LGBTQ often experience in schools. The scene began with several students sitting together in a classroom, talking about their summers and their girlfriends. Another student enters and sits down next to them. The group of girls whispered, "That's the new girl. I hear she's straight." Seemingly oblivious, the new girl tapped the popular girl on the shoulder and asked, "Do you have a pencil I could borrow?" The popular girl recoiled, stood up and shouted, "Oh no, she didn't touch me!" The other girls chimed in, "You're gonna turn straight now!" The popular girl announced, "I've got to go to the nurse to get something so I don't turn straight!" The new girl put her hands over face and began to cry. As the scene ended, all the characters turned toward the camera and said in unison: "Bullying is wrong, no matter who is in that seat."

The second group decided to take a more straightforward, informational approach, rather than a performance or skit. They wondered, *do people know what LGBTQ means*? They felt that some foundational knowledge about, and the demystifying of, this acronym was important. Each member of the group took one of the letters in the acronym and created note cards that indicated what that particular letter meant. As the PSA began, the students sat side by side in four chairs, holding their index cards. The camera panned slowly from student to student allowing for the viewer to read the definitions provided on the index cards: "L is for Lesbian. It means I like other girls." "G is for Gay." "B is for Bi-sexual." "T is for transgender."

The third group produced a PSA that combined a skit with straightforward informational elements. This group also addressed the prevalent theme of bullying, "othering," and pathologizing queerness in schools, supporting their message with statistics that communicated the material impact of hurtful and exclusionary behavior rooted in homophobic/transphobic ideologies. The PSA began with three students eating lunch in the cafeteria. When a student who identified as gay attempted to sit at their table, the other students yelled, "Ew, you are gay!" and told her she couldn't sit with them. The whole group then turned to the camera, and the young women each held up signs that communicated tragic statistics[1]: more than 50% of girls and 30% of boys identifying as LGBTQ had reported attempting suicide, and nearly three quarters of LGBTQ youth had considered doing so. As the PSA ended, the camera panned across a banner that read: "Don't Judge by Sexual Orientation. Peace, Love, Acceptance."

As the course sequence reached the conclusion of our six weeks together, I asked the class how they would like to present what was learned at the program showcase, a concluding course experience to be held at the end of the final week. Although we covered several other topics concerning social justice in schools, such as the school to prison pipeline, language discrimination, and "white-washed" curriculum, the class unanimously wanted to revisit their PSA videos regarding gender and sexuality. For them, these videos were powerful for multiple reasons. The PSAs provided educational opportunities they believed were necessary as a starting point to raise awareness of the ways heterosexism and homophobia operate in schools and the physical and mental harm caused by bullying, exclusion, and othering, as well as provide basic information about the LGBTQ community. The PSAs also provided an entry point into different potentialities for what might be considered "normal," glimpses of a virtual with ways of being and expressing one's identity and sexuality that exceed the traditional gender binary categories and normative construction of heterosexuality. We all decided that we would combine all of the PSAs into one video, edit it to include transitions and titles, and we would share this as our final project at the showcase. After we viewed the edited video (which the girls elected to set to Michael Jackson's "Human Nature") we reflected on our mutual learning. The students commented that it was a "good learning experience," "It opened my mind for the better," and "I realized that school should really be the safest place for LGBTQ teens."

For me, I had brought my own limited understandings into composition with these girls, their experiences, and together we had produced ourselves differently—a "making with" (Haraway, 2016) that produced us in solidarity with each other and forged connections across a continuum of gender expressions and sexual identifications. It also disrupted traditional modes of teaching. Rather than imposing my own agenda, which, because it came from my own (straight) perspective did not connect with their experience, we formed a teaching assemblage in which I provided some structure and facilitation while the students produced the content from their own experiences, interests, and aspirations for a different world. This alliance between heterogenous elements—myself and my knowledge, the program, a social justice agenda, the students, their experiences—created lines of flight, forging new territories of possibility for their own subjectivities-in-formation, and mine, in what I suggest is a pedagogy of virtualities.

POSITIVE DIFFERENCE AND A PEDAGOGY
OF VIRTUALITIES

In Western society, commonsense binary thinking forces us into categories that are not just reductive in the face of the immense complexity and non-linearity of the world, but also actively cause material harm—as, for example, shown by the statistics my students had found regarding the drastically high numbers of LGBTQ youth who had considered suicide or actually took their own lives. This "commonsense" thinking, over time, has become taken-for-granted as the correct way of seeing the world, and any idea or body that exceeds the binaries it creates is seen as an aberration, a problem to be fixed, disciplined into submission to the norm, or even erased completely (Braidotti, 2013). However, as I have argued throughout this chapter, there *are* different ways of thinking and being available to us, ones that break away from the value for sameness (and sameness as defined by the dominant culture), and instead start from "the principle of not-one" (Braidotti, 2013, p. 96)—difference.

From the perspective of dominant thought, the young people in my summer class had only two choices in terms of selves: they could conform to what was right (cisgender heterosexuality) or they could be the less-than-human, deviant other, their bodies subject to bullying, internal pathologizing, and other forms of harm. However, with a starting point of difference—and difference defined as productive—the students could be produced in innumerable and perhaps even as-yet-unthought-of ways: their bodies not fixed into static sex and gender formations, but rather complex assemblages of potentialities (Braidotti, 2013). This notion of productive difference moves us away from focusing on what bodies are (or are supposed to be) or how they fit (or do not fit) preordained categories of boy/girl, straight/gay, and so on, and instead, prods us to focus on what bodies can do. Rather than coding our students from birth into particular formations of self, we would only know what they were capable of becoming as they continued to form assemblages with other bodies, materialities, and forces (Deleuze & Guattari, 1987).

As teachers and teacher educators, we can become-ally and forge alliances with our students by adopting a pedagogy of virtualities—that is, a pedagogy that allows for the actualization of students' and teachers' potentialities through joint activity—in our work with students. We need to adopt a starting point of difference and multiplicity, and understand our work as sympoiesis (Haraway, 2016), a making with students. From this perspective, our teaching only crystallizes into such in composition with our students— that is, teaching is a joint production emerging from a heterogeneous assemblage (Strom, 2015).

At the same time, we must account for ourselves. As educators and teacher educators, we are embodied and embedded, and speak from particular geo-political locations in particular configurations of space-time-matter (Barad, 2007; Braidotti, 2013). Our syllabi and the lesson plans we create also are concrete manifestations of these specific perspectives, and we must account for them as such, while keeping them unfinished and open enough to be able to connect with students' lives and experiences. For example, my syllabi and lessons for the EYLP was an instantiation of my understanding of social justice issues from my experiences as a White, straight, cis, middle class teacher and teacher educator whose background included teaching mostly multilingual immigrant students. Therefore, in my syllabus, I focused in on class, race, and language, which were issues I had direct experience confronting in the classroom. It was not until I brought these plans into composition with a specific group of students that it became clear that my perspective was incomplete, and indeed, by virtue of that partiality, could have reinforced the heteronormative status quo by imposing a straight gaze on the students, rendering their experiences invisible, and denying them a space to engage in binary-pushing explorations of who they were becoming.

Because our embodied-and-embeddedness (Braidotti, 2013) binds us and our teaching in particular ways, we can only create pedagogies of the virtual by coming into composition with students in ways that connect and move outward, jointly constructing and expanding on original plans. This entails a fundamental decentering of the teacher-self, disrupting the normalized category of "teacher" as the holder of knowledge and doer of action, and instead becoming an ally (becoming-ally), adopting teaching as a fundamental act of alliance. Such a pedagogy cannot be completely planned out, nor follow any kind of set formula: "it experiments rather than standardizes, producing ever-new alignments, linkages, and connections" (Grosz, 1993). Since we cannot know in advance what these virtualities might entail, we must be open and flexible with our ideas and seek to provide structures that can respond to students' current realities while providing entry points into mapping out new potentialities. This means that teachers must be comfortable in turning toward the unknown, embracing uncertainty, and understanding that pedagogy must be co-constructed in the moment of encounter (Strom & Martin, 2013). However, I do not suggest that teachers enter their classrooms unprepared—merely that their "plans" be unfinished and flexible to allow for co-creation and co-emergence.

To develop teachers—and indeed, teacher educators—capable of forging alliances with students and reimagining teaching as an act of coming into composition, of making-with, requires that we push on current patterns of curriculum and practice in teacher education. Teacher educators must guide teacher candidates to develop and practice a politics of location (Haraway, 1988; Rich, 1984)—that is, creating a practice of critically examining and articulating the ways our perspectives are shaped by our geo-political, material, and temporal positioning in the world. These positionings will shape their teaching practices, their curriculum, and their interactions with students, which will, in turn, affect students in material ways. To develop this kind of perspective means fundamentally disrupting notions of neutrality and transcendence in teacher education, and emphasizing that our teaching practices spring from our bodies and backgrounds, and are political, whether we want them to be or not (Strom, 2017).

As teacher educators we also need to provide explicit opportunities to problematize not just often-internalized, traditional discourses of the teacher as both the holder of knowledge and the controller of classroom activity (Freire, 1970), but binary logic itself, and the ways these reinforce harmful status quos of heteronormativity, heterosexism, and other material-discursive formations in classrooms that uphold inequality. Recognizing and problematizing dualistic worldviews in teacher preparation programs can provide an entry point to a more decentered way of seeing the craft of teaching, moving away from an individualistic perspective to one that casts the classroom as multiplicity (Strom, 2015). Further, teacher candidates need opportunities to probe the self/other (or self/world) binary to develop an understanding of difference as positive and productive, rather than negative (Braidotti, 2013). Being able to view difference as a creative force is imperative for teachers to value a range of ways of knowing and being in the world, particularly those that exceed normative labels. While fostering these shifts in the thinking of teacher candidates might seem like a tall order, pursuing a fundamental ontological interruption to dominant, rational humanist understandings of the world is necessary if teachers are to work together with their students in ways that help create a more just world (Martin & Strom, 2015).

In addition to engaging in learning to develop decentered, multiplistic understandings of teaching and value for plurality (i.e., ontologies beyond the heteronormative gaze), teachers also need ample time to put these ideas to work, recursively, in a supported environment. These practice opportunities must explicitly attend to continuing to develop curriculum and teaching practices together with students, and appropriate guidance to begin to develop comfort with ambiguity and openness in the classroom. In this way, teacher educators can engage in pedagogies that foster ally subjectivities and advance understandings of schools and classrooms as LGBTQ-inclusive and affirmative contexts.

Although most teacher preparation programs have moved to more social understandings of teaching and learning (Cochran-Smith & Villegas, 2016), opportunities to learn about theory/methods and practice those are still separate, and time devoted to practice in a supported manner is often short or, with the advent of alternate route programs, completely absent (Zeichner, 2010). Models of teacher preparation that mesh teacher learning and practice, such as urban teacher residencies (e.g., Klein et al., 2013; Zeichner, 2010), may offer more ecological possibilities where teacher candidates can have extended opportunities to practice co-creating with students in a supported environment.

This critical reflection about my work with my former students highlights how, by engaging with critical posthuman theoretical frameworks, and analyzing my teaching/learning experiences via this lens, I gained important insight regarding teaching social justice from a more intersectional and inclusive lens, coming together with students to forge pedagogical alliances—pedagogies of the virtual—which co-produced new modes of being and exceeding-subject for all of us, including my own line of becoming-ally. I suggest that posthuman concepts, if translated carefully and deliberately scaffolded (Strom & Lupinacci, in press), might assist teacher candidates (and teacher educators) to consider themselves beyond normative constructions of what it means to be an educator, as well as examine the implications of our teaching, our scholarship, and our service in relation to LGBTQ members of the school community. Ultimately, for those who seek to advance equity and social justice in education—but especially for those who benefit from straight/cis-gendered privilege—engaging in processes of becoming-ally is integral to co-create classrooms that are affirmative spaces for students along the LGBTQ and gender/sexuality expression continuum.

NOTE

1. Students retrieved these statistics from Internet sources in July of 2011. For more current figures regarding LGBTQ teen suicide and other health risk factors, see the Center for Disease Control's Youth Risk Surveillance System (CDC, 2015) or the Gay, Lesbian & Straight Education Network's (GLSEN, 2016) report on educational exclusion.

REFERENCES

Barad, K. (2007). *Meeting the universe halfway.* Durham, NC: Duke University Press.
Boal, A. (2005). *Games for actors and non-actors.* New York, NY: Routledge.
Braidotti, R. (2013). *The posthuman.* Cambridge, MA: Polity Press.

Braidotti, R. (2017). The posthuman condition. Presentation at the University of Utrecht, Netherlands, August 2017.

Center for Disease Control. (2015). Youth risk surveillance system. Retrieved from https://www.cdc.gov/healthyyouth/data/yrbs/index.htm.

Cochran-Smith, M., Villegas, A. M., Abrams, L., Chavez Moreno, L., Mills, T., & Stern, R. (2016). Research on teacher preparation: Charting the process of a sprawling field. In D. Gitomer & C. Bell (Eds.), *Handbook of research on teaching* (pp. 439–548). Washington, DC: AERA.

Deleuze, G., & Guattari, F. (1987). *A thousand plateaus: Capitalism and schizophrenia* (B. Massumi, Trans.). Minneapolis: University of Minnesota Press.

Deleuze, G. (1988). *Spinoza: Practical philosophy.* San Francisco, CA: City Lights Books.

Freire, P. (1970). *Pedagogy of the oppressed.* New York, NY: Continuum.

Gay, Lesbian & Straight Education Network. (2016). Educational exclusion: Drop out, push out, and the school-to-prison pipeline among LGBTQ youth. Retrieved from https://www.glsen.org/sites/default/files/Educational%20Exclusion_Report_6-28-16_v4_WEB_READY_PDF.pdf

Grosz, E. (1993). A thousand tiny sexes: Feminism and rhizomatics. In C. Boundas & D. Olkowski (Eds.), *Deleuze and the theatre of philosophy* (pp. 187–210). New York, NY: Routledge.

Haraway, D. J. (1988) Situated knowledges: The science question in feminism and the privilege of partial perspective. *Feminist Studies, 14*(3), 575–599. doi:10.2307/3178066

Haraway, D. J. (2016) *Staying with the trouble: Making kin in the chthulucene.* Durham, NC: Duke University Press.

Klein, E. J., Taylor, M., Onore, C., Strom, K., & Abrams, L. (2013). Finding a third space in teacher education: Creating an urban teacher residency with Montclair State University and the Newark public schools. *Teaching Education, 24*(1), 27–57. doi:10.1080/10476210.2012.711305

Ladson-Billings, G. (1994). *The dreamkeepers: Successful teachers of African-American children.* San Francisco, CA: Jossey-Bass.

Ladson Billings, G., & Tate, W. (1995). Toward a critical race theory of education. *Teachers College Record, 97*(1), 47–64.

Lloyd, G. (2002). *The man of reason: "Male" and "female" in western philosophy.* New York, NY: Routledge.

Lucas, T., Villegas, A. M., & Freedson-Gonzalez, M. (2008). Linguistically responsive teacher education: Preparing classroom teachers to teach English language learners. *Journal of Teacher Education, 59*(4), 361–373. doi:10.1177/0022487108322110

McIntosh, P. (1988). *White privilege and male privilege: A personal account of coming to see correspondence through work in women's studies* (Working Paper 189:1–20). Wellesley, MA: Wellesley Center for Research on Women.

Martin, A., & Strom, K. (2015). Neoliberalism and the teaching of English learners: Decentering the teacher and student subject. *SoJo Journal, 1*(1), 23–43.

Oakes, J. (2005). *Keeping track* (2nd ed). New Haven, CT: Yale University Press.

Paris, D., & Alim, H. S. (Eds.). (2017). *Culturally sustaining pedagogies: Teaching and learning for justice in a changing world.* New York, NY: Teachers College Press.

Rich, A. (1984) Notes towards a politics of location. In R. Lewis & S. Mills (Eds.), *Feminist postcolonial theory: A reader* (pp. 29–42). New York, NY: Routledge.

St. Pierre, E. (2000). Poststructural feminism in education: An overview. *Qualitative Studies in Education, 13*(5), 477–515. doi:10.1080/09518390050156422

Strom, K., & Lupinacci, J. (in press). Posthuman pedagogies in two educational leadership program qualitative research sequences. In C. Taylor & A. Bayley (Eds.), *Posthumanism and higher education: Reimagining pedagogy, practice and research*. London, England: Palgrave.

Strom, K. J., & Martin, A. D. (2013). Putting philosophy to work in the classroom: Using rhizomatics to deterritorialize neoliberal thought and practice. *Studying Teacher Education, 9*(3), 219–235. doi:10.1080/17425964.2013.830970

Strom, K., & Martin, A. (2017). Thinking with theory in an era of Trump. *Issues in Teacher Education, 26*(3), 3–22.

Strom, K. (2015). Teaching as assemblage: Negotiating practice in the first year of teaching. *Journal of Teacher Education, 66*(4), 321–333. doi:10.1177/00224 87115589990

Strom, K. (2017). Creating new futures: Thinking differently to build a better world. Paper presented at the Carnegie Project on the Educational Doctorate (CPED) biannual convening, Oakland, CA

Villegas, A. M., & Lucas, T. (2002). *Culturally responsive teaching: A coherent approach.* Albany: State University of New York Press.

Zeichner, K. (2010). Rethinking the connections between campus courses and field experiences in college- and university-based teacher education. *Journal of Teacher Education, 61*(2), 89–99. doi:10.1177/0022487109347671

CHAPTER 9

BATTLING HETERONORMATIVITY IN TEACHER EDUCATION

Reflections on a Human Development Course from a Teacher and Student

Peggy Shannon-Baker and Ingrid Wagner

ABSTRACT

Teachers, due to their position of power in knowledge construction processes, can reinforce, deconstruct, and/or disrupt heteronormative discourse.
Teacher educators in particular are positioned to train future teachers in how
to identify, critique, and disrupt such discourse. The purpose of this chapter
is to discuss the anti-heteronormative pedagogy that Peggy used in an undergraduate course on human development. We also share the implications of
this pedagogy based on Ingrid's experiences as a student in the class. This
work is based on interactionist theory, queer theory, and nonunitary subjectivity. We used a practitioner-based approach to analyze course materials
(e.g., assessments, syllabus), teacher journals, and student assignments. We
grouped our understandings into three major areas: an intentionally anti-

---

Exploring Gender and LGBTQ Issues in K–12 and Teacher Education, pages 147–162

heteronormative pedagogical approach; assignments and activities that promote dialogue, critical reflection, and investigation into the lived experiences of intersex, trans, and gender nonconforming children; and the implications for a student's future teaching practice.

> *By most counts, U.S. teachers in K–12 settings are woefully ill prepared to teach LGBTQ and non-gender conforming youth and to work against heterosexism and homophobia in schools.*
> —Clark, 2010, p. 711

Although written nearly 10 years ago, this quote still rings true today. Within the United States, LGBTQ topics are addressed sparingly if at all as it relates to children and young adults (e.g., Myers & Raymond, 2010). This lack of discussion and limited preparation for future teachers remains an issue internationally as well (e.g., Bartholomaeus, Riggs, & Andrew, 2017; Magnus & Lundin, 2016) as schools attempt to move beyond "tolerance" rhetoric toward disrupting the discrimination and harassment LGBTQ students face (Bradley-Johnston, 2017; DePalma & Atkinson, 2009; Paterson, 2014). However, LGBTQ topics are "decontextualized" (Gorski, Davis, & Reiter, 2013, p. 224) or invisible in teacher education courses on diversity despite the use of such courses to prepare teachers to work cross-culturally (Shannon-Baker, 2018).

Diversity-related courses (Clark, 2010; Gorski et al., 2013) should not be the only place to engage with gender, LGBTQ, and intersex issues. Instead, teacher educators must engage with these issues throughout the curriculum because these reflect the lived experiences of K–12 students. However some preservice teachers argue that addressing LGBTQ issues is "irrelevant" because they assume that their k–12 students will be heterosexual (Szalacha, 2004). We suspect that these reactions are the result of teaching about non-heteronormative experiences primarily within an "intervention" or workshop-based capacity (i.e., in a single diversity-oriented course). In other words, only "adding in" narratives about LGBTQ topics in a few places in their training demonstrates that it is not relevant to the whole teacher (education) experience.

Teacher education programs need to better prepare future teachers to not only work with LGBTQ youth, but also actively disrupt heterosexism, homophobia, and heteronormativity. We believe that this work starts with a critical introspection about how teacher education—without conscious intention otherwise—maintains heteronormativity. We define heteronormativity as the hegemonic belief that gender is a dichotomy (woman and man), that one's gender prescribes a heterosexual orientation, and that all representations of family, desire, and sexuality are built on assumed heterosexual and gender norm relationships (Magnus & Lundin, 2016).

Specifically addressing LGBTQ, intersex, and gender-based experiences is especially important in courses addressing youths' social, emotional, physical, and cognitive development. In their review of 23 textbooks, Young and Middleton (2002) found that although references were made to LGB (and sometimes trans) issues, many of these instances came after or before discussions about sexually transmitted diseases and "non-marital lifestyles." Such presentations present LGBTQ people as diseased and deviant. Young and Middleton also found that references to LGB issues were primarily discussed in relation to social and emotional development in "early adulthood" (p. 93) that is, not related to younger children nor to other domains of development. Young and Middleton conclude that teacher educators must include outside source material to address the gaps in pre-assigned textbooks. We maintain, however, that even such add-ins are troubling without also a discussion of what it means to include/keep out the experiences of LGBTQ and intersex people from textbooks, and how such texts, taught on their own, otherwise maintain a heteronormative discourse about human development.

Teachers, in their position of power, can reinforce (Kedley, 2015), deconstruct, or actively disrupt heteronormative discourse through their interaction with students, selection of course materials, and design of activities. This is especially important in education programs where teacher educators are vital to the disruption of heteronormative discourse in the field, as well as to the training of future teachers in how to identify, critique, and combat such discourse. Thus, the purpose of this chapter is to share the anti-heteronormative practices Peggy (a teacher educator) used while teaching a course on human development, as well as the implications for the future professional practices of Ingrid (an early childhood preservice teacher who took the course).

To discuss how our course disrupted heteronormativity in teacher education, we first outline the various theoretical frameworks upon which we built our writing, thinking, and practices. These theories include interactionist theory, queer theory, and the notion of nonunitary subjectivity. Next, we identify the methods that we used to reflect upon and write about our course on human development. We also provide contextual information about the course, such as how it fit within various teacher education programs. We then share our narratives and experiences within four major sections. First, Peggy details her anti-heteronormative pedagogical stance. Second, we describe the various assignments and activities from the course that focused on the lived experiences of LGBTQ and intersex youth. Third, Ingrid shares her learning and the implications of this course for her subsequent teacher education coursework and future teaching practices. Finally, we identify several key areas where the course's anti-heteronormative approach could be improved in future iterations. We conclude with summative reflections on the course, as well as our advice for teacher educators and P–12 teachers interested in disrupting heteronormativity in their own classrooms.

THEORETICAL FRAMEWORK

This work is informed by interactionist theory, queer theory, and the notion of nonunitary subjectivity. Historically, an interactionist approach theorizes that our sense of gender is influenced by interactions, and our interactions are influenced by our sense of gender, especially those that embody power differentials (Ridgeway & Smith-Lovin, 1999). As a "background identity," gender is "enmeshed" with other forms of identity (e.g., race, socioeconomic class; Ridgeway & Smith-Lovin, 1999, p. 193). However, what is missing from this interactionist approach is just how other forms of identity impact gendered interactions and social hierarchies. This is where queer theory is particularly important.

As Green (2007) argues, queer theory and interpretivist frameworks such as interactionism share a "sustained commitment to deconstruction" and to living "*in tension*" (emphasis in original, p. 27). Both frameworks see language as playing a central role in constructing our subjectivities. Both also utilize investigations of the self while rejecting a self that is predetermined (Green, 2007). Interactionists argue that our sense of gender identity—both for ourselves and writ large—are maintained by a "feedback loop" where our interactions represent a power imbalance and lead us to believe that future interactions will also be imbalanced (Gussak, 2008).

Some queer theorists, on the other hand, disrupt such normalized power imbalances by highlighting non-heteronormative practices and identities (Green, 2007). Other queer theorists further deconstruct identity and representational politics to identify the intersectional nature of queerness with race, socioeconomic class, nationality, and capitalism (Cohen, 1997; Hennessy, 2000) as well as White supremacy and settler colonialism (Smith, 2010).

Queer theorists in the area of disability studies redirect the conversation to the body, flesh, and embodied lived experience (McRuer, 2006; Plummer, 2003). Combining these two areas of thought highlight how bodies are normalized, and those bodies outside of the norm are pathologized (Sherry, 2004). Refocusing on the body is especially important in biologically driven fields like that of human development. Countering heteronormative discourse in human development coursework entails addressing both biological diversity and the symbolism of gender and sexuality (Butler, 1990), and how norms about biology, gender, and sexuality are used as a means for social control, or in this case through the discourses in teacher education. Further, by also considering the theory of nonunitary subjectivity (Bloom,

1996), this work disrupts the traditional notion of subjectivity by embracing fragmentation and multiplicity; that one's subjectivity can change over time and in relation to systems of dominance.

METHODS

This work utilized a practitioner-based approach (Cochran-Smith & Lytle, 2009; Howard, 2003; Hubbard & Powers, 2003; Schön, 1987) within a teacher-student collaboration (e.g., Cohen et al., 2013). About one year after the course on human development ended, Peggy proposed to Ingrid that we write together about the course on human development given our shared interests in multicultural education issues. Ingrid had already taken other courses with Peggy, and we had otherwise been in touch about Ingrid's professional development as a future teacher. We then began to meet regularly via video conferencing to have critical conversations (e.g., Schuck, Aubusson, & Buchanan, 2008) about course materials such as the textbook (Berk, 2014), PowerPoint lectures, assignment prompts, Peggy's teaching notes, and Ingrid's own assignment products. After reviewing all of the course materials and Ingrid's work in particular, we identified several key classroom activities, source materials, and assignments that stood out in how they addressed an anti-heteronormative approach. We then discussed these items in more depth, journaled individually, and identified the implications this class had for our current practices. We understood these conversations to be "mutually empowering" (Miller & Stiver, 1997) and based in relational learning (Buber, 1970).

The course was offered as part of a year-long sequence covering human development from the neonatal stage through adulthood and death. This particular course covered neonatal to early adolescent development (age 11). For early childhood education majors, this course was a replacement option for another human development course that covered a longer time span in one semester. This course also fulfilled requirements for students in speech pathology and nursing majors. The basic syllabus and core textbook (Berk, 2014) were established by the education department, though each instructor was allowed to add additional materials and/or assessments at their discretion. Peggy taught the course, and Ingrid was one of the nine students. The discussion below illuminates Ingrid's perspective on the course; it is important to note, however, that her voice does not speak for all nine students.

OUR UNDERSTANDINGS

We grouped our understandings about how this teacher education course on human development disrupted heteronormative discourse into three major areas: an intentionally anti-heteronormative pedagogy; assignments and activities that were based on the lived experiences of intersex, trans, and gender nonconforming children; and a student's learning from her reflections on the course material and implications for her professional practice. We follow these discussions with a critical introspection about the course and how it could be improved in the future.

Anti-Heteronormative Pedagogy

As a queer, anti-racist feminist educator, I (Peggy) embodied a pedagogical approach to this course that reflected both "anti-work" and "ally-work" (Clark, 2010, p. 705). According to Clark (2010), whereas "anti-work" is focused on the disruption of "racist, heterosexist and homophobic discourses," "ally-work" engages in critical dialogue aimed at interrogating difference in order to create "productive alliances" (p. 705). The notion of allies has also been investigated, where even "ally-work" has been broken down into that which serves as an "affirmation" of those in the non-dominant group to someone who takes "informed action" steps (Brown & Ostrove, 2013, p. 2220). Although the distinctions between "anti-work" and "ally-work" are important, we believe that both are necessary to scaffold teacher candidates' understandings.

This anti-heteronormative approach entailed a close reading of the required course text (Berk, 2014) that found little to no positive representations of gender nonconforming, LGBTQ, and intersex children. Although the text did address how gender roles and stereotypes are learned in early childhood, it favored biologically driven theories: "Biology *clearly* affects children's gender typing, channeling boys toward active, competitive play and girls toward quieter, more intimate interaction" (Berk, 2014, p. 217; emphasis added). Additionally, in the text's subject index, "gay, lesbian, and bisexual people" included subheadings on eating disorders, suicide, partner abuse, and cohabitation, as well as parenthood, friendships, healthcare decisions, and marriage (p. SI–13). Experiences of children who are trans and intersex were not represented.

After analyzing the textbook and considering my own positionalities, I designed the course to address the development of trans and intersex children directly, not as a separate unit but throughout the semester as we progressed through each new age-based developmental stage. Thus, similar to other teacher educators (Young & Middleton, 2002), I researched other resources (e.g., Herndon, 2006) to use with the textbook. For example, when I introduced the role of genetics in neonatal development during the second week of class, we also discussed the difference between sex (as biologically based) and gender (as a social construction). Since the text tended to conflate sex and gender, it was important for me to establish that sociologically driven theories differentiate the two. This then led to a discussion about the "impact" of chromosomal makeup on development, where I included videos about being intersex and perspectives on the difference between choosing one's gender identity versus being assigned an identity. I also provided links to the Intersex Society of North America (www.isna.org) and their pamphlet "Teaching Intersex Issues" (Herndon, 2006). Finally, the journal assignment for that week asked students to critically reflect on how the textbook did not discuss people who are intersex. This journal extended our in-class discussions about identifying how sex, gender, and heteronormativity are interwoven in American discourse around neonatal, early childhood, and later development.

Beyond identifying such discourse, my pedagogy also integrated intersectional (Crenshaw, 1991) narratives. This meant that we considered the intersectional impact of multiple identities on development, such as refugee status, race, disability, socioeconomic class, national origin, language, gender, and sexuality. Although intersectional identities were addressed throughout the semester, one important example came from Week 10 when we discussed the emotional and social development of 2–6 year-olds. In this case, we investigated the identity development of Ryland, a 6-year old transgender boy who has cochlear implants. This story was especially important for the course not only because it shared Ryland's experience from prenatal development to kindergarten, but it also shared how he knew he was a boy before he could talk. In Ryland's case in particular, his positive development was aided by his parents' and community support (The Whittington Family, 2014). This lesson built on previous ones addressing the differences between sex and gender as well as how to identify self-awareness in young children.

As a teacher educator, I also shared these practices with the class, including the research strategies I used to locate and select resources that moved beyond the hyper-sexualization and subtly negative portrayals of LGBTQ people (Young & Middleton, 2002). I also shared with the students that as a queer person and an ally it was important for me to disrupt the erasure and negative portrayals of intersex and trans people, especially in spaces that would otherwise perpetuate this discourse. I shared these practices with the class for two reasons. I saw this as a way to model anti-heteronormative pedagogy in a way that demonstrated how theory and practice can be intimately tied together. In addition to learning about the lived experiences of young trans and intersex people, the teacher candidates also learned through observation and hearing my critical reflections about how to enact a culturally responsive pedagogy (Howard, 2003; Ladson-Billings, 2011; Shannon-Baker, 2018).

CRITICAL ASSIGNMENTS AND ACTIVITIES
ABOUT LIVED EXPERIENCES

I (Peggy) also designed several activities, discussion formats, and assignments that encouraged students to reflect on their own beliefs and stereotypes in order to practice strategies for disrupting heteronormative discourse. In addition to reflecting on my own experiences as a queer person
(Kedley, 2015), I incorporated videos and guest speakers to demonstrate
how our theoretical discussions about development had lived implications.
In class, we watched videos from young adults who are intersex sharing
how they were subjected to genital surgery to assign them a sex, sometimes
without consent from their parents (BuzzFeed Presents, 2015). Then we
discussed how identities are shaped, both by assignment from others and
via one's agency in self-identification. Subsequently, I wrote some of the
summative mid-term and final exam questions based on these discussions.
These questions asked the students to reflect on a video or narrative about
a life experience and then relate it to developmental theories. Thus, the
students not only learned theoretically how parental support or peer bullying impacts gender nonconforming children, but they based this learning
on hearing stories of this development.

When some students seemed hesitant to discuss a particular topic, we
used *think-pair-share* and exit-slip formats. The *think-pair-share* format engages both cognitive and social learning skills (Carss, 2007), and provides time
for students to consider the question or problem and discuss it in a more
intimate paired setting before sharing with the larger class. In one example
from the class, after watching a video about the non-profit organization
Team Up for Youth that addresses access to after-school sports for "under-
privileged" girls (Hey You Up There, 2010), the students considered the
following question: how does participation in sports effect development?
The students then compared their notes with a partner. Finally, we compiled a larger list as a class including how sports can help build social and
leadership skills, improve sleep, and teach strategic thinking. The larger
discussion also helped the class make connections to how the political nature of Title IX funding for athletic programs have personal consequences
for girls' development. In this example, the *think-pair-share* format provided
a formative assessment of their understanding of how gender-based differences in school funding impacts development.

I also assigned occasional exit slips, which are a question-based strategy
typically used at the end of a class session to check students' understanding
(Garrison & Ehringhaus, 2009). I used exit slips to provide another space
to check in with each student and/or address any potential apprehension
I read from students' limited participation in a discussion. For example,
when we watched the video about Ryland's story (The Whittington Family,

2014) during Week 11, we had a discussion after about the students' reactions. This led to numerous questions, including some about being trans, sexuality, and what happens during puberty. In my journaling about the course, I documented that I "wanted to hear from everyone so I had them do an exit slip on their reactions and questions they had." As a result, I learned that the students wanted to know more about being trans through puberty, and used this information to change my later lesson plans. From Ingrid's perspective, these exit slips provided a safe space to clarify misconceptions without peer judgement. As we can see from Ingrid's perspective below, the variety of discussion and media formats encouraged us as a class to deeply engage in various topics about LGBTQ, gender nonconforming, and intersex children's development.

A Preservice Teacher's Perspective

As a preservice teacher studying education, I (Ingrid) feel that these topics should be discussed more frequently in teacher education programs because of their tremendous effect on the development of the student and their caregivers. Often in education courses, discussions address how to create a classroom where diverse families are welcomed and respected, and encouraging family involvement in classroom events and activities. Creating an anti-heteronormative environment would fall in line with these discussions, especially because "children understand their gender identity as young as age 2" (Rose, 2017, para. 23). Gender identity is a large part of child development as it impacts the child's physical, emotional, cognitive, and social development. By understanding the importance of creating an anti-heteronormative environment in our classrooms, we can help support the development of students who are a part of the LGBTQ community. Going beyond the individual student, an anti-heteronormative classroom reaches their siblings and parents, allowing them to recognize and support their family's diversity.

Let's examine the story of Isabel Rose, a mother of a transgender daughter, who "allowed" her then son Samuel to "play as he saw fit in his early years (which) paved the path for later emotional security" (Rose, 2017, para. 17). When Samuel was 4 years old, Isabel discovered him playing in the backyard wearing a princess dress. Positively encouraging such play was like a rebirth. Now, Sadie is an 8 year old girl "who greets each day with excitement" (Rose, 2017, para. 19). Isabel occasionally finds herself wondering what would have happened had she punished Sadie for wearing the princess dress. However, because Isabel allowed for Sadie's gender exploration at a young age, she now has daughter who "felt safe enough to transition" (Rose, 2017, para. 18). Isabel states, "most children lack the vocabulary to articulate how they feel when they are so young. Their only recourse at gaining understanding may be to don a tutu as a boy, or to wear a Superman costume as a girl" (Rose, 2017, para. 24). As an early childhood education major, I feel that this information is important in order to fully support the development of children in my future classroom. When in a classroom, it is important to be perceptive of both the verbal and nonverbal communication from your students.

Throughout Peggy's course, Human Development, we were constantly engaged in critical thinking through class discussions and weekly journals. For each class, the expectation was that we read the materials required in order to have a discussion based on the content presented for each day. As an education student, I could quickly and accurately draw from my notes and readings and apply it to a lived experience about LGBTQ issues in the scenarios we discussed. As an educator, having the skill to critically think about these lived experiences, I feel more prepared for situations I may face in elementary classroom.

Through our weekly journals, the critical conversation continued. We expressed our critical thoughts on how being an intersex, trans, or gender nonconforming child would interact with their development across four domains: cognitive, social, physical, and emotional. Reflecting on my journals from the class, I have included the following excerpt that demonstrates my critical thinking throughout the course:

> In my opinion, being intersex would have a huge impact on an individual's development. First of all, it would have a major affect [sic] on their physical development. Because they were born with anatomy that doesn't fit the typical definition of a male or female, they will have trouble finding answers for the unanswered questions of their body... As their peers go through puberty, intersex individuals won't be able to relate, which affects their social development... Intersex individuals are often advised not to talk about their differences, which can be really hard when they are searching to feel accepted among their peers. This in turn can have effect on them emotionally. They can feel lost and alone, which can lead to anxiety and depression. Lastly, these physical, emotional, and social changes and pressures can affect their cognitive development. They are so focused on the changes in their physical body and hormones that they cannot focus on their intellectual development.

This journal demonstrates how I brought together all of the stages of development. One domain of development does not stand alone. This journal entry also demonstrates how we were encouraged to apply our knowledge from the textbook to the lived experience of intersex children.

Beyond these critical discussions, Peggy's pedagogy modeled anti-heteronormative practices. She created a classroom that made students more engaged because she was excited to teach the material presented, and she believed the information she taught was important in our future occupations. Our class was a judgement free zone where we could ask the hard questions—questions we may have been eager to ask, but never found the right person or time to ask. As a student, I wanted to be prepared for class each day because I wanted to learn from the discussions and ask questions. This safe and anti-heteronormative space made me a more motivated student, which in turn, makes me a more motivated teacher. I am more motivated to learn about how I can provide an anti-heteronormative environment in my elementary classroom.

Discussion: Critiques for Future Iterations

Although it is important to identify what practices and activities worked well, we believe it is equally important to be critical of this work and Peggy's practices in order to identify what could be improved for future iterations of the course. Together, we identified three key areas that warrant further discussion: the importance of communication and language, extending the knowledge learned to skills that the preservice teachers can use, and locating intersectional resources about LGBTQ and intersex children.

Based on our critical discussions about the course, the importance of communication and use of appropriate language was important from both the teacher and student perspectives. Our close re-reading of Peggy's assignment prompts and exam questions revealed that, even despite maintaining an anti-heteronormative pedagogical stance, some prompts still alluded to a heteronormative discourse. Take for example the following: "Intersex people are those people whose gender does not match their sex." Peggy designed this as a true/false question on the midterm to measure if students understood the definition of "intersex." However, the prompt's wording still maintained the normative view that gender and sex must "match." From Ingrid's perspective, teachers must learn how our language as a trusted adult could affect a child. Teachers and teacher educators must maintain a vigilance in identifying how our own work is still influenced by unconscious and learned heteronormative motivations (and other hegemonic discourses) despite our intentions otherwise. This means that we need to know not only how to identify such microaggressions (Sue et al., 2007), but also (re)learn inclusive and appropriate ways to communicate.

In our critical discussions about Ingrid's learning after the course, it surfaced that she felt comfortable with her knowledge about LGBTQ and intersex development but "not 100%" in operationalizing that knowledge. Although the course did a lot of "affirmation" based ally-work, a future version of the course should include more activities and assignments that had students doing "informed action" ally-work (Brown & Ostrove, 2013). For example, Ingrid identified that a later journal could build on the first journal entry that assessed students' theoretical understanding about intersex children's development. This subsequent assignment could ask students to research more narratives and write a children's story that includes positive narratives. In-class activities could have students write scenarios based on experiences shared in a video and have their peers in the class act out and reflect on how they would approach the scenario. Such activities and assessments would then build on their knowledge about LGBTQ and intersex children's development by practicing skills they would use in their future professions.

Finally, in reflecting on the design and implementation of the course, and reviewing Peggy's notebook where she journaled about teaching the course, a key issue was in locating intersectional resources. Although more attention is being paid to considering the development of young people who are LGBTQ or intersex (The National, 2015), and more videos and news stories are being circulated about their lived experiences (Rose, 2017), most of these stories focus on young LGBTQ people who are White, many of whom also come from middle- to upper-class backgrounds. Just as we need to reflect on how we participate in the maintenance of heteronormativity in teacher education (Jennings, 2015), we must also interrogate if our inclusion of LGBTQ narratives maintains White supremacist and classist discourses. Similarly, we need to share, create, and support more intersectional representations of young LGBTQ and intersex lives.

CONCLUSION

Practically, this chapter shares the planning, implementation, and implications of a human development class that sought to disrupt heteronormative discourse in teacher education. We wanted to go beyond just identifying that heteronormativity is systemic within teacher education, or enacting what Sedgwick (1990) might call a "paranoid reading" of curricula (p. 127). A look at local teacher education course programs while writing this chapter in early 2017 showed us that few classes if any explicitly address LGBTQ experiences. Such hegemony, however, is already known to queer students, teachers, and scholars. As Clark (2010) similarly argues, identifying the existence of a discourse may not be enough to fight its persistence. Instead, we must *also* develop, share, and build upon specific practices and activities that actively disrupt heteronormativity.

We need a broad conception of the "ally-work" (Brown & Ostrove, 2013; Clark, 2010) that LGBTQ and non-LGBTQ people do in teacher education. We also need to disrupt the gendered notion that a "good teacher" is one that "supports" LGBTQ students, reifying that these students live in a constant state of victimhood (Smith, 2015). As Smith (2015) argues, "Framing pro-LGBTQ work strictly in the safety and care discourses allows teachers to sidestep the stigmatization of their work" (p. 239). This will only serve to reinforce the belief that because they are approaching teaching with care, they are must be doing good work, rather than encouraging a critical reflection on one's pedagogical practices and strategies to work with LGBTQ students.

Rather, as teachers and teacher educators, we must recognize our own positionalities and the discourses within which we operate. The critical reflections we provide here aim to do that. Additionally, we encourage more such work to utilize collaborations between students and teachers. It embodies a "radically inclusive teaching" practice (Lesnick & Cook-Sather, 2010) by encouraging teacher and student to share the roles of "teacher, learner, and colleague" (p. 3). Future collaborations between teachers and students might bring in more perspectives on such anti-heteronormative approaches to teaching and teacher education. Whereas our chapter focused on the perspective of one student, other research might try to incorporate divergent views on the impact of such courses. However, Ingrid's perspective highlights the potential that deep engagement with the material and critical discussions about lived experiences can promote critical thinking and practices that disrupt heteronormativity in the classroom. Further, continued engagement with these discussions in such a partnership can help to address the lack of systemic discussions on LGBTQ, gender nonconforming, and intersex topics in teacher education.

REFERENCES

Bartholomaeus, C., Riggs, D. W., & Andrew, Y. (2017). The capacity of South Australian primary school teachers and preservice teachers to work with trans and gender diverse students. *Teaching and Teacher Education, 65,* 127–135. doi:10.1016/j.tate.2017.03.006

Berk, L. (2014). *Exploring lifespan development* (3rd Ed.). Boston, MA: Allyn & Bacon.

Bloom, L. R. (1996). Stories of one's own: Nonunitary subjectivity in narrative representation. *Qualitative Inquiry, 2*(2), 176–197. doi:10.1177/107780049600200203

Bradley-Johnston, N. (2017). Embracing the rainbow: Approaches to exploring issues concerning the LGBT community in primary schools in Northern Ireland. *The STeP Journal: Student Teacher Perspectives, 4*(2), 19-35. Retrieved from http://ojs.cumbria.ac.uk/index.php/step/article/view/400

Brown, K. T., & Ostrove, J. M. (2013). What does it mean to be an ally?: The perception of allies from the perspective of people of color. *Journal of Applied Social Psychology, 43*(11), 2211–2222. doi:10.1111/jasp.12172

Buber, M. (1970). *I and thou* [trans. by W. Kaufmann]. New York, NY: Charles Scribner's Sons.

Butler, J. (1990). *Gender trouble: Feminism and the subversion of identity*. New York, NY: Routledge.

BuzzFeed Presents. (2015, March 28). What it's like to be intersex [Video file]. Retrieved from https://www.youtube.com/watch?v=cAUDKEI4QKI

Carss, W. D. (2007). *The effects of using Think-Pair-Share during guided reading lessons* (Unpublished thesis). The University of Waikato, Hamilton, New Zealand. Retrieved from http://hdl.handle.net/10289/2233

Clark, C. T. (2010). Preparing LGBTQ-allies and combating homophobia in a US teacher education program. *Teaching and Teacher Education, 26*(3), 704–713. doi:10.1016/j.tate.2009.10.006

Cochran-Smith, M., & Lytle, S. L. (2009). *Inquiry as stance: Practitioner research for the next generation*. New York, NY: Teachers College Press.

Cohen, C. J. (1997). Punks, bulldaggers, and welfare queens: The radical potential of queer politics? *GLQ: A Journal of Lesbian and Gay Studies, 3*(4), 437–465.

Cohen, J., Cook-Sather, A., Lesnick, A., Alter, Z., Awkward, R., Decius, F., & Mengesha, L. (2013). Students as leaders and learners: Towards self-authorship and social change on a college campus. *Innovations in education and teaching international, 50*(1), 3-13. doi:10.1080/14703297.2012.746511

Crenshaw, K. (1991). Mapping the margins: Intersectionality, identity politics, and violence against women of color. *Stanford Law Review, 43*(6), 1241–1299. Retrieved from http://www.jstor.org/stable/1229039

DePalma, R., & Atkinson, E. (2009). "No Outsiders": Moving beyond a discourse of tolerance to challenge heteronormativity in primary schools. *British Educational Research Journal, 35*(6), 837–855. doi:10.1080/01411920802688705

Garrison, C., & Ehringhaus, M. (2009). Formative and summative assessment in the classroom. *National Middle School Association*. Retrieved from: http://schools.nyc.gov/NR/rdonlyres/33148188-6FB5-4593-A8DF-8EAB8CA002AA/0/2010_11_Formative_Summative_Assessment.pdf

Gorski, P. C., Davis, S. N., & Reiter, A. (2013). An examination of the (in)visibility of sexual orientation, heterosexism, homophobia, and other LGBTQ concerns in US multicultural teacher education coursework. *Journal of LGBT Youth, 10*(3), 224–248. doi:10.1080/19361653.2013.798986

Green, A. I. (2007). Queer theory and sociology: Locating the subject and the self in sexuality studies. *Sociological Theory, 25*(1), 26–45. doi:10.1111/j.1467-9558.2007.00296

Gussak, D. (2008). An interactionist perspective on understanding gender identity in art therapy. *Art Therapy: Journal of the American Art Therapy Association, 25*(2), 64–69. doi:10.1080/07421656.2008.10129414

Hennessy, R. (2000). *Profit and pleasure: Sexual identities in late capitalism*. New York, NY: Routledge.

Herndon, A. (2006). Teaching intersex issues. *Intersex Society of North America*. Retrieved from http://www.isna.org/files/teaching_packet.pdf

Hey You Up There. (2010, June 18). The game plan for girls sports – Highlights [Video file]. Retrieved from https://www.youtube.com/watch?v=CZQRryhS1eo&list=PLF79CD5EEC86A08D3

Howard, T. C. (2003). Culturally relevant pedagogy: Ingredients for critical teacher reflection. *Theory into Practice, 42*(3), 195–202. doi:10.1207/s15430421 tip4203_5

Hubbard, R. S., & Powers, B. M. (2003). *The art of classroom inquiry: A handbook for teacher-researchers.* Portsmouth, NH: Heinemann.

Jennings, T. (2015). Teaching transgressive representations of LGBTQ people in educator preparation: Is conformity required for inclusion? *The Educational Forum, 79*(4), 451–458. doi:10.1080/00131725.2015.1068420

Kedley, K. E. (2015). Queering the teacher as a text in the English Language Arts classroom: Beyond books, identity work and teacher preparation. *Sex Education, 15*(4), 364–377. doi:10.1080/14681811.2015.1027762

Ladson-Billings, G. (2011). "Yes, but how do we do it?": Practicing culturally relevant pedagogy. In J. G. Landsman & C. W. Lewis (Eds.), *White teachers / diverse classrooms: Creating inclusive schools, building on students' diversity, and providing true educational equity* (pp. 33–46). Sterling, VA: Stylus.

Lesnick, A., & Cook-Sather, A. (2010). Building civic capacity on campus through a radically inclusive teaching and learning initiative. *Innovative Higher Education, 35*(1), 3-17. doi:10.1007/s10755-009-9122-3

Magnus, C. D., & Lundin, M. (2016). Challenging norms: University students' views on heteronormativity as a matter of diversity and inclusion in initial teacher education. *International Journal of Educational Research, 79*, 76–85. doi:10.1016/j.ijer.2016.06.006

McRuer, R. (2006). *Crip theory: Cultural signs of queerness and disability.* New York, NY: New York University Press.

Miller, J. B., & Stiver, I. P. (1997). *The healing connection: How women form relationships in therapy and in life.* Boston, MA: Beacon Press.

Myers, K., & Raymond, L. (2010). Elementary school girls and heteronormativity: The girl project. *Gender & Society, 24*(2), 167–188. doi:10.1177/0891243209358579

Paterson, K. (2014). "It's harder to catch a boy because they're tougher": Using fairytales in the classroom to explore children's understandings of gender. *Alberta Journal of Educational Research, 60*(3), 474–490. Retrieved from https://ajer.journalhosting.ucalgary.ca/index.php/ajer/article/view/1368

Plummer, K. (2003). Queers, bodies and postmodern sexualities: A note on revisiting the "sexual" in symbolic interactionism. *Qualitative Sociology, 26*(4), 515–530. doi:10.1023/B:QUAS.0000005055.16811.1c

Ridgeway, C. L., & Smith-Lovin, L. (1999). The gender system and interaction. *Annual Review of Sociology, 25*(1), 191–216. doi:10.1146/annurev.soc.25.1.191

Rose, I. (2017, March 28). Transgender child's mom: Love your kids, period [Op ed]. *CNN.* Retrieved from http://www.cnn.com/2017/03/28/opinions/reconsidering-indulgence-isabel-rose-opinion/index.html

Sedgwick, E. K. (1990). *The epistemology of the closet.* Los Angeles: University of California Press.

Schön, D. (1987). *Educating the reflective practitioner: Toward a new design for teaching and learning in the professions.* San Francisco, CA: Jossey Bass.

Schuck, S., Aubusson, P., & Buchanan, J. (2008). Enhancing teacher education practice through professional learning conversations. *European Journal of Teacher Education, 31*(2), 215–227. doi:10.1080/02619760802000297

Shannon-Baker, P. (2018). A multicultural education praxis: Integrating past and present, living theories, and practice. *International Journal of Multicultural Education, 20*(1), 48–66. doi:10.18251/ijme.v20i1.1518

Sherry, M. (2004). Overlaps and contradictions between queer theory and disability studies. *Disability & Society, 19*(7), 769–783. doi:10.1080/0968759042000284231

Smith, A. (2010). Queer theory and Native Studies: The heteronormativity of settler colonialism. *GLQ: A Journal of Lesbian and Gay Studies, 16*(1–2), 41–68. doi:10.1215/10642684-2009-012

Smith, M. J. (2015). It's a balancing act: The good teacher and ally identity. *Educational Studies, 51*(3), 223–243. doi:10.1080/00131946.2015.1033517

Sue, D. W., Capodilupo, C. M., Torino, G. C., Bucceri, J. M., Holder, A. M. B., Nadal, K. L., & Esquilin, M. (2007). Racial microaggressions in everyday life: Implications for clinical practice. *American Psychologist, 62*(4), 271–286. doi:10.1037/0003-066X.62.4.271

Szalacha, L. A. (2004). Educating teachers on LGBTQ issues: A review of research and program evaluations. *Journal of Gay & Lesbian Issues in Education, 1*(4), 67–79. doi:10.1300/J367v01n04_07

The National. (2015, July 27). *Transgender in Texas* [Video file]. Retrieved from https://www.youtube.com/watch?v=0B60EoINkXc

The Whittington Family. (2014, May 27). *The Whittington family: Ryland's story* [Video file]. Retrieved from https://www.youtube.com/watch?v=yAHCqnux2fk

Young, A. J., & Middleton, M. J. (2002). The gay ghetto in the geography of education textbooks. In R. M. Kissen (Ed.), *Getting ready for Benjamin: Preparing teachers for sexual diversity in the classroom* (pp. 91–102). Lanham, MD: Rowman & Littlefield.

CHAPTER 10

AN INTERGENERATIONAL SELF-STUDY OF NARRATIVE REFLECTIONS ON LITERATURE, GENDER, AND LGBTQ IDENTITIES

Adrian D. Martin and Monica Taylor

ABSTRACT

This chapter reports on a self-study conducted by two teacher educators in the Northeastern United States who investigated critical narratives about their lived experiences and professional practices in relation to literary works, gender and LGBTQ issues in education. Employing elements of narrative inquiry, autoethnography and co/autoethnography, the authors connected their analysis with prior research conducted with a focus group session of young adults. Findings suggest that teacher educators must consider how time and space mitigate understandings of gender and LGBTQ issues and identities, and the need for teacher educators to better incorporate ally identities as a salient element of the professional self.

Exploring Gender and LGBTQ Issues in K–12 and Teacher Education, pages 163–182

Globally, advances have been made in the struggle for LGBTQ equity and social justice. An increasing number of nations have instituted de jure marriage equality and have provided employment and housing protection for LGBTQ individuals (Roth, 2015). The media presence of LGBTQ characters and a focus on issues relevant to the lives of LGBTQ communities has proliferated in recent years and can be seen in multiple films, television programs, and theatrical presentations (Human Rights Campaign, 2014). This combined visibility of LGBTQ individuals and issues in both current events and entertainment programming, in conjunction with the proliferation and accessibility of multiple platforms for the dissemination of such content (e.g., mobile devices), has enabled an emergent discourse at the onset of the 21st century wherein LGBTQ individuals, communities, topics, and themes have become a staple of the mainstream (Ghaziani, 2011; Ng, 2013; Seidman, 2003).

As promising as this trend may seem, visibility in and of itself is not synonymous with equity. LGBTQ individuals continue to struggle for recognition, equality, and basic human rights. Furthermore, in contrast to the increased presence of LGBTQ matters in mainstream media, attention to such topics continues to be marginalized in curriculum, classroom discourse, and learning opportunities both for teachers and students (Gorski, Davis, & Reiter, 2013; Marshall & Hernandez, 2013; Martin, 2014a; Martin & Kitchen, in press; Taylor, Meyer, Peter, Ristock, Short, & Campbell, 2016; Vavrus, 2009). As education researchers and teacher educators, we attend to gender and LGBTQ issues in our scholarship and pedagogy with our students (Martin, 2014b; Taylor & Coia, 2014). We are committed to engaging with the scholarly and academic community to combat heteronormativity, transphobia, and the dominance of patriarchy. We strive to include LGBTQ and gender issues as central to the learning experiences of our preservice/inservice teachers. As such, we have interrogated our own practices to identify how we contribute to and can continue to contribute towards such an aim in our work. For us, a central element in this process has been to actively reflect upon and consider how our own positionalities, time, and contexts inform the values we possess and bring to our work in our scholarship and in our classrooms.

For Adrian, this suggests reflecting on his working-class background, experiences growing up as the child of Cuban immigrants to the United States, prior years of professional practice as an elementary and early childhood educator, and living as a gay man in an era of growing conservatism. For Monica this entails examining her past experiences as a young girl witnessing her mother being abused by a closeted gay father, as an urban middle school teacher and teacher educator, her current position as a mother of gay son, and her lifetime of becoming a feminist in a patriarchal society.

Who we are, who we were, and who we seek to be informs our professional identities and our professional practice (Martin & Strom, 2017; Taylor & Coia, 2006). As educators cognizant that students in our courses identify or will identify as LGBTQ, we are conscious of the imperative to engage in a pedagogy that affirms and is inclusive of LGBTQ identities and provides learning experiences to promote ally identities among non-LGBTQ students. Having initially met in the doctoral program at Monica's institution, we draw from our shared interest in gender and LGBTQ issues in education combined with an interest (and love for) creative works of literature. Our identities and experiences as teachers and students have been shaped and enriched by poetry, novels, short stories, and plays. In other words, who we are is equally influenced by what we read. The works of A.S. Byatt, Marge Piercy, Adrienne Rich, Patti Smith, and Audre Lorde, for Monica, and Armistead Maupin, Tennessee Williams, E.M. Forster, and Madeleine L'Engle, for Adrian, have been both life changing and life affirmative. We concur with Julia Kristeva that literature and language are both transformative and can serve as mirrors to interrogate identities, to educate, and to shed light on the realities (and possibilities) for one's ontological capacities (Kristeva, 1984). As educators and researchers conscious of the effects of patriarchy and heteronormativity and committed to social justice and educational equity, we acknowledge the power of literature as a tool to stimulate students' thinking and critical consciousness. For us, writing and sharing our own narratives has been a meaningful front in our professional development. This is because "Stories and narrative, whether personal or fictional, provide meaning and belonging in our lives. They attach us to others and to our own histories by providing a tapestry rich with threads of time, place, character, and even advice on what we might do with our lives" (Witherell & Noddings, 1991, p. 1).

In this chapter, we report on a self-study of our own critical narratives in relation to our work relative to gender and LGBTQ issues in education. Our narrative inquiry focused on our experiences as students, teachers, and teacher educators, and how we grappled with LGBTQ and gender issues in K–12 and teacher education contexts. In addition, we considered how literature and creative works informed this understanding. We connect this inquiry with a focus group discussion on LGBTQ discourses we previously conducted with young adults with the purpose of gaining a sense of how these discourses have changed from our own schooling and early teaching years. We approached the writing of this chapter as an opportunity to share our meaning-making of our individual stories and the narrative of our joint endeavors. We begin with a discussion of queer theory as the theoretical outlook that informs this work, the methodological approach to this self-study, and the analysis of our narratives. We share our individual and joint narratives, attentive to critical moments and how these connect with literary texts. We conclude with a discussion and consider pedagogical possibilities that can be taken up by members of the teacher education and education community at large.

QUEER SPECTACLES

We engaged in this inquiry on our narratives as LGBTQ advocates and allies over the course of a year. During that time we experimented with and employed multiple theoretical frameworks to guide our thinking, inform our meaning-making of these stories, and support the trustworthiness of the work. Our aim was to put theory and philosophy to work for us (Strom & Martin, 2017), to facilitate a consideration of our experiences and our identities from multiple perspectives. The different theories were akin to spectacles (Martin, 2014a), attuning us to "see" varied aspects of ourselves, our work, and our stories in myriad ways. As analytic devices/spectacles, applying, working with, and "seeing" our data (our narratives) through multiple frames of thought (e.g., feminist perspectives [Weedon, 1987], new materialism [Fox & Alldred, 2014], post-structuralism [St. Pierre, 2000]) highlighted the complexity, nuances, and contradictions inherent in the messy and morphic flows of events we sought to understand and interpret. Our use of these diverse frameworks (or spectacles) illuminated past conceptualizations of LGBTQ issues in schooling, current circumstances and realities, and possibilities for future practice, advocacy, and research. In this chapter, we concentrate on the use of queer theory as a productive lens.

Queer theory is an umbrella term for multiple conceptual frames, analytic tools, notions, perspectives, and critiques that aim to disrupt (to deconstruct) normative gender and sexual identities as well as institutions, structures, and discourses that undergird and sustain these views (Alexander, 2008; Wilchins, 2014). Seeking to push the boundaries of what has been conceived in terms of ontological interpretations of self as gendered and sexual identities manifest as a binary (male/female, heterosexual/homosexual), queer theory highlights the genealogical unfolding that perpetuates these status quo assumptions (Butler, 1990; Sedgwick, 1990) and, ultimately, the performative qualities that characterizes and stabilizes as fixed, esstentialist identities (Carpenter & Lee, 2010). It provides a theoretical and conceptual landscape to think beyond/outside binary constructions of the material world towards new constructions and interpretations of our embodied experiences as sentient, conscious beings (Muñoz, 1999; Pascoe, 2012; Warner, 1999). In relation to education research, the productiveness of engaging with queer theory to analyze systems of schooling, teaching, and learning has been demonstrated by academics in diverse contexts (see this volume).

In this inquiry we "wore" queer theory spectacles to identify how our narratives attended to constructions of self that deviated from heteronormative/heterosexist and patriarchal discourses in relation to our life experiences as students, teachers, and teacher educators. Further, queer theory was productive to meditate upon literary works and the presence/absence of bodies in these works that extend beyond binary conceptions of gender and/or sexuality. Queer theory opened up intellectual and affective spaces we had previously not considered (in our lives, those of our students, and in the literature we read), and enabled the decentering of heteronormative and patriarchal "norms" from the margins of our thought.

METHODOLOGY

Our qualitative self-study drew elements from narrative inquiry (Clandinin, 2013), autoethnographic research (Adams, Jones, & Ellis, 2015) and co/autoethnographic investigations (Taylor & Coia, 2009). As with our prior discussion on the affordances of experimenting with varied theoretical frames, drawing from diverse methodological approaches facilitated analysis of our narratives. The autoethnographic elements allowed us to attend to self in our contexts (past, present, and future). Co/auto-ethnographic elements supported a consideration of self and other (Monica and Adrian) in relation to setting, and narrative inquiry provided the analytic basis to make sense of our stories and our stories in relation to literary works. In essence, this experimentation served to queer methodology, to make it strange and new, and to put methodology to work for us (Koro-Ljungberg, 2016).

Data sources for this inquiry were an online journal wherein we wrote narratives about ourselves, our teaching experiences, and our meaning-making of self in relation to gender and sexual identities. We reflected upon and analyzed the connections/disconnections in the narratives (Alvermann, 2000), identifying how queer theory informed our interpretation of these and literary texts of personal significance. We met in person once a semester, furthering our insights from our online communication, sharing other new narratives of our professional and personal experiences, and how we understood queer theory in relation to these.

We also connected this work to a focus group session with young adults that we previously conducted. Personal notes from the focus group session served as analytic memos (Cresswell, 2012). The focus group session methodologically anchored us in the present understanding of LGBTQ issues and themes among young adults, thus enabling us to connect our past histories and understandings as students and teachers with those of today. We maintained individual journals to document our own thought processes, our meaning-making of our pedagogical and academic experiences, and our reflections on gender and LGBTQ issues in education. These provided an additional analytic outlet to attend to, process, and reflect upon in our conversations and discussion about our lives, our teaching, and our scholarship.

Analysis involved recursive examinations of our data through our "queer spectacles," identifying emergent themes in our stories and salient moments of insight. We considered how we ourselves were positioned as gendered individuals, as an ally and feminist (Monica) and as a gay person (Adrian). We further considered how others were positioned (students, members of the academic community). As we examined how our narratives (and the narratives that surfaced in the focus group session) differed contingent with time and space, we recognized a need to move beyond fixed, static interpretations on what it means to engage with LGBTQ themes in our teaching and scholarship, towards a realization that the constant flux of social activity/life experience suggests a need to consistently rethink and refashion pedagogy/scholarship to advance equity and social justice in an ever changing world.

NARRATIVE FINDINGS

In the following, we present critical incidents that illustrate the insights we gained from this work. These are initially presented as the meaning-making of our individuals narratives, and subsequently that of our joint work with the youth group discussion. We recognize that our experiences as students, teachers, and teacher educators coalesced to inform how we conceive of engaging with gender and LGBTQ issues in our work, and thus this account is partial, rooted in our values, and is a corollary of our positionalities. Furthermore, our recognition of time and context as mediators in this work shaped our conception of future practice and scholarship.

Adrian's Narratives

I grew up in an urban neighborhood right outside of New York City. The community was predominantly made up of immigrant residents with a rapidly increasing number of Caribbean, Central, and South American residents, many who were native speakers of Spanish engaged in the process/ struggle to learn the English language. My home reflected this linguistic scenario, and my earliest recollections are in Spanish, from the sound of my mother's voice, the call and response during Sunday mass, and the choruses of what would now be considered classic salsa music played on the radio. I remember how my mother and I would visit the local library. I recall the children's section and what seemed like endless stretches of books that ensconced the room. The floor was covered with a brightly colored woven rug, bean bags accessible to sit back in, and plush toy animals to snuggle with as the librarian read during the story time hour. Turning the pages of those trade books, tracing the print of the big books on display, and indulging in the illustrations of stories by Beatrix Potter, Maurice Sendak, and Dr. Seuss brought me joy, opened up new worlds beyond my immediate community, and served as the beginning of a life-long love for literature and the written word.

Yet despite my enthusiasm for books, to read (and to be read to), I failed to find texts that reflected who I was, adults like my parents, or homes like my own. Where were the stories about children growing up in urban areas? Where were the stories with grown-ups who spoke languages other than English? Where were the stories about *mamis* and *papis* (not mommies and daddies) who went to the *bodega* (not the supermarket) and relished suppers of *carne ripillada y arroz con frijoles* (shredded beef with rice and beans) instead of meatloaf, pot roast, or sirloin steak? The library opened up worlds for me, yet not the world that I was living in.

Years passed and, despite this lack of recognition in the printed page, my love for reading continued. I graduated from wordless texts and picture books to the *Hardy Boys*, L. Frank Baum's land of Oz, Madeline L'Engle's *Time Quartet*, and Beverly Cleary's precocious Ramona Quimby. As in my early childhood, books provided fantasy from life and expanded my worldview, but someone like myself was still absent from the page. And, while I always recognized that I was somehow different from most of the other boys around me, it was not until adolescence that I began to better understand who I was and recognize that the identity of gay male reflected this. Once again, I turned to the library, to the printed page seeking a character, a context, anything with which to identify and connect with. I wanted to know that I was not alone and that others were experiencing the world (and engaging with the world) in ways like myself. Literature continued to provide escapism and whimsy, but left me longing and unfulfilled. At five, I was missing from the texts. At fifteen, I could not be found.

An affordance of living close to a major city was that I was within reach of enclaves with those who did reflect who I was identifying as. I began to regularly spend time in Greenwich Village, Chelsea, and the lower East side of Manhattan, neighborhoods that celebrated a rich and long queer history with a strong and vibrant LGBTQ community. By my college years, I could frequently be found perusing the stacks and reading in "A Different Light" or "The Oscar Wilde Bookshop," independent bookstores that specialized in LGBTQ literature. It was then, as a young man, that I began to see myself in the books I held and in the pages that I turned. For the first time, literature resonated as more than fantasy or the world beyond the horizon, but as a mirror of myself and the possibilities for my lived experience.

When I began my work as an urban early childhood and elementary educator, I was cognizant of the need to include texts in my classroom to reflect who my students were, their identities, and their communities. This was a proactive and conscious process of seeking and adding such books to my own classroom library. I nonetheless, however, failed to consider the need to include books with LGBTQ characters and diverse representations of families.

I remember one student who spoke of her mother and her mother's partner as being part of the family and living in the same household. The partner would usually accompany the mother to school events such as concerts and performances. Other parents, other mothers and fathers, would parade towards the front of the auditorium with camera in hand ready to capture those precious moments when their children were performing. This student's mother did so also. And yet, her other parent, her other mother, waited in the back of the auditorium either unwilling, or more likely feeling unable, to stand next to her partner in celebration of their child.

Potentially, many of the adults at this school performance lived with the tacit assumption that heterosexuality was normal and natural, and any deviance from this a pathology. These two women may have been aware of the need to maintain a certain space or abstain from demonstrations of affection at a school function. While there was no openly notable hostility or dislike demonstrated at the event, these women nonetheless tempered physical proximity and contact in ways that would never need to be considered by a heterosexual couple.

As I reflected on these and other experiences as a Hispanic gay male who worked in P–12 urban education, Monica shared a text that was significant in her own life. I listened to her enthusiasm for *Free to Be... You and Me* (1974), a collection of poems and puns by Marlo Thomas and colleagues. Monica shared the significance of this book in her upbringing and how it offered varied observations and commentary relevant to gender norms and diverse representations. I obtained a copy of my own and found that one of the poems, Dan Greenburg's "My Dog is a Plumber" stood out. It humorously captures a child's internal dialogue as she/he contemplates gender roles. The child's dog (who is a boy) enjoys playing with pots and pans. The child's father can't throw a ball or climb a fence, and the mother drives a van. Through lyrical verse, Greenburg's speaker concludes that determining an individual's gender on the basis of what he or she does is futile. Gender stereotypes would prohibit boys from playing with dolls, girls from wearing pants, men from staying home to take care of their children, or women from driving race cars or fixing fire trucks. The reality is that men, women, boys, girls, intersex, and all genders can engage and participate in all of these activities without these activities defining who they are. From a queer theory lens, they are all performative. I cannot help but wonder, were I to have included such a text and materials in my classroom, how might it have facilitated my students' awareness that the world is full of diverse individuals? What might such a text, or a text with diverse representation of family, have meant to that girl with two mothers, and to the many other students who came from LGBTQ headed households that I taught?

I am surprised that even now, in today's day and age of *Transparent*, *The New Normal*, Lavergne Cox and the increased media presence of LGBTQ individuals and issues, many of my former P12 students and current preservice teacher students reference the "normalcy" of traditional gender roles. LGBTQ representations aside, for many of them, boys are boys, girls are girls, and what is good for one is not necessarily good for the other. It is a struggle to get preservice (and in-service) teachers to recognize the salience of engaging with LGBTQ themes and issues in their own classrooms. Texts such as *Free to Be Me... You and Me* may provide a starting point to delve into this critical area of focus. And certainly, the proliferation of LGBTQ themed children's texts (see this volume) provides a multitude of opportunities available to educators today that were not accessible during my K-12 professional years and certainly not available in my own childhood and adolescence. As an urban teacher educator, many of my students readily acknowledge the salience and imperative to engage in culturally responsive pedagogies. Why not LGBTQ responsive pedagogies as well?

Monica's Narratives

Free to Be... You and Me was one of the most significant texts of my childhood. In fact, it was THE soundtrack to which I grew up. Marlo Thomas, who conceived the collection, was my idol and professed the same beliefs as my mom. As a little girl, pictures of Indira Gandhi and Gloria Steinem were above the bathtub and as my mom washed my hair she would say, "One day you could be anything that you want to be." But I also grew up in the context of watching my vocal feminist mom muster up the strength to escape a physically abusive husband. My father felt rage at the imposed patriarchy in which he had to live as a closeted gay man. He turned to drugs and alcohol as a means of survival, of repressing his body and emotions, and yet the physical anger was difficult to contain. I understood in theory that, like Helen Reddy sang, "I could do anything," but I also knew from a very young age that that those ideals were easier said than done.

It was hooks (2013) who wrote: "patriarchy begins at home... It is the one dominator culture that we tend to learn from family, from folks who purport to care about us " (p. 34). This was my reality too—the dominance of patriarchy started in my home. Even with her professed ideals, my mom struggled to model relationships and behaviors that disrupted the traditional notions of gender. The mixed message was it is important to be successful in a man's world, but to remember that getting married needed to come first. But just as home is where patriarchy can start, it is also where it can be dismantled through words, but more importantly through actions. If the patriarchy starts in the home, then perhaps my home, the one I have created with my husband for my sons, provides them space to be free to be who they want to be. What do these ideals look like in schools? How many generations does it take to dismantle the patriarchy?

About ten years ago, I returned to *Free to Be...You and Me* when my own children, Michael and Griffin, were young. I wanted to raise boys who understood that they could be whoever they want to be. And this is exactly what Thomas and her colleagues wanted. She writes in the 35th anniversary (2008) edition, "If you are a grown-up who first read this book 34 years ago—and are now opening to this page, possibly with your own child snuggled on your lap—welcome back!" (p. 4). This book was created because "celebrating individuality and challenging stereotypes empowers both children and adults with the freedom to be who they want to be and to have compassion and empathy for others" (p. 4). What does this look like and how is it realized? Did *Free to Be...You and Me* help me to find my voice and become empathetic? Has it influenced my children to be individuals?

Beyond the home, I believe that schools, especially at the preschool and elementary level, provide children with a foundation to construct a positive self-concept and develop a stance of compassion, acceptance, and understanding of others. Lucky for me and my two sons, we found Playhouse, a parent cooperative preschool that actively seeks to create a school community that welcomes diverse families regardless of race, class, ethnicity, gender, religion, sexual orientation, family make-up, language, or ability. Since its founding in 1951, this has always been the mission of the school. As one of founders explained, they hoped "to give our children a different life than we had with wars and there was going to be peace forever. We wanted the best for our children" (Taylor, 2017, p. 31). In order to do this, much attention was paid to how families were recruited, welcomed, and integrated into the school. Additionally, Playhouse established a tuition sliding scale so that families of various economic levels could have access to the school. They also included the following in their mission statement:

{ESX}Playhouse hopes to arrive at a kind of global peace in a world of discord through creating a diverse community where the child's self-concept is strong. Participating in this type of community sows the seeds of compassion, acceptance, and understanding of others. The roots of peace and the acknowledgement of others begins with the first experience of the child. These experiences influence a child's future beliefs about social justice. (Playhouse School, 2018)

Playhouse was the perfect fit for my family as I hoped my children would, at an early age, build a worldview of openness and acceptance. In some ways I thought that Playhouse would be a school experience that resembled *Free to be You... and Me*. As I reflected, "I had a hunch that learning alongside children whose families encompassed many races, classes, languages, abilities, religions, and sexual orientations would influence Michael and Griffin, but I had no idea how deep their social justice root would grow" (Taylor, 2017, p. 59).

My son Michael spent three years at Playhouse and then entered kindergarten at our neighborhood public school. One day, he invited two of his friends, Olivia and Kyle, over for a play date. After I prepared lunch, I left the kitchen to give them some privacy and sat at the dining room table in the room adjacent. I was in the perfect spot to eavesdrop on their oh-so-honest conversation. The kids started to list the children in their classes and whom they liked and loved:

> **Olivia:** Well, what about Brendan M.?
>
> **Michael:** Well, I like him as a friend.
>
> **Kyle:** Yeah. He is really smart.
>
> **Olivia:** What about Olivia W.? Do you like her as more than a friend, Michael?
>
> **Michael:** (giggle, giggle) No. She's, she's just a friend.
> (I knew he had a little crush on her.)
>
> **Kyle:** I don't really know her.
>
> **Olivia:** I think she likes David as more than a friend.
>
> **Kyle:** And Lucas?
>
> **Olivia:** He's okay. I don't see him at school much. Michael, you just like him as a friend, right?
>
> **Michael:** Yeah, he's just a friend. But you know, two boys can love each other. It doesn't have to be a boy and a girl.
> (Okay, that really peaked my interest. I couldn't wait to hear how Michael was going to explain this.)
>
> **Michael:** You know, you can have all different kinds of families. Two boys can love each other, two girls can love each other, or a boy and a girl can love each other.
>
> **Olivia:** Yeah. I know.
>
> **Kyle:** Really? But how do two boys or two girls have babies? I thought you needed a mom and a dad.
> (At this point, Michael used his expert voice, a common tone for him)
>
> **Michael:** That's easy. If a family has two dads or two moms, then they can adopt a baby. It's no big deal. One of my friends at Playhouse has two moms.
>
> **Olivia:** Yeah. It's really no biggie. (Taylor, 2017, pp. 59–61)

In that moment, I felt a mixture of great joy and pride. Michael essentially stated that he was an advocate for same-sex families. We had never really had a direct conversation about the makeup of different families, but clearly it was something that he had thought a bit about. Later, when he was alone, I asked him quietly if he had ever talked about this at Playhouse, but his memory seemed foggy. Writing this twelve years later, I reminded him of the conversation, hoping for some insight, but I get none. The only thing he tells me with quiet emotion is that it bothers him when people use the word "gay" as an insult.

This shy expression of protest warms my heart, especially because of the past headlines about the bullying and harassment of gay teenagers inside and outside of school that have led to their suicides. Learning of some the suicide stories of Asher Brown (thirteen years old), Billy Lucas (fifteen years old), Justin Aaberg (fifteen years old), Seth Walsh (thirteen years old), and Tyler Clementi at Rutgers University has saddened me terribly. Nationally, we spent late June of 2016 grieving the loss of 50 lives at Pulse, the LGBTQ night club in Orlando, Florida. How could this have happened, and during Pride month no less? As we were reminded by the talented Lin Manuel Miranda (2016), "Love is love is love is love."

Nine years later, as a freshman, Michael joined the Gay Straight Alliance at his school as an act of solidarity. When I asked him about his choice, he said, "Isn't this what you raised me to do? Isn't this about social justice?" And these ideals have governed his time in high school, befriending and supporting peers because of shared interests and not based on judgment around non-conformity to gender and sexuality norms. I know in my heart that Michael will continue to feel strongly about his convictions and will advocate for others who are being ostracized.

Three years later my youngest son, Griffin, at the age of thirteen came out to us at home and to his friends and teachers at school. We were incredibly proud of his courage and self- confidence, especially at such a young age, but we were also worried about what this would mean for his life as he moved forward into the world. It was emotional too for me as I thought about the cycle we were breaking—that we had created a home environment where our children could be themselves and not feel pressured to hide their identities or conform to the socialized notions of masculinity and heteronormativity. I grieved too for my father whose own journey had been so different and wrought with self-hatred and anger.

Both Michael and Griffin were influenced by their experiences at Playhouse. Can I solely attribute this awareness of a world beyond gender stereotypes to Playhouse? Probably not, but I do believe that being in a school where the values of compassion, individualism, and understanding what it means to be in someone else's shoes are the foundation and can lead to a stance that challenges the status quo.

Narrative Reflections on the Youth Group Discussion

As we reflected upon our individual narratives, we often wondered how teachers (and future teachers) can address LGBTQ and gender issues in their own classrooms. Analyzing our lived experiences via the sharing of our stories with one another was productive, providing insight on how our past informs our present, and how literature served as a catalyst for particular forms of understanding. Yet, we also recognized that today's rapidly changing socio-political context suggest that our current students may possess lived experiences and understandings of gender and LGBTQ identities different from our own. To gain insight on this, we decided to build upon our own reflective contemplations by having a shared dialogue with young adults to discuss gender and LGBTQ issues.

We were eager to engage with young people and learn from their perspectives. Having previously discussed *Free to Be . . . You and Me*, we decided to use some of the poems as a starting point for our discussion group. We wondered if these texts would still be relevant to today's youth. Would the poems provoke dialogue? Would the young people in the discussion find them to be outdated? These were questions that brewed for us as we began to organize a discussion group.

Because Monica works closely with a local urban magnet school for the performing arts, she asked a few of the teachers with whom she collaborates if they might be interested in organizing a focus group. The teachers were enthusiastic and eagerly helped to draft a parental permission slip and set up a time, date, and location for the volunteers to meet with us. Prior to the discussion, as we planned and selected the literature, we made a conscious decision to let go of our own preconceived agendas about how the discussion might unfold. We wanted the young people to feel as comfortable as possible to discuss these issues in a relaxed, safe, and affirmative environment. We decided that we would introduce ourselves, ask the young people to do so also, and then read and discuss each poem. We did not design a list of questions to provoke conversation. We hoped that the dialogue would be as natural as possible. We didn't know where we were going to end up but we were eager, open, and curious.

Our group consisted of seven young women, two young men, one teacher, and the two of us. We chose three poems from *Free to Be . . . You and Me* that we thought would open the dialogue in our small focus group. We began our conversation with Greenburg's "Don't Dress Your Cat in an Apron" which focused on breaking out of traditional roles. We then moved to "My Dog is a Plumber," another Greenburg poem, and then finally we read "No One Else" by Elaine Laron. The students were eager to read the poems and share and express their views and thoughts. Over the course of our conversation, we reviewed the poems, providing an opportunity for multiple oral readings and some think time to allow participants to gather their thoughts. We were struck by how open, how receptive, and how welcoming they were.

Engaging in this process heightened awareness of gender and sexuality issues not only for the participants in our group, but for ourselves as well. Our intention was to provide a safe space for an open and frank discussion. We found as the conversation progressed that for the participants, LGBTQ and gender issues were deeply intertwined with their racial backgrounds and religious affiliations (our participants were predominantly youth of color from working and lower-class backgrounds). We recall many expressed how their parents' religious convictions "bumped heads" with their views and feelings about LGBTQ issues and stereotypic gender expectations. One young man related how concerned his father was that he not be gay. Another student reflected that while her mother was a star athlete in her own country, once in the United States, it was unthinkable that her own daughter would want to excel at sports. This young woman, regardless of her own gender or sexual identity, was encouraged by her mother to have a boyfriend as a cure to her athletic interests. As we reflected on the myriad responses these young adults provided, we realized these deeply personal challenges and struggles they faced were refreshingly countered by the affirmative stance on accepting each other and being friends with one another regardless of gender and/or sexual identity.

Reflecting on our discussion, we realized that sexual identity and gender expression are not aspects of self that emerge within a vacuum, but rather are realized and expressed through language, culture, and community norms. While the narratives on ourselves highlighted how personal experience and encounters with literature shed light on who we are and our meaning-making of LGBTQ and gender discourses, our engagement with the discussion group highlighted the intersectionality (particularly race and religion) of identities and relevant LGTBQ and gender discourses. For young people who recognize themselves as non-gender conforming or as sexual minorities, bullying and social ostracization are a result not only of identities and expressions outside of faith-based views of normalcy, but also of divergence from culturally sanctioned and approved expressions of masculinity and femininity.

FROM THE PAST, TO THE PRESENT, TO A QUEER FUTURE

Our work in this narrative self-study and engagement with the group discussion has called us to posit how we could better facilitate instructional contexts and learning experiences that are affirmative safe spaces not only for GLBTQ youth, but for all young people to explore the complex and highly personal intersectionality of the identities they claim and those that are socially ascribed to them. From a queer theory perspective, our discussion enabled an open dialogue that queered, or disrupted the hegemony of normative gender and sexual identity categories that are routinely positioned as natural and desirable in schooling and social contexts (Endo & Miller, 2014; Shlasko, 2005). Both our narrative inquiry and subsequent work with the discussion group enabled the examination of gender and LGBTQ issues in relation to literary works and in relation to lived experiences.

Collectively, these opened up possibilities for non-heteronormative discourses in schools and literature as possessing the agentic capacity to center what had previously remained on the margins of thought. We learned that today's youth are coming of age in a world of heightened LGBTQ and gender expansive identity visibility. The discourses on non-normative gender/ sexual identities that queer theory has sought to advance are not as queer today as they were twenty or even ten years ago. Our analysis of our work with the discussion group and ongoing reflections of work with our current students suggests that media, particularly social media, is a virtual doorway (and in ways, a virtual text) that can facilitate representations and reflections of self that were absent in each of our early schooling and professional experiences. Thus, for youth of the 21st century, gender expansive identities and LGBTQ issues of invisibility may not be as salient an issue as in the past. Rather, for some, the challenges of today stem from the pervasive influence of LGBTQ and gender oppressive discourses frequently associated with particular religious or cultural norms, mitigating the likelihood that teachers (or future teachers) will take up LGBTQ affirmative practices in their classrooms (Martin & Kitchen, in press).

Given this context, we contemplate our future practice as teacher educators and scholars, to consider the possibilities in our own future practice with preservice and in-service teachers to serve as allies for LGBTQ and gender diverse youth and enable classroom contexts where all students are free to be who they are and who they choose to become. We envision queer futurities (acknowledging the multiplicity of identities and life experiences), queer spaces (educative environments unencumbered by heteronormative and patriarchal restraints) and queer narratives (the recollection, collection, and sharing of stories that suggest the possibilities for imminent experience beyond heteronormativity). To advance towards such a context, we provide the following suggestions that can be taken up by teachers and teacher educators in their classrooms.

Educators must possess a clear understanding of their views, beliefs, and values relevant to gender equity and LGBTQ inclusiveness. They need to engage in deep reflection and study of self as a gendered person and in terms of sexual identity. Just as our own self-study work and the investigation of our narratives promoted insights on our positionalities and our work as researcher and teacher educators, others in the field may also benefit from such systematic inquiry on the self. Such work has enabled some teacher educators to better attend to gender and LGBTQ issues in their classrooms (Cosier & Sanders, 2007; DeJean, 2010; Whitlock, 2010). In addition, educators in P–12 and teacher education should promote similar inquiry among students (Blackburn, Clark, Kenney, & Smith, 2010). Given that many cultural, social, and political discourses perpetuate biases and the marginalization of gender diversity and LGBTQ identities, such reflective experiences and critical examinations on these issues may contribute to inclusive dispositions and an advocacy perspective (Goldstein, Russell, & Daley, 2007).

We also argue that educators must be aware that they have (or will have) students who identify beyond the gender binary or as LGBTQ. Drawing from such an awareness, it is vital to articulate that the classroom context is a welcoming space for all students. Explicitly relate this and maintain this value, especially during any dialogue about gender and LGBTQ issues. This can contribute to a safe, comfortable, relaxed and affirmative environment. Ultimately, it is not enough to discuss these issues in classrooms (Mcconaghy, 2004; Robinson & Ferfolja, 2001). All students (LGBTQ and non) need teacher models who are advocates for gender equity and LGBTQ inclusiveness and who take pride in such a disposition.

Queer conversations and critical discussions are challenging for many. To facilitate these, it is incumbent upon teachers to enable safe spaces by openly and explicitly relating that the setting for such dialogues is a place free of judgments or evaluations. The intent of the discussion is to promote understanding among all members of the classroom, not to label, single out or critique any one person's views or beliefs. Nonetheless, we argue that it is necessary for teachers and teacher educators to affirm their dispositions for gender equity and as LGBTQ allies. Comments, feedback, and input that is sexist, homophobic, transphobic, or serves to further marginalize gender diverse and LGBTQ individuals should be called out for what it is (Grace & Benson, 2000). While all students should be included and affirmed in classrooms, discourses and commentary that serve to further marginalize others should be critiqued. This can serve as a learning opportunity for all members of the classroom community.

Further, in acknowledgment of the power of literature, texts should be employed to shed light and inform the meaning making of gender and LGBTQ identities, we suggest that literary works can serve as entry points for discussions and pedagogical activities on these issues. Potentially, students might identify and select texts to discuss. Literature can serve as the entry point for gender and LGBTQ centered discussions. In addition, discussion norms can be crafted to enable those in the discussion to navigate the flow of conversation with the teacher acting as facilitator. A strength of our dialogue (and the students mentioned this) was that *they* were in command and geared the conversation toward those areas of concern most important to them. Setting up the environment and affirming our safe space was our main responsibility, but the conversation ultimately belonged to the students.

Clearly, classroom environments should be constructed to promote gender equity and LGBTQ inclusiveness. Instances of gender and sexual marginalization should be used as pedagogical moments to further advance equity and inclusion. Nonetheless, educators must be sensitive and aware of the fact that some students may be indecisive about or uncomfortable with discussing their own sexuality. No member of the classroom community should be coerced or forced to share or discuss facets of self when not yet ready to do so. Part of facilitating a safe space and allowing students to take ownership of the conversation is to recognize that there might be group participants who are more quiet than talkative. To insist upon having a student share when not ready or willing to can have dire consequences, the least of which might be feeling a lack of trust toward the teacher who initially declared the setting as a "safe space." For young people who are or will identify as GLBTQ (and for straight youth as well) teachers need to expect moments of silence, uncertainty, and welcome the potential opportunities for learning and development these moments present.

CONCLUSION

This inquiry enabled us to learn more about our own identities as researchers and teacher educators in relation to gender and LGBTQ issues and how the youth of today make meaning of these issues and what it means to identify as male, female, gay, straight, or none of these. Furthermore, it also provided insight on potential pedagogical approaches that could be used to support instructional contexts that proactively seek to affirm all members of the classroom community. In this way, this project contributes to the emergent body of knowledge on pedagogical practices, school systems, and policy initiatives needed to advance academic and learning contexts that embrace all members of the school community and affirm gender and LGBTQ identities.

We encourage our fellow teacher educators and education researchers to take up the recommendations in this chapter. Should these recommendations move beyond the margins of pedagogical and research practice towards increased implementation, they may serve as a means to combat heteronormativity and patriarchy in schools and contribute towards the proliferation of queer affirmative classrooms. Furthermore, these may promote widespread insight on the social construction of gender and sexuality. For educators and teacher educators committed to equity and social justice, such practice should be an integral component of their pedagogical repertoires.

REFERENCES

Adams, T. E., Linn, H. J., & Ellis, C. (2015). *Autoethnography*. Oxford, England: Oxford University Press.

Alexander, B. K. (2008). Queer(y)ing the postcolonial through the west(ern). In N. K. Denzin, Y. S. Lincoln, & L. T. Smith (Eds.), *Handbook of critical and indigenous methodologies* (pp. 101–134). Thousand Oaks, CA: SAGE.

Alvermann, D. (2000). Researching libraries, literacies, and lives: A rhizoanalysis. In E. S. Pierre & W. S. Pillow (Eds.), *Working the ruins: Feminist poststructural theory and methods in education* (pp. 114–129). New York, NY: Routledge.

Blackburn, M. V., Clark, C. T., Kenney, L. M., & Smith, J. M. (Eds.). (2010). *Acting out! Combating homophobia through teacher activism*. New York, NY: Teachers College Press.

Butler, J. (1990). *Gender trouble: Feminism and the subversion of identity*. New York, NY: Routledge.

Carpenter, V. M., & Lee, D. (2010). Teacher education and the hidden curriculum of heteronormativity. *Curriculum Matters, 6*, 99–119.

Clandinin, D. J. (2013). *Engaging in narrative inquiry*. London, England: Routledge.

Cosier, K., & Sanders, J. H. (2007). Queering art teacher education. *International Journal of Art & Design Education, 26*(1), 21–30. doi:10.1111/j.1476-8070.2007.00506.x

Cresswell, J. W. (2012). *Qualitative inquiry and research design: Choosing among five approaches* (3rd ed.). Los Angeles, CA: SAGE.

Dejean, W. (2010). Courageous conversations: Reflections on a queer life narrative model. *The Teacher Educator, 45*(4), 233–243. doi:10.1080/08878730.2010.508262

Endo, H., & Miller, P. C. (Eds.). (2014). *Queer voices from the classroom*. Charlotte, NC: Information Age.

Fox, N. J., & Alldred, P. (2014). New materialist social inquiry: Designs, methods and the research-assemblage. *International Journal of Social Research Methodology, 18*(4), 399–414. doi:10.1080/13645579.2014.921458

hooks, b. (2013). *Writing beyond race: Living theory and practice*. New York, NY: Routledge.

Ghaziani, A. (2011). Post-gay collective identity construction. *Social Problems, 58*(1), 99–125. doi:10.1525/sp.2011.58.1.99

Goldstein, T., Russell, V., & Daley, A. (2007). Safe, positive and queering moments in teaching education and schooling: A conceptual framework. *Teaching Education, 18*(3), 183–199. doi:10.1080/10476210701533035

Gorski, P. C., Davis, S. N., & Reiter, A. (2013). An examination of the (in)visibility of sexual orientation, heterosexism, homophobia, and other LGBTQ concerns in U.S. *Journal of LGBT Youth, 10*, 224–248. doi: 10.1080/19361653.2013.798986

Grace, A. P., & Benson, F. J. (2000). Using autobiographical queer life narratives of teachers to connect personal, political and pedagogical spaces. *International Journal of Inclusive Education, 4*(2), 89–109. doi:10.1080/136031100284830

Greenburg, D. (1974). Don't dress your cat in an apron. In M. Thomas (Ed.), *Free to be...you and me* (pp. 46–47). New York, NY: McGraw-Hill.

Greenburg, D. (1974). My dog is a plumber. In M. Thomas (Ed.), *Free to be...you and me.* (pp. 86–87). New York, NY: McGraw-Hill.

Human Rights Campaign. (2014, January 30). *Growing presence of LGBT characters on TV.* Retrieved from https://www.hrc.org/blog/growing-presence-of-lgbt-characters-on-tv

Koro-Ljungberg, M. (2016). *Reconceptualizing qualitative research: Methodologies without methodology.* Los Angeles, CA: SAGE.

Kristeva, J. (1984). *Revolution in poetic language.* New York, NY: Columbia University Press.

Laron, E. (1974). No one else. In M. Thomas (Ed.), *Free to be . . . you and me* (pp. 12–113). New York, NY: McGraw-Hill.

Marshall, J. M., & Hernandez, F. (2013). "I would not consider myself a homophobe": Learning and teaching about sexual orientation in a principal preparation program. *Educational Administration Quarterly, 49*(3), 451–488.

Martin, A. D. (2014a). From Adam and Eve to Dick and Jane: A literary nomadic inquiry on gender and sexuality in teaching and teacher education. In M. Taylor & L. Coia (Eds.), *Gender, feminism and queer theory in the self-study of teacher education practices* (pp. 143–156). Boston, MA: Sense Publishers.

Martin, A. D. (2014b). Kaleidoscopic musings on a queer praxis. In H. Endo & P. C. Miller (Eds.), *Queer voices from the classroom* (pp. 169–175). Charlotte, NC: Information Age.

Martin, A. D., & Kitchen, J. (in press). LGBTQ themes in the self-study of teacher educator practices: A queer review of the literature. In J. Kitchen, M. Berry, H. Guojonsdottir, S. M. Bullock, M. Taylor, & A. R. Crowe (Eds.), *International handbook of self-study of teaching and teacher educator practices* (2nd ed.). Dordrecht, The Netherlands: Springer.

Martin, A. D., & Strom, K. J. (2017). Using multiple technologies to put rhizomatics to work in self-study. In A. Ovens & D. Garbett (Eds.), *Being self-study researchers in a digital world: Future oriented pedagogy and teaching in teacher education* (Vol. 16, Self-study of Teaching and Teacher Education Practices, pp. 151–163). Dordrecht, The Netherlands: Springer. doi:10.1007/978-3-319-39478-7_11

Mcconaghy, C. (2004). On cartographies of anti-homophobia in teacher education (and the crisis of witnessing rural student teacher refusals). *Teaching Education, 15*(1), 63–79. doi:10.1080/1047621042000179998

Miranda, L. M. (2016). Love makes the world go 'round [Recorded by Lin Manuel Miranda and Jennifer Lopez, MP3]. New York, NY: Epic Records.

Muñoz, J. E. (1999). *Disidentifications queers of color and the performance of politics.* Minneapolis: University of Minnesota Press.

Ng, E. (2013). A "post-gay" era? Media gaystreaming, homonormativity, and the politics of LGBT integration. *Communication, Culture & Critique, 6*(2), 258–283. doi:10.1111/cccr.12013

Pascoe, C. J. (2012). *Dude, you're a fag: Masculinity and sexuality in high school* (2nd ed.). Berkeley: University of California Press.

Playhouse School. (2018). *Diversity: Commitment to diversity.* Retrieved from http://www.playhouseonline.org/about-us/diversity

Robinson, K. H., & Ferfolja, T. (2001). "What are we doing this for?": Dealing with lesbian and gay issues in teacher education. *British Journal of Sociology of Education, 22*(1), 121–133. doi:10.1080/01425690124146

Roth, K. (2015, January 23). LGBT: *Moving towards equality*. Retrieved from https://www.hrw.org/news/2015/01/23/lgbt-moving-towards-equality

St Pierre, E. A. (2000). Poststructural feminism in education: An overview. *International Journal of Qualitative Studies in Education, 13*(5), 477–515. doi:10.1080/09518390050156422

Sedgwick, E. K. (1990). *Epistemology of the closet*. Berkeley: University of California Press.

Seidman, S. (2003). *Beyond the closet: The transformation of gay and lesbian life*. New York, NY: Routledge.

Shlasko, G. D. (2005). Queer (.) pedagogy. *Equity & Excellence in Education, 38*(2), 123–134. doi:10.1080/10665680590935098

Strom, K. J., & Martin, A. D. (2017). *Becoming-teacher: A rhizomatic look at first-year teaching*. Rotterdam, The Netherlands: Sense Publishers.

Taylor, M. (2017). *Playhouse: Optimistic stories of real hope for families of little children*. New York, NY: Garn Press

Taylor, M., & Coia, L. (2006). Revisiting feminist authority through a co/autoethnographic lens. In D. Tidwell & L. Fitzgerald (Eds.), *Self-study research and issues of diversity* (pp. 51–70). Rotterdam, The Netherlands: Sense Publishers.

Taylor, M., & Coia, L. (2009). Co/autoethnography: Investigating teachers in relation. In C. Lassonde, S. Gallman, & C. Kosnik (Eds.), *Self-Study research methodologies for teacher educators* (pp. 169–186). Rotterdam, The Netherlands: Sense.

Taylor, M., & Coia, L. (Eds.). (2014). *Gender, feminism and queer theory in the self-study of teacher education practices*. Rotterdam, The Netherlands: Sense Publishers.

Taylor, C. G., Meyer, E. J., Peter, T., Ristock, J., Short, D., & Campbell, C. (2016). Gaps between beliefs, perceptions, and practices: The Every Teacher Project on LGBTQ-inclusive education in Canadian schools. *Journal of LGBT Youth, 13*(1–2), 112–140.

Thomas, M. (Ed.) (1974). *Free to be . . . you and me*. New York, NY: McGraw-Hill.

Thomas, M. (Ed.) (2008). *Free to be . . . you and me*. Philadelphia, PA: Running Press Kids.

Vavrus, M. (2009). Sexuality, schooling, and teacher identity formation: A critical pedagogy for teacher education. *Teaching and Teacher Education, 25*(3), 383–390.

Warner, M. (1999). *The trouble with normal: Sex, politics, and the ethics of queer life*. Cambridge, MA: Harvard University Press.

Weedon, C. (1987). *Feminist practice and poststructuralist theory*. Oxford, England: Blackwell.

Whitlock, R. U. (2010). Getting queer: Teacher education, gender studies, and the cross disciplinary quest for queer pedagogies. *Issues in Teacher Education, 19*(2), 81–104.

Wilchins, R. A. (2014). *Queer theory, gender theory: An instant primer* (2nd ed.). Bronx, NY: Magnus Books.

Witherell, C., & Noddings, N. (Eds.). (1991). *Stories lives tell: Narrative and dialogue in education*. New York, NY: Teachers College Press.

ABOUT THE EDITORS

Adrian D. Martin, PhD, is an assistant professor at New Jersey City University. Previously, he was an English language arts department chair and an urban elementary classroom teacher for more than ten years. His research interests are informed by his professional experiences and attend to issues of equity, diversity, and social justice in education. His current scholarship examines the ways that educators understand their professional identities as teachers in addition to ways K–12 education and teacher education can promote the affirmative inclusion of LGBTQ members of the school community. As a qualitative methodologist, Adrian investigates emergent forms of qualitative and post-qualitative inquiry informed by post-structural, postmodern, and posthuman philosophies. His research has been published in numerous peer-reviewed journals, including *Teachers College Record, Critical Inquiry in Language Studies,* and *International Journal of Qualitative Studies in Education.*

Kathryn J. Strom, PhD, is an assistant professor in the Educational Leadership Department at California State University, East Bay and teaches in the Educational Leadership for Social Justice EdD program. Her research interests include culturally and linguistically responsive teaching and educator preparation, critical posthuman/neo-materialist theoretical perspectives on pedagogical learning/practice, and post-qualitative methods of inquiry. Dr. Strom received her PhD at Montclair State University in Teacher Education and Teacher Development. Her research has appeared in multiple peer-reviewed journals, including the *Journal of Teacher Education, Equity and Excellence in Education,* and is the author of the book *Becoming-Teacher: A Rhizomatic Look at First Year Teaching.* She also serves as a member of the

Exploring Gender and LGBTQ Issues in K–12 and Teacher Education, pages 183–184
Copyright © 2019 by Information Age Publishing
183

research team of the International Consortium of Multi-Lingual Excellence in Education (ICMEE), a federally-funded effort to develop, implement, and research online, collaborative language-learner focused teacher professional development across the US and Europe. Before joining the faculty at CSU East Bay, Dr. Strom, as a research associate at WestEd's Quality Teaching for English Learners (QTEL) initiative, also worked with leaders and teachers in school districts nationwide to develop equitable pedagogies for language learners. Prior to pursuing her doctorate, Dr. Strom was a history teacher and school leader in southern California.

ABOUT THE CONTRIBUTORS

Michael D. Bartone, PhD, is an assistant professor of elementary education in the Department of Literacy, Elementary, & Early Childhood Education at Central Connecticut State University. His work examines the intersections of race and sexuality in schools and in education. He is also interested in understanding how elementary school teachers understand identity and whose identities they in/exclude in their instruction.

Lynn Bravewomon, EdD, earned her doctorate in Educational Leadership for Social Justice from California State University- East Bay. She holds a Masters of Arts in Teaching and a BA in psychology from Beloit College. Dr. Bravewomon is the Coordinator of Safe and Inclusive Schools Program and an educational consultant with public and private schools. Dr. Bravewomon is passionate about, and recognized, for her work towards developing K–12 school systems in which all students benefit as LGBTQ students and families are met with a thriving school culture of inclusion and respect.

Hidehiro Endo, PhD, is Associate Professor of the Teacher Licensure Program at Akita International University in Japan, where he teaches courses to pre-service teachers. His research interests focus on social justice issues pertaining to LGBT youth, Asian youth, and English language learners. His scholarly work appears in *Multicultural Education, International Journal of Critical Pedagogy*, and *Teaching and Teacher Education*, as well as in several books and book chapters. He is also co-editor of the book series *Research in Queer Studies*, published by Information Age.

Exploring Gender and LGBTQ Issues in K–12 and Teacher Education, pages 185–188
Copyright © 2019 by Information Age Publishing
185

Göran Gerdin, PhD, is a Senior Lecturer in the Department of Sport Science at Linnaeus University, Sweden. His research focuses on how issues of gender, bodies, spaces and (dis)pleasures shape students' participation, enjoyment and identities in school health and physical education. Lately, he has also been researching the practices and enactment of socially-critical perspectives in teacher education and physical education with a focus on inclusion, democracy, equity and social justice. In his work, Göran draws on qualitative and participatory visual methodologies as informed by poststructural, Foucauldian and Butlerian thinking.

Paul Hartman, PhD, taught in the Chicago Public Schools for thirteen years as an elementary and ESL classroom teacher. Currently he is an assistant professor in the School of Teaching and Learning at Illinois State University where he teaches courses on early childhood and elementary literacy education. His research focuses on the intersection of literacy, race, language, gender, and sexuality. He is particularly interested in exploring how literacy can be used as a way to critically understand and change the world, especially in the primary grades.

Paul Chamness Iida, PhD, is Professor of International Liberal Arts at Akita International University in Japan, where he teaches undergraduate writing courses and a teacher preparation course on using pop culture to teach language. His scholarship focuses on two areas: instructional methods of language learning and teaching, and the critical examination of under-represented groups of learners and teachers in the K–12 setting. His scholarly work can be seen in such journals as *Multicultural Education, International Journal of Critical Pedagogy, Teaching and Teacher Education, International Journal of Educational Research*, and *Journal of Thought*, as well as in several books and book chapters.

Amanda Mooney, PhD, is a Senior Lecturer in Education (Health and Physical Education) at Deakin University, Australia. Drawing on qualitative methodologies, Amanda's research examines cultural and societal factors, particularly gender, in relation to identities, professional practice and pedagogies in Physical Education, Health and Sport. Spanning various contexts including school-based Health and Physical Education, community sporting clubs and Physical Education Teacher Education settings, this work seeks to promote more equitable, enjoyable and meaningful experiences for youth in physical education and sport. Amanda's more recent work explores cultural practices that shape identities, health and wellbeing amongst young people in rural and regional contexts.

Mara Sapon-Shevin, EdD, is Professor of Inclusive Education at Syracuse University. Their areas of specialization include teaching social justice, embodied pedagogy, anti-oppressive education, and using the arts for social justice. Mara is also a faculty member in Disability Studies, Women and Gender Studies, and Programs in the Analysis and Resolution of Conflict and Collaboration. Their most recent publications include (with Diana Lawrence-Brown), *Condition Critical: Key Principles for Equi*table *and Inclusive Education* (Teachers College Press) and *Because We Can Change the World: A Practical Guide to Building Cooperative, Inclusive Classroom Communities, 2nd Edition* (Corwin Press). Mara can frequently be found singing for social justice, standing on street corners protesting, leading Let Your Yoga Dance or making quilts.

Peggy Shannon-Baker PhD, is an assistant professor in the Department of Curriculum, Foundations, and Reading at Georgia Southern University. Peggy is a specialist in international education, multicultural education, and mixed methods research. Peggy's current scholarship addresses global multicultural education and heteronormativity in teacher education. This work has been published in the *International Journal of Multicultural Education, International Journal of Qualitative Methods,* and elsewhere, as well as a co-authored chapter in *RIP Jim Crow: Fighting racism through higher education policy, curriculum, and cultural interventions.* Peggy has also taught in K–12 schools in urban and rural locations in the USA, Ecuador, and Tanzania.

Ashley Lauren Sullivan, PhD, is an Assistant Professor of Early Childhood Education at Penn State Erie, The Behrend College. Ashley has published in *The Bank Street College of Education Occasional Paper Series* and *The Journal of Poverty.* Her chapter, *Kindergartners Studying Trans* Issues Through I Am Jazz,* was included in the award-winning text, *Teaching, Affirming, and Recognizing Trans and Gender Creative Youth: A Queer Literacy Framework.* Ashley's upcoming books include *Voices of Children in Early Childhood Education: Reflections on Resistance and Resiliency* (co-authored with Laurie Urraro) and *Introducing Critical Childhood Perspectives: Reconceptualist Thought, Diversity, and Social Justice Expectations* (co-authored with Gaile Cannella).

Monica Taylor, PhD, is a feminist teacher educator, social justice advocate, and parent activist. She is a professor in the Department of Secondary and Special Education at Montclair State University. She has several publications on feminist pedagogy and research methodologies, teaching for social justice, teacher leadership, and urban teacher education. Her recent book, *Playhouse: Optimistic stories of real hope for families with little children,* describes a progressive parent cooperative school through the interwoven narratives of her own children and those of families for the last sixty years. Her commitments to fighting sexism, heteronormativity, and racism manifest in all aspects of her life.

Laurie Lynn Urraro, PhD, teaches Spanish at Penn State Erie, the Behrend College. Her areas of expertise include contemporary female-authored Spanish drama and gender theories. She has published articles and book reviews on contemporary female-authored Spanish drama and co-authored a recent article with Dr. Ashley Sullivan titled "Missing Person's Report: Where are the Transgender Characters in Children's Picture Books?." In 2016 her co-authored book *Medical Spanish for Nurses: A Self-Teaching Guide* was published. In addition to collaborating on early childhood education issues that involve the LGBTQ community, she is working on her own book project dealing with contemporary Spanish theater.

Ingrid Wagner, BA, graduated summa cum laude from the University of Cincinnati with a Bachelor's degree in Early Childhood Education. Throughout her college career, she enjoyed being a member of the University Honors Program which gave her learning experiences in Ecuador, Costa Rica, and in the Greater Cincinnati community. Ingrid is in her second year as a teaching fellow in English Language Arts for a summer enrichment program for underserved youth called Breakthrough Cincinnati. She is looking to continue her career as a teacher in an urban setting and pursuing a graduate degree in the future.